Arsenic Was Her Weapon

Also by Brian Jenkins
and from McFarland

The Trial of Emma Cunningham: Murder and Scandal in the Victorian Era (2020)

Madeleine Smith on Trial: A Glasgow Murder and the Young Woman Too Respectable to Convict (2019)

Arsenic Was Her Weapon

*Women Poisoners
of 19th Century Britain*

BRIAN JENKINS

McFarland & Company, Inc., Publishers
Jefferson, North Carolina

ISBN (print) 978-1-4766-9507-5
ISBN (ebook) 978-1-4766-5624-3

Library of Congress cataloging data are available

Library of Congress Control Number 2025024930

© 2025 Brian Jenkins. All rights reserved

No part of this book may be reproduced or transmitted in any form or by any means, electronic or mechanical, including photocopying or recording, or by any information storage and retrieval system, without permission in writing from the publisher.

Front cover image: © AI Shutterstock Generator.

Printed in the United States of America

*McFarland & Company, Inc., Publishers
Box 611, Jefferson, North Carolina 28640
www.mcfarlandpub.com*

Table of Contents

Preface 1

Introduction 3

ONE
Early Female Murderers 9

TWO
A Rising Tide of Arsenic 30

THREE
A Plague of Poisoners 46

FOUR
A Form of Clemency 75

FIVE
A Question of Class 97

SIX
Class Beyond Question 120

SEVEN
Class Has Limits 143

EIGHT
Late-Century Female Poisoners 170

Conclusion 190

Chapter Notes 193

Bibliography 205

Index 211

Preface

THIS BOOK IS IN SOME SENSE an extension of my interest in the sensational crimes—murders—committed by Madeleine Smith and, 30 years later, Florence Maybrick. Maybrick's case was unique in that she was convicted despite her gender and standing in society. These upper middle class women were but two of the multitude of females who in the 19th century were charged with willful murder by poisoning. Indeed, such murderesses were so numerous that poisoning was considered a woman's crime whereas there was no shortage of male poisoners. The century ended as it had begun with the execution of a female murderer. Yet it saw the emergence of Britain as the first industrialized nation and with it the multiplication of the middle classes and the creation of vast wealth. Why in this booming society did so many women resort to homicide? This question the book seeks to answer.

Undoubtedly, the ill-distribution of the affluence provides an important clue. The "lower orders" were society's vast underprivileged majority. For many of them the basic conditions of life were an unaffordable daily cost. Also, the bonds of matrimony among the laboring classes were often frayed, and the physical violence of husbands and the temptations of adultery became motives to kill.

The lower orders who found themselves afoul of the criminal law long received "rough justice." Rapid trials without the defense of legal counsel often ended in lightning convictions and bungled public executions before celebratory crowds. Fearful these demonstrations would undermine public support for capital punishment, the practice's supporters closed them to the public in 1868. Not that this improved the treatment of the condemned. However middle class women were generally considered incapable of murder and had little reason to anticipate the terror of a horrific public death. In those few cases where the evidence required that charges be brought, defendants usually escaped conviction thanks to purported lunacy serving as a compelling reason for clemency. In the Maybrick case the judge steered the jury to a conviction.

However, during the second half of the century the lower orders were in capital cases provided with counsel by the presiding judge, not that this gave them equality with their social superiors or certainty of an acquittal.

That the press played an important role in the system of justice was an undeniable fact, and its influence grew in the second half of the century with the arrival of popular newspapers and the expansion of the reading public. Crime was a staple of the press since it boosted circulation. The national and metropolitan media concentrated on the truly sensational cases, especially those of middle class women, which they reported in great detail. Working class murders were rarely considered of national importance, so their reporting was left to the regional and local press. They disputed the justice of convictions and influenced the commutation of death sentences. This continued for years after Maybrick's death sentence was commuted to penal servitude for life. She was released after 20 years. That she remained imprisoned for so long despite the agitation, which included that of the American government and press, for she had been born an American citizen, was probably due to the rigid opposition of Queen Victoria to further leniency, and the belief of a succession of home secretaries who investigated the case that she had been guilty.

The accused murderers are discussed in two distinctive ways. The eight middle class women who went to trial are bundled together in three chapters and examined separately from the mass of poisoners belonging to the lower orders of society. For the latter, I have chosen a more pedestrian approach, with narrative and analysis advancing more or less chronologically. This ensured that not many escaped notice and that not all of them merited examination. Those discussed in detail had some lasting significance in a society undergoing change. I benefited from the work of earlier authors who have published books on the more chilling individuals. The availability of those detailed accounts permitted discussion of the changing attitude towards women in the second half of the century, as Victorian opposition to the execution of females deepened and there was much talk, which the government felt obliged to contradict, that the capital punishment of women was about to be abolished. They had to wait until 1969, and the abolition applied to both genders.

This is another family endeavor. My wife, Jean, was a constant supporter and careful editor. Son Maldwyn found a way to convert the language of the written text to American English. His brother, Owen, found an image that McFarland with some modification has accepted as the cover for the book.

Introduction

BRITAIN UNDERWENT AN ECONOMIC, social, and political transformation during the 19th century. From the previous century it inherited an "overwhelming increase in population" made possible by a sufficient supply of the simplest food necessary to support life. That increase became even more startling from 1800. According to the census of the following year the total population stood at near 9 million, by mid-century the figure approached 18 million, and in 1881 the number stood at 26 million. Among the contributory factors was the increase in the birth rate that went hand in hand with a lowering of the age at which women married and the many pregnancies outside of marriage.

There was a correlation between the ever-growing population, the migration of marginal agricultural laborers to towns and cities, and the establishment of urban industries. These had sprung up during the late years of the 18th century. This continued during the first half of the 19th century, and while by mid-century Britain had emerged as the first industrial nation, half of the workforce still worked on the land. Coincidentally immigrants poured into urban Britain. Among them were the victims of the Irish famine as the potato crops failed and the British government mismanaged its inadequate relief policies. Between 1841 and 1851, 400,000 Irish arrived, and a decade later 600,000 were existing in the mill centers and factories of Lancashire and Cheshire. Suitable housing was in short supply, and the Irish shared with English migrants spaces in attics and cellars, where they lacked water and sanitation. Up to four families were required to divide rooms no more than 10 feet by 10 feet. On ground floors, cesspools and drinking wells were often perilously close to one another, thereby contributing to an environment in which disease, political agitation, and crime thrived. In his 1853 book *Crime: Its Amount, Causes and Remedies*, former prison inspector Frederic Hill described these lower orders, or laboring classes, as "herded together in lodging houses, the very hotbeds of immorality, ill-fed, badly clothed and worse educated." Week after week they toiled for their daily bread, discovering that almost all their earnings necessarily went to pay for their miserable room and board. Not surprisingly, many sought escape in cheap alcohol.[1]

Epidemics of measles, smallpox, whooping cough, consumption, influenza, typhus, typhoid, and cholera swept through the urban areas. Although vaccination eventually brought smallpox under better control, they encountered a popular resistance familiar to us in the 21st century. Inoculations were made mandatory for very young infants in 1853 only to be resisted by fearful parents notwithstanding the appointment of special officers to enforce prosecutions for noncompliance. By mid-century Dr. John Snow identified cholera, one of the more terrifying epidemics of disease, as waterborne, only for his innovative research and findings to be resisted by leading lights of the medical profession. Not until 1890 were all towns required to take "responsibility for the basic provision of pure water supply and proper sanitary decisions."

State intervention, both in the economy and public health, was long resisted. Belief that government interference and expenditure was likely to be interested, incompetent, and corrupt was another legacy of the previous century. So also was the dislike of centralization. Who wanted a central organ of the state empowered to meddle and impose a common standard on the entire country? In the vanguard of the resistance was much of the middle class. They swelled in number during industrialization. Socially, they held the central ground between the privileged minority of aristocracy and landed gentry and the vast majority of the nation at society's base. Who were the middle classes? They were the liberal professions, the Church, the law, medicine and banking and the multiplying businessmen. Annual income often defined their status. A lesser annual income, perhaps £60, often distinguished the lower middle class from the masses beneath them. They were owners of small businesses, shopkeepers, farmers, clerks, and teachers, and were more formal in behavior and dress than their social inferiors.[2]

Certain characteristics became identified with the middle class. Reputation and respectability were proclaimed the foundations of business success. Sobriety of conduct was hailed as a vital step towards personal fortune, and those who adhered to this standard considered themselves the vanguard of the nation's progress. Morality was the guide of both their personal and public lives, although as many as 57 shops in the capital were doing a brisk trade in pornography. At much the same time, the Society for the Suppression of Vice sought the expulsion of whores, brawlers, and braggarts from the streets of cities and towns in the hope of ensuring the safety of middle class pedestrians. However, the trial, conviction, and execution of Dr. William Palmer, accused of murder by poisoning in 1856, challenged the moral complacency of the middle class to which he belonged. A legal scholar who attended the trial concluded that this serial killer was proof of a fact that many kindhearted people seemed to doubt, namely, that such a thing as atrocious wickedness was consistent with good education, perfect sanity, and everything that deprives men of all excuse of crime. Up to this point it had been the fixed opinion of the middle classes that homicides were committed only by the lower orders.

Palmer's poison trial nourished doubts about the infallibility of expert scientific witnesses. The prosecution's expert toxicologist, Alfred Swaine Taylor, failed to detect the strychnine that was supposed to have caused the death. Then a pair of defense experts, one of them William Herapath, disputed the quality of his scientific analysis and his competence. Summing up the evidence, the lord chief justice dismissed them, both men of distinction, as mere hired partisans of the prisoner. In short, these scientists were suspected of abandoning objective analysis in their pursuit of financial gain and/or professional advancement. Yet an "ascendant middle-class morality" had been identified as the "best hope of vanquishing the contemporary domestic poisoner." The great advantage middle class poisoners had over those of the lower orders was their ability to retain the best barristers to explain or exploit the differences between toxicologists and thus carry their case, whether defense or prosecution, with the jury.[3]

In 1847 a high court judge deplored the "fearful and appalling" increase in crime. Running through it, or so it seemed, was a "crimson thread." He may have read the annual statistics that recorded a sevenfold jump in felonies between 1808 and 1842. Frederic Hill sought to reassure his middle class readers, asserting that crimes were steadily decreasing in number and taking a milder and milder form. The vast majority were petty offenses and the lower orders, the laboring classes, were less violent than they had been. He blamed Irish immigrants and foreigners for the most heinous offenses. There was thankfully at the end of this dark tunnel a desire of the English "to see others obtain by gradual and secure means, those blessings which we ourselves enjoy." The working classes should be lifted out of destitution and educated. No less important, Hill recommended the "adoption of such means for apprehension, trial, and punishment of offenders as shall secure, as far as practicable, that every offence be followed by immediate detection and certain conviction."[4]

Effective police forces were an obvious means of crime prevention and perhaps solution. The 18th century had decided that the threat of execution was the best deterrent of crime. It bequeathed to the following century the "Bloody Code" in which almost 200 crimes, many of them minor, were punishable by death. These were slowly slashed in number until, in 1861, only three remained, the principal being murder. Homicides reported by the police between 1857 and the century's end rarely exceeded 400. By this time a "new police" had been organized. Their founding was the establishment of London's Metropolitan Police in 1829, and legislation in 1856 required all municipal authorities to act. A force's efficiency was then assessed by Inspectors of Constabulary, and upon receipt of a passing grade the local authority was partially recompensed by the central government. Not that distinctively uniformed officers inspired the public with confidence as gatherers of evidence, for all too often the suspected criminals they detained were immediately released by magistrates. By 1869 the estimated cost of policing was three million pounds annually while the losses from crime were put at double that figure. Not surprisingly local rate payers who funded the local police sought an alternative to the supposed prevention of crime by the distinctively clothed men who patrolled the streets. Sensationalist murders and the attempted assassinations of Queen Victoria—and there were, in all, seven—provided the impetus for the creation of detective departments. Famous authors, especially Charles Dickens, assured the middle classes that detectives would protect them from the dangerous lower orders.[5]

Once successfully arrested, an accused entered a complex system of criminal justice of which the English were somewhat excessively proud. Lord Palmerston, while briefly serving as home secretary, and confident he was the "intensest Englishman in English public life," boasted of the human quality of English justice. The innocent, he declared, had "every possible security which human institutions can [provide] for freedom from unjust punishment." Medical men were duty bound to give certificates of death, and by 1836 there was a national register of deaths. If a doctor suspected a death was unnatural, he was expected to inform the local coroner, who along with his inquest jury investigated both it and any suspiciously sudden demise. Physicians who gave evidence at an inquest received a very modest payment that was doubled if they performed a postmortem or a toxicological analysis. Should the jury return a verdict of willful murder, the accused appeared before magistrates who decided whether or not to commit him or her for trial at the next assizes. There the prisoner had the presumption of innocence and the case had to be proved beyond a reasonable doubt. The jury, dubbed the palladium of British liberties, was ostensibly the "final adjudicator on the facts of the case." On the jury sat 12 men between the ages of 21 and 60 and possessed of minor property qualifications that excluded the lowest of the low. Jurors were not truly reflective of society. The affluent middle classes were usually successful in ensuring their own exclusion with the result that tradesmen and farmers usually dominated the membership. Their levels of education made it unlikely that they would be able to follow and understand fully the evidence of eminent medical scientists. As one senior judge—who, as such, was upper middle class—gave vent to his social prejudice with his opinion that men who labored with their hands all day long lacked the memory, mental power, and habits of thought "necessary to retain, analyze, and arrange [in their own minds] the evidence of, say, twenty witnesses to a number of minute facts given on two or three different days." A decision to convict required the unanimity of the 12. Hence many judges were inclined to tell juries how to vote.[6]

That criminal justice was exclusively male—coroners, juries, solicitors, magistrates, barristers, judges—reflected the extent to which women of all classes were members of a society in which their position was distinctly inferior. In marriage they were devoid of legal independence; wife and husband were in law one person, and that individual was the husband. That subject position did slowly change during the second half of the century. Middle class spouses came to be hailed as the symbolic keepers of society's values, embodiments of a greater, nurturing goodness, of purity and morality. Yet the first four decades of the century saw 131 women executed for murder, and three quarters of them were indicted for the killing of a newborn child. Infanticide continued to emerge as a persistent crime among the lower orders, but the law on this crime was at best hazy and its punishment by no means consistent.

"An Act to Prevent the Destroying and Murthering of Bastard Children" had been placed on the statute book the better part of two centuries earlier. Concealment of an illegitimate birth became a presumption of guilt of murder. However, the severity of the law induced courts and juries to treat the accused with greater compassion during the third quarter of the 18th century. There was a deeper understanding of the motives of mothers who killed—poverty, shame, despair, and preserving honor. Evidence—in the form of baby clothes and linen—that it was the mother's intention to keep and care for the child often sufficed to save her from the gallows. Moreover, surgeons contended that a woman in strong labor was not always possessed of her faculties of reason. She was a special case within the category of insanity. Exhausted by the labor of delivery, unable to sleep, she might kill the child to which she had given birth whilst experiencing a temporary frenzy.

Another important and influential player in the criminal process was the press. Heavy taxation had restricted the growth of the newspaper industry during the first half of the century at a price that would attract a large readership. Instead, single broadsides carried accounts of trials and executions and cost at most a penny. But technological developments, such as steam presses, and the reduction of taxation early in the second half of the century made possible mass production at a price within reach of an ever-expanding sector of society. Improvements in education and the passage of legislation in 1870 further enlarged the literate public. Newspapers, national and provincial, thrived. Sensational murders, inquests, and capital trials were heavily reported and were devoured by this new audience. As a result, the fourth estate frequently played a large role in whether or not sentences of death were commuted. Among the condemned, the press had the easiest time arousing public sympathy for a certain class of women, even in those cases where their victims were their husbands. Consequently, gender and class did on occasion win for the wife a measure of compassion.[7]

CHAPTER ONE

Early Female Murderers

THE FIRST FEMALE POISONER OF THE 19th century, Mary Voce, was executed on Nottingham's Gallows Hill on March 16, 1802. Prior to her trial a handful of young unmarried women had been charged with the willful murder of their infant children. Some were acquitted, and several underwent public execution. All resorted to cruder methods of disposing of the child than poison. Elizabeth Jarvis threw her unwanted child into a pond; Alice Clark buried her baby face down in a dung heap; and Mary Thorpe dropped the weighted bundle holding her week-old baby—whom she lacked the means to support—into a river in Sheffield. Like many young girls from the humblest class of society, she found employment at an early age, in her case 14, in the hard grind of domestic service. Yet few had a harsh word for her. Ever amiable and good-tempered, she exuded "happiness and respectability," which may have made her an inviting target for the man who seduced and betrayed her. She was charged with the "wilful murder of a male bastard child," and her defense—milk fever, which occasionally was likened to a form of temporary insanity—was rejected. She was hanged at York on March 17, 1800, and had the unwelcome distinction of being the first woman so executed in the 19th century. Unlike the unmarried young women, Mary Voce was a wife and a mother.

Mary was born in 1778 in a village outside the city of Nottingham, and the premature deaths of her parents led to her being raised by close relatives. Contemplating her adult life, she thought she would have greater stability and security if she married. She chose Thomas Voce, a former soldier, as her husband, and they had a son. Their life together was reflective of their class, one of poverty and violence. When Thomas left to pursue a military pension, Mary took in lodgers to scrape together a small income and became pregnant by one of them. When he returned, Thomas deserted her, for the duration of his absence meant that he could not be the unborn child's father. She persuaded him to return only for him to convince himself that he had not fathered the earlier child. Mary was, after all, an attractive young woman "in the prime of life and comeliness of person," and she lacked a commitment to fidelity. Penniless, abandoned by her husband, betrayed by her lover, and faced with the prospect of supporting two children on her own, she contemplated prostitution before deciding to poison her infant daughter. The infant's screams of agony brought neighbors rushing to her room; an inquest convicted her of murder and sent her for trial at Nottingham Assizes. Without legal representation, and notwithstanding her vehement protestations of innocence, she was swiftly convicted. Her improbable defense was that, during her brief absence while breakfasting with a neighbor, a mature child had entered her room and, unaware of what the bottle of water contained, administered it to the restless and noisy infant. She had mixed arsenic with the water. The judge exhibited some sympathy in his summation, referring to the violence she had suffered at the hands of her husband only to contend that her infidelity had given Thomas ample reason to punish her. Furthermore, her maternal grief during the infant's fatal illness told him that she had not lost her reason. He thereby disqualified a defense of insanity and thus a measure of clemency.[1]

Deadly poisons were readily available, for in most homes there was ample reason for them to be on hand. Mercuric chloride was a strong laxative and a useful antiseptic credited with the suppression of biting bedbugs and the relief of syphilis. But its metallic taste discouraged its adoption by poisoners of humans. More fatal still was Prussic acid—cyanide—which also had therapeutic uses. Doctors prescribed it for dyspepsia, neuralgia, earache, and skin rashes. Again there was a drawback for the poisoner: its distinctive odor of bitter almonds. Largely odorless, strychnine was an equally swift and efficient killer and another therapy for dyspepsia and constipation. It was arsenic, though, that became the poisoner's first choice. A remedy for a multitude of domestic ailments, it was also used extensively in agriculture. It had no distinctive odor, and a lethal dose might cost no more than a penny. The purchaser could give as a reason for its acquisition the elimination of the large and aggressive rats that had arrived from Norway almost a century earlier. Moreover, in diluted doses arsenic could be employed as a cosmetic with benefits to physique, respiration, and physical appearance. Hence the reputed emergence of arsenic eaters who took it as a tonic or a sexual stimulant. Fowler's solution was a popular arsenic-based tonic first marketed the previous century. Another attraction for the poisoner was the ease of its addition to food and drink. The death, on the other hand, whether accidental or designed, was excruciatingly painful, as the screams of Mary Voce's young child testified.[2]

No one could draw a definite boundary between a poison and

a medicine. the famed toxicologist, Alfred Swaine Taylor, acknowledged. That doctors prescribed medical doses of poisons such as mercuric chloride, excited public as well as legal and scientific concern. In response Taylor stressed the necessity of medical men knowing what dose and in what time it would prove fatal.

The failure of early Stuart legislation to curtail illegitimate births by severely punishing unwed mothers who killed their newborn infants eventually led to its attempted amendment. Lord Ellenborough introduced in 1803 the Malicious Shooting and Stabbing Act. Frightened by the radical revolution in France, he quit the more liberal English Whigs and joined the Conservatives. The legislation made abortion unlawful, whether induced by medicine or any other means, and repealed the 1624 infanticide act. Concealment of a birth, previously judged an admission of intent to murder the newborn, was downgraded to a crime punishable by a sentence of up to two years in a house of correction. Of course, the presumption of innocence lifted the onus of proof from the defendant and placed it where it belonged, on the prosecution. "There was little contemporary understanding of the separation of the body of mother and child, and over the point at which neglect, or an act that resulted in death, became murder with intent." The first defendant tried for willful murder of an infant following the new law's passage was acquitted. Over the next four decades, 48 women were tried at the Old Bailey for murder or manslaughter. Thirteen of them were convicted and sentenced for the lesser crime of concealment of the birth, two were executed, and 33 were acquitted. Meanwhile, in the provinces mothers or wives who murdered more crudely received harsher treatment. Sentences of death were restricted to the most provocative cases in which the defense offered "could not be believed."[3]

From Mary Voce's execution in 1802 until the early spring of 1809, poison did not become the preferred instrument of death of either the unmarried young women about to give birth or those wives who killed abusive husbands. "In the catalogue of human crimes, none manifested so much depravity as that of poisoning," thundered the prosecutor of Mary Bateman, wife and mother of several children, at the opening of her trial for willful murder. "It is one of those of which the commission was most easy and the prevention most difficult," he continued. "When we received injury through the medium of that food, from whence we sought refreshment, or that medicine to which we looked for relief in sickness, we might be truly said to be every hour in danger, and in the midst of life to be in death." Poisoning was always premeditated. Mary Bateman was one of six children whose parents, the Harkers, were respectable and responsible farming folk. She exhibited a "very sharp and active disposition" and gave evidence of intelligence. By the age of 12 she had mastered reading and writing, probably at a Sunday school. Her literacy made her a highly unusual child of so low a social class raised in an agricultural community. The "knavish and vicious disposition" she allegedly possessed during these formative years was in all likelihood the backdating of the evidence given at her trial. While living at home she mixed with the gypsies drawn to the local fair where they told fortunes, presumably for a small fee. In their company, she came to understand how gullible simple folk were and how simple it was to relieve them of what little they possessed. She saw in fraud a comfortable life.[4]

Parents of large families and very limited means farmed out young daughters as domestic servants, and Mary was packed off to the neighboring town of Thirsk four miles away. She became at the age of 12 literally a "maid of all work." Her payment for seemingly endless days of drudgery was bed and board only, so she compensated herself with small thefts. This became a repeated pattern in house after house as she was released from one and moved on to another. Eventually, there was no employment for her in Thirsk. Her next port of call was York, where, caught stealing clothes, she slipped away to the much larger industrializing city of Leeds. Seeking a softer, less dangerous life than that in the mills, she took up the trade of making mantuas, the overgowns of fashionable women. In 1792, after an accelerated courtship, she married John Bateman. He was an astute choice. Physically attractive, he promised to be a sensible husband for a woman aged 24 still finding her way in life. A wheelwright in the age of the wooden wheel, employed for 15 years by a single master and known for the sobriety of his personal life, he was a man of "irreproachable character." He would be able to support his wife and any children, and they were to have five. Beyond that, the acute Mary realized he was not a husband who would interfere when her activities went beyond those of housewife and mother. What began as a sideline, telling fortunes and selling love potions, became a full-time occupation. Her motive for a career of deception and theft was primarily greed enhanced by the sense of power she derived and enjoyed from its success. Then there was her apparent immunity to punishment. Whenever she became notorious in a local community, she and her family, at little inconvenience, moved on to another. When caught thieving small amounts of money from lodgers, she carefully avoided prosecution by returning the sum taken. The Criminal Code still listed an absurdly large number of minor crimes as capital offenses. Certain of her own cleverness, and overconfident, she set her acquisitive sights on the more affluent targets higher up the social ladder.[5]

A pair of Quaker sisters named Kitchen ran a small drapery store. When one of them fell ill, Mary Bateman brought to the store medicines allegedly prescribed by a "country doctor," only for the patient to die less than a week later. This grim news brought the Quaker mother down from Wakefield only for her and the surviving daughter then to fall ill. The ever-present Mary administered their food and medicines, and within 10 days they died. All three Kitchens were buried, and *cholera morbus* was believed to have been the cause. The similarity of their symptoms to those of arsenical poisoning excited the suspicion of a local physician who had briefly treated one of the women; in his opinion her death had "proceeded from poison." He recommended an autopsy, but no family member survived to authorize it, so there was no medical examination of a body. The sisters' creditors soon discovered that the house had been emptied of its contents, and this at a time when the dead women's good friend Mary had sole access to it. She fulfilled the three requirements for a charge of homicide—motive, opportunity, and means in the ready availability of arsenic. She escaped an inquiry into the deaths but aroused a similar suspicion of poisoning five years later. The near fatal poisoning of Joseph Gosling, his wife, and their four children was traced to a cake they had all eaten. It had been left for them by an anonymous donor, perhaps Mary. Happily, a surgeon was on hand, and he saved their lives with large doses of emetics. Analysis detected arsenic in the remnants of the cake. One year after the Gosling episode, Mary Bateman was charged with willful murder of another female.[6]

Her trial opened at York Castle on March 17, 1809. Mr. Justice Le Blanc, who in the past had been a target of the press for allegedly perverting justice out of mistaken humanity, presided. Bateman stood indicted of defrauding, over the course of two full years, the middle class Perigos, William and Rebecca. The total amount was £70 in cash along with clothes and furniture worth a "considerable amount." The understanding was that the "property should be restored." Bateman pretended to consult her spirit medium, the fictional Miss Blythe of Scarborough. Letters "purporting to come" from the medium gave instructions for relieving Rebecca Perigo of the "evil wish" under which she was convinced she labored. When the time came for the restoration to the Perigos of their pledges of money and property Mary Bateman introduced poison into their food. The husband escaped death by not eating it, and, following his wife's demise, he arranged to meet the fraudster and for her to be arrested. Found on her person was a bottle filled with a "deadly mixture." Her motives, the prosecuting counsel argued, were the avoidance of public exposure as an impostor and a cheat and the evasion of punishment. Hence her early requirement that all of the alleged Blythe letters be burned on receipt, thereby ensuring there was no trace of the communications. But one or two escaped destruction.[7]

The trial witnesses included Sarah Stead, who had suggested to her aunt Rebecca that she approach Mary Bateman. She possessed the power, it was believed, to overcome the evil spirits to which a country doctor had attributed Rebecca's worrying "fluttering in her side." In return the Perigos had forwarded cash, clothes, valuable household effects, items of furniture, and a bedstead. They received six bags of powder with a schedule for their addition to a daily diet of Yorkshire pudding. The last bag was the largest, and both Perigos became sick once its powder was added to the pudding. Rebecca ate far more than William, who had disliked the taste, and she vomited. Should they become unwell, they were instructed to take teaspoonfuls of the recuperative honey with which the prisoner had mixed the charm allegedly sent to her by Blythe. The condition of the couple continued to deteriorate, though that of the husband less critically, since he had again taken far less than his wife. She would not allow him to call a doctor, impressed as she had been by the accused's warning that this would vitiate the magical therapies. She died in great pain with severe headaches, diarrhea, yellow vomit, green froth, a heavily swollen tongue, and breathing difficulties. William Perigo did then consult a local surgeon, Thomas Chorley, who, on hearing his symptoms—numbness in his extremities, fever, and pain in the bowels—developed a paste out of the remnants of the flour of the final pudding. He concluded that the couple had been poisoned. Now reduced almost to poverty, Perigo opened the silk purses in which the accused had apparently sown guinea notes and gold as part of the charm process. Instead, their contents were worthless. His confidence in Mary Bateman at last obliterated, he went to the authorities, and she was arrested. The death had not been natural, three medical witnesses testified, naming mercuric chloride as the poison they had identified. Its strong metallic taste may have been the reason why William Perigo took so little of the Yorkshire pudding and the honey. Evidence was also introduced showing that Blythe's letters were in Bateman's handwriting, and that there was no such woman living in Scarborough.[8]

Although she had extracted £70 in cash from the Perigos and had pawned many of the items of furniture and other household goods the couple had surrendered, Mary Bateman had no defense counsel. There was no cross-examination of the widower on his seemingly supernatural ability to remember in precise detail the destroyed letters supposedly received from Blythe. There was no evidence of the accused's purchase of mercuric chloride or of it being found in the Batemans' household. All she offered in her defense was a denial of the charge and its supporting evidence. In summing up, the judge was astonished that in contemporary Britain any individual could be the dupe of the prisoner's frauds. Notwithstanding William Perigo's "extraordinary credulity," the judge was impressed with the widower's clear memory of the destroyed letters. He was critical of the absence of an inquest into the death and of the want of a full examination of the corpse. The black spots of gangrene on the body and an odor so foul that heavy smoking of tobacco would have been required to mask it may have been the explanation. Found guilty by the jury and sentenced to death, Bateman immediately entered a plea of the belly. The judge instructed the sheriff to empanel 12 matrons to decide if she was "with quick child." Several women scuttled out of the court before the doors were locked, and the 12 who failed to flee announced that she was not with child.[9]

Escorted to her cell, the condemned mother suckled the young child she had carried to the prison. The Rev. George Brown, the ordinary (or chaplain), strove without success to convince her to confess her crimes, and on taking communion she carefully omitted the confession. To her husband, who did not visit her after she was convicted, she lamented in a message the disgrace he had suffered, admitted to a great many frauds, denied she had committed murder, and surrendered her wedding ring. When the prison chaplain alluded to the deaths of the Kitchens, her denial of their deaths was ambiguous, and Mary maintained her innocence of murder even as she stood entirely composed on the gallows. Before a crowd that was estimated at 20,000, many of whom had hiked from the area where she had been born and initially raised, she was hanged on March 20, 1809. Her body was cut down after an hour and then dispatched to the Leeds Infirmary for dissection. Before the autopsy there was a public crush to see the body, each viewer paying threepence, thereby raising £30 for charity. Medical students were each charged a half-guinea to observe the initial stages of the dissection. Local medical men paid five guineas, and the grand total so raised was £80. Strips of her skin were tanned into leather and sold, appropriately under the circumstances, as magic charms to ward off evil spirits.[10]

Mary Bateman was a distinctive poisoner. She was not one of the great number compelled by poverty to kill and belonged, as time was to show, to those whose motivation was almost exclusively greed. She preyed initially upon the desperate poor, robbing them of what little they had. The Kitchens stood above this class of society, and had she been convicted of their deaths she might have been considered the first female serial poisoner of the century. The instrument of death according to their symptoms was arsenic, whose lethal use far exceeded that of the other poisons. For the elimination of the Perigos she turned to mercuric chloride despite the difficulty of its administration without its recognition by the victim. She was, as were many female poisoners, a product of that class of society whose struggle to survive was beyond hard. Yet it was one from which she had partially escaped. What Mary Bateman had exhibited was an inability to control her impulses, emotional resilience, an absence of moral judgment, and an aggressive pursuit of benefits without a hint of concern for her victims. Philippe Pinel, a contemporary French scientist, would have diagnosed "moral idiocy."[11]

The lives of very young children of the poor in particular were frequently short. "Wasting diseases," birth injuries, maternal exhaustion, respiratory disorders such as bronchitis and pneumonia, malnourishment, and the common infectious diseases that prospered in their squalid and unhygienic living conditions were all killers. Needy parents farmed them out when still young to work in mines, mills, and domestic service. Consequently, their lives were less than precious. Sad supporting evidence of this came four months later with the trial at the Old Bailey of Rebecca Merrin for the "willful murder of her own child." She was convicted of concealment, not murder, and punished as the Ellenborough Act required. Her fine was one shilling, one twentieth of a pound, and detention for six months in the house of correction. Little had changed, as the women tried in the provinces for murdering their illegitimate children quickly learned. Most had been driven by want to this extreme, and many paid the ultimate penalty following their betrayal by the men who shared the responsibility. The males invariably escaped criminal punishment. The means of death were desperate and brutish. Unwanted children continued to be beaten to death, thrown into ponds and streams, or dropped into privies with female garters tied around their necks. There were exceptions to these run-of-the-mill violent deaths. Jane Cox administered arsenic to her son of 15 months. She did so at the urging of the father, and he paid her a pound as an additional inducement to kill. He was a farmer and a single parent with eight legitimate children to support and was acquitted of complicity. She was hanged by the neck at Exeter on August 12, 1811. Mary Cook's story was much the same. She drowned her illegitimate daughter of 18 months, for the father was another married farmer with legitimate offspring, and was executed at Dorchester on August 1, 1814.[12]

Seven months later the Turners, law stationers on London's Chancery Lane, sat down to dine at their combined residence and place of business. They had four servants, two apprentices, a cook, and a maid, who ate as was usual an hour earlier. Three Turners sat at the dinner table. Orlibar Turner, the senior partner, who now resided with his wife across the Thames in Lambeth. His son and junior partner, Robert, and his heavily pregnant wife, Charlotte, occupied the other chairs. On their menu was rump steak, potatoes, and dumplings, but no sooner had they begun to eat than all three became seriously ill. One of the apprentices, Thomas King, who had not sampled the dumplings and was not unwell, summoned local apothecary Henry Ogilvy. On arrival he probably suspected food poisoning, a common enough complaint, and responded "most judiciously." He evacuated and washed out the stomachs of the victims with "sugar and water mixed with milk and a full dose of castor oil." Having seemingly stabilized them, he left the house. More than four hours later a family friend and a surgeon, John Marshall, appeared on the scene. He found the cook lying on the stairs, she and the other apprentice having tasted or tested the suspect dumplings. In great agony she complained of burning pains in her stomach, of violent retching, severe headache, and great thirst. He instructed her to drink milk and water and then went upstairs to care for the family members. There he found the senior Mrs. Turner, who had come from Lambeth on hearing from the second apprentice of the emergency. She assured Marshall that the suffering of the family members was far worse than that of the cook. Their bowel evacuations were in color a "bright homogeneous green"; he later argued they resembled those produced from a solution of arsenic. He persisted with the apothecary's therapies and sought to relieve the thirst of which all complained by washing out their mouths with cold water. The following morning, March 22, after a restless night, the Turners were all recovering. The vomiting had diminished, and although they still suffered from violent stomach pains, their bowel motions were at least closer to the proper color despite the streaks of green.[13]

Marshall's initial treatment of the Turners appears to have planted in his mind the suspicion that arsenic was the cause of their severe illness. This was strengthened by his friend Orlibar the following day. He drew the surgeon's attention to the white powder he had produced by a simple washing of the contents of the pan in which the dumplings had been cooked. Eliza Fenning, the cook who prepared the ill-fated meal, became an immediate focus of interest. Her family was working class, and of 10 children she alone had survived, which may have convinced her that she was in some way special. Farmed out to domestic service by her parents as a young girl of 14, she impressed one employer as a "hoity-toity, wild, giddy, unsettled sort of girl, curious and inquisitive, and minding what did not concern her." She was unusually literate for a girl of her class and was inclined to exhibit attitudes above those characteristic of her lowly social station. This bred tension within the small servant community. Her treatment of Sarah Peer, who had been the Turners' maid far longer than Eliza had been the cook, was often cavalier. Pretty and petite, Eliza may also have tortured the young apprentices with flirtatious behavior, and her mistress, Charlotte Turner, had witnessed her leaving their room not fully dressed. Sharply reprimanded and provisionally dismissed, her termination was rescinded on the advice of the senior Mrs. Turner. This did not improve the relationship between Charlotte and Eliza. The mistress of the house found the cook, who was about the same age as herself, insubordinate and since the reversed dismissal even wanting in due respect. The cook ignored her objections and prepared yeast dumplings for the dinner on March 21. Two days after the suspected poisoning Orlibar and Marshall informed a magistrate at Hatton Garden Public Office of their suspicions of the cook. He issued a warrant for her arrest on a charge of attempted murder, a capital offense, and it was immediately enforced.[14]

Still ill, Eliza was transported to Clerkenwell Prison's infirmary. Four days later, on March 30, she was back before the magistrate and heard the depositions of the principal witnesses in support of the charge. They were Orlibar Turner, John Marshall, and Charlotte Turner, whose sworn depositions were recorded by the clerk to the several magistrates, he another friend of the Turners. Orlibar Turner recounted the dinner and the serious illness of those who had eaten the dumplings. Apprentice Roger Gadsen had been tempted while in the kitchen by what remained of the dumplings only for the cook to strive to dissuade him from sampling them. He ignored the caution and, eating a piece no larger than a nut, was swiftly "seized with violent vomitings." This did not prevent his dispatch to Fulham to bring the other Mrs. Turner to the house. The cook, Orlibar continued, made no inquiry about the ill and did nothing to assist them. To get around the fact that she was also seriously ill, having for reasons known only to herself eaten a portion of the suspect dumplings, he stated that she partook of them afterwards and "was in consequence seized with similar vomiting." Suspicious of her, Orlibar went in search of the arsenic kept in an office drawer for the purpose of suppressing vermin that destroyed paper. He discovered the poison missing. So he went to the kitchen, where he found the brown pan in which the dumplings were mixed. This he briefly examined with the aid of water and saw a powder that appeared to have separated from the dough. This finding he intended to draw to the attention of the medical men, emphasizing that no one but the cook had made the dumplings.

One. Early Female Murderers

John Marshall recounted his late evening call to the Turner household, where the severely ill included the cook and the apprentice Gadsen. The surgeon's suspicion of arsenic as the cause was confirmed by his examination of the dish handed to him by the senior Turner the following day, which had in his opinion a "quantity of arsenic at the bottom of it." He separated the poison from the dough "by the usual method." When the dough was dissolved in warm water, the poison fell to the bottom. This was one of the relatively rudimentary methods to isolate and analyze arsenic, and none of them were truly reassuring at a time when expert medical evidence was becoming central if not vital in poisoning cases. As chemist Joseph Hume had asserted several years earlier, "all the measures taken to ascertain its presence failed, and where [even] the most delicate tests were ineffectual." However, he had shown by experiments that his test was "greatly superior." Drop by drop a weak solution of ammonia was added to a solution of silver nitrate, and this eventually produced a "bright yellow precipitate of silver arsenic." To his credit, Marshall had called upon Hume's aid, for the silver test required the skill of a chemist. "A novice in chemistry, he warned, might, without unjust design, occasion the death of an innocent person, by want of skill in investigation." But a critic who did not share Hume's confidence that the test was effectively foolproof commented, "I cannot think we shall be justified in influencing the opinion of a jury by tests of this kind until the subject has been much more investigated." Neither Marshall nor Ogilvy was a qualified expert.

Eliza Fenning would go to trial at a time when the medical hierarchy was being more clearly defined in the Apothecaries Act of 1815. Apothecaries traditionally catered to the lower middle class and the lower orders, and while Marshall was always referred to as a surgeon, a step above an apothecary, he was one of the latter who had taken the opportunity with the establishment of the College of Surgeons in 1800 to secure a license from it as an additional qualification. By 1815 surgeon-apothecaries were "the most numerous part of the Profession in Town and Country." The Act added a fourth step to the medical hierarchy of physician, surgeon, and apothecary, which was "chymists and druggists," shopkeepers from whom apothecaries wished to be clearly distinguished.[15]

The case made before the magistrates became a committal hearing, notwithstanding the highly circumstantial nature of the evidence. Charlotte Turner announced that the prisoner had been employed for a little more than six weeks and attributed the souring of their relationship to the cook's indelicacy of conduct, alluding to her exit from the apprentices' room, and the warning she gave her to quit as a consequence. This she compassionately lifted, she claimed. Subsequently, the suspect persistently sought permission to make yeast dumplings, a task at which she claimed to excel. The cook ordered yeast without first consulting her, so she permitted her to make them for the fateful dinner, but on seeing the dough she "firmly believed the deleterious ingredients were then mixed in it" for it was "flat, heavy and black." The young Mrs. Turner was followed by her mother-in-law, who reported arriving at the house at eight o'clock that evening. She encountered the cook on the "stair foot" and commented on the dumplings. The prisoner blamed the ill effects on the milk the maid had fetched and with which "Mrs. Robert [Turner] made the sauce."

The son backed his father's evidence, adding that his personal condition had been far worse than that of the others though he had not tasted the sauce. Roger Gadsen also corroborated the senior partner's testimony. Sarah Peer, who had been a maid of the younger Turners for almost a year, provided the cook with a possible motive. After her near dismissal, Eliza had said that she would never like the family anymore, implying a grievance that might spark revenge. Peer denied entering the kitchen while the dumplings were being made and stated that she never tasted them, had permission to spend the day out from dinner onwards, and had not returned until nine o'clock that evening. When his turn came, William Thiselton, the Hatton Garden police officer, declared that he had apprehended the prisoner and had searched her "box," in which he found nothing suspicious. She had suggested that the poison may have been in the yeast or had been added to the milk by the "very sly and artful" maid. Absent any investigation of either possibility the prisoner was committed to trial on the capital crime. At this point Eliza might have secured bail with two sureties each of £50, or have accepted remand in Clerkenwell Prison for a lengthy period. Her third option was to stand trial rapidly at the Old Bailey. Probably confident that the largely circumstantial case to which she had listened was far from conclusive, undoubtedly unwilling to sit in a Clerkenwell cell for months until the next session of the court, and knowing her parents could not raise the money for bail, she selected the third option, and her trial opened less than two weeks later. Her choice proved to be a calamitous mistake.

At this time justice was on occasion a rare commodity at the Old Bailey. Among its principal performers there was much conviviality. Twice every day, at three o'clock and again two hours later, they were invited by the sheriffs to splendid dinners in the room above the court. The ample food and excellent wines attracted the attention of cynics. The unfortunate wretches on trial, they quipped, were speedily convicted, sentenced to death and hanged or transported to the other side of the world to ensure the meals did not spoil. The Reverend Cotton, the ordinary, whose rubicund visage "betokened the enjoyment of the good things of this life" rather than renunciation of earthly pleasures, "was ever punctual in his attendance at both dinners." The city judges rushed from the dinner table to their seats on the bench, and leading counsels scurried after them. The recorder of London, the Old Bailey's senior judge, Sir John Silvester, had a reputation for being "uncouth and overly severe." He presided over the Fenning trial, but she professed to fear nothing. Her parents had scraped together two guineas to retain a "counselor" to plead on her behalf, and her conscience told her she was not guilty. Her counsel was an Irishman who combined rough manners and gentlemanly feelings, which led him to the sands of Calais across the Channel to fight a duel with his chief competitor for court business. Afterwards they became friends. Peter Alley had a large business in the criminal courts, which he usually handled well. He had secured an acquittal nine years earlier in a similar case, that of Henry Wyatt. A boy of 15, he had been accused by his employer of seeking to poison him, his wife, and his spinster sister by adding arsenic to their coffee. The evidence was entirely circumstantial, Wyatt also drank the coffee and fell ill, and the only medical witness, a Clerkenwell apothecary, identified as arsenic the white substance found in the coffee grounds. His confirmatory test was far from convincing, however, and Alley walked away with much of the credit for the jury's verdict.[16]

At the Fenning trial the witnesses who had given evidence before the magistrates in the form of depositions amplified them with the plain intent to confirm the cook's guilt. Charlotte Turner isolated Eliza in the kitchen with the six dumplings, apart from her own occasional visits. The dough did not rise as it ought and when made was black and heavy instead of white and light. All being very ill they sent for the nearest medical man, the apothecary, and subsequently for the surgeon. Peter Alley in cross-examining her had clearly been told by his client of a coal delivery on the fateful day that would have obliged her to leave the kitchen, thereby giving another access to it and perhaps to the dumplings. This delivery Charlotte denied. Her father-in-law, the senior Turner, followed her into the box and insisted that the accused did not give the "smallest" assistance to the ill, including her heavily pregnant young mistress, and was apparently unconcerned with the family's plight. He immediately suspected arsenic, but was not asked why, and his little experiment the following morning produced a white powder. This was, of course, a common description of the poison. Arsenic had been kept in an office, Orlibar continued, but went missing about two weeks earlier. Although office and drawer were accessible to all, only the accused went there frequently for paper to light the office fire, and, being literate, she could understand the stern written warning on the bottle about the toxicity of its contents. On asking the cook an accusatory question about the malign ingredients she had introduced into the dumplings, she replied that they must have been in the milk brought by Sarah Peer, and that no one but herself had anything to do with the dumplings.

Gadsen's account of the arsenic did not differ significantly from that of the senior master. He went on to say that he ate a walnut-sized piece of the dumpling he discovered in the kitchen—notwithstanding the cook's warning not to do so—and sopped up the remaining sauce with bread. In 10 minutes although very ill he was dispatched to Lambeth to bring the senior Mrs. Turner to the house. He was very sick on the way there and back. He, the maid, and the cook had supped on dumplings the previous evening, which were light, white, and good. He agreed, when asked by the judge, that he would not consider it extraordinary to see the cook go to the office drawer in which poison and paper were kept. The senior Mrs. Turner remembered on her arrival remarking to the prisoner that the "devilish" dumplings had done the mischief. Eliza insisted yet again that instead it was the milk fetched by the maid to make the sauce, and for it her young mistress had been responsible. This the elder Mrs. Turner rejected, and Robert Turner was again quick to support his wife and mother. He had eaten more dumplings than anyone else and had suffered more, he continued to claim, and he denied eating the sauce.

There could be no mistaking Sarah Peer's dislike of the accused. Following the incident over the latter's exit from the apprentices' room, she recalled the cook snapping that she no longer had any liking of the young Turners. She was never in the kitchen during the making of the dumplings, the maid asserted, and went on to corroborate the mistress's denial of a coal delivery on March 21. One had indeed been made, as Eliza clearly informed her counsel, and had he taken the trouble to contact the coal merchant he would have been in a position to point out that neither Charlotte Turner nor Sarah Peer could have been in ignorance of it. This would have cast doubt on the accuracy of their evidence. She was seldom in the office, Peer swore, and was unaware of poison and paper in the drawer. Alley obliged her to admit that she and the accused were rarely on good terms. William Thiselton recalled that the accused had not suspected the flour. She had used it to bake the pie that the apprentices and servants ate without ill effect on March 21 and then used the same flour to make the dumplings. The yeast was a different matter altogether, for after its use she spotted a red sediment at the bottom of it. Delivered two days before the dinner, she had handed it to the maid. Prompted by the judge, Peer insisted that she gave it to Fenning and "saw no more of it." The final witness was the surgeon apothecary. Surprisingly, the first medical man summoned to the house, the apothecary, was not called as a witness. Equally surprising was Alley's failure to cross-examine Marshall, for his belief that the ill had been victims of arsenical poisoning was at best superficial. No less questionable was the surgeon's opinion that a knife used to cut arsenic would be blackened. His statement that he had found arsenic in neither the yeast nor the flour ought to have led to questions about how he reached these decisions.

Eliza Fenning made a short statement in which, following her affirmation of complete innocence, she made five points. She liked and was very comfortable in her place in the Turner household. Her emergence from the apprentices' room "undressed" was a consequence of Gadsen's improper behavior in seeking to take liberties with her. The furious younger Mrs. Turner had intended to dismiss her, but she looked to the elder Mrs. Turner as her real mistress and it was she who quietly secured the threat's removal. The accusation of her master, the senior Turner, that she had failed to assist him when he was seriously ill was unjust because she was herself violently ill. Nor had she any "concern" with the office drawer holding the arsenic, for when in need of paper to light the office fire she simply requested it. Five witnesses introduced by Alley had known Eliza for lengthy periods of time, and they testified to her excellent character, honesty, disposition, and behavior.

While this was happening in the courtroom, William Fenning, the accused's illiterate father, was across the street in a public house seeking someone to write out for him an item of evidence on a piece of paper. It was that his daughter had sent for him on the afternoon of March 21 but this had slipped his mind until that evening. He went to the Turners after nine o' clock and before 10 o' clock, rang the bell, and told the maid who opened the door that his daughter wished to see him. Peer sent him away with a flea in his ear, telling him that Eliza had been sent "upon a particular message by the mistress." No mention was made of his daughter's illness. To ensure this information was heard in court he passed the written note to Alley, who drew it to the attention of the judge, but neither of them paid it any further notice. The agitated father wished to enter the witness box to report that he was denied access to his daughter at a time when she was lying in great agony at the foot of the stairs. The judge declined to hear him out and instructed him to leave the box. Gadsen was recalled, presumably by the judge, only for

Eliza to point out it was not he but the elder apprentice, Thomas King, whom she wanted questioned. He knew, she explained, that she never went to the now notorious office drawer, and when she needed paper to light the fire he handed it to her. The judge declined to hear this witness, despite his important defense evidence. Instead, he encouraged King to contradict her. He and Gadsen had seen her go often to the drawer, King suddenly remembered.

With such decisions Mr. Justice Silvester hampered the defense, and in his summing up he was conspicuously antagonistic to the accused. He stressed the maid's testimony of the prisoner's comment to her that she "should not like Mr and Mrs Turner anymore," of her persistent requests for permission to prepare yeast dumplings, and her warning to Gadsen not to eat the remnants of one because it was "cold and heavy and would do him no good." The poison was conveniently at hand, bought to suppress the vermin that ate the valuable vellum and parchment, but the judge ignored the senior Turner's comment that rats and mice had not been a problem for 18 months. What he chose to dwell upon was the accused's knowledge, her literacy, and that the powder in the wrappings was a deadly poison. He then defined for the jury the two questions they would need to answer. Was arsenic administered to the four victims, and, if so, by whose hand? That the arsenic was in the dough had in his opinion been "fully proved" by the surgeon, who on examining the remnants found that the powder in the bottom of the dish was arsenic. This water test was by no means conclusive, nor were any of the others, including Hume's silver test. This important point escaped the judge's notice. The possibility of poison in the flour, the yeast, or the sauce was reasoned away. But it was another two decades before there was scientific proof of the presence of arsenic. However, in the quantities guessed or estimated by Marshall, the poison would have proven fatal to those who ate the dumplings, yet all had survived. The apothecary who was first on the scene had treated the ill successfully with a therapy similarly employed in cases of common food poisoning. He was not called to give evidence. With the dumplings named by the judge as the intended instrument of death, the identity of the responsible person was a foregone conclusion. The cook, he reminded the jury, had given no assistance to the master and mistress. That she was very ill herself escaped his notice. He admitted that the evidence was entirely circumstantial but assured the 12 occupants of the jury box that often "circumstances were more conclusive than the most positive testimony." The jurors wasted no time convicting Eliza Fenning of attempted murder. She considered the verdict unjust and anticipated a sentence of at least six months imprisonment. Then, on April 14, the judge sentenced her to be hanged. Stunned, she was carried from the dock "convulsed with agony and uttering frightful screams." Her remaining hope was a commutation of the death sentence and perhaps transportation to a colony, although she thought death would be preferable to life in another country with "such depraved wretches."[17]

More than three months were to elapse before Eliza mounted the gallows at Newgate Prison on July 26. During this long delay her case was taken up by important elements of the press, and their attitudes were partisan. Those supportive of the Conservative government were hostile to the condemned woman, and one in particular, the *Observer*, relentlessly blackened her character. Published weekly, it thrived on crime. Newspapers somewhat aligned with the more liberal Whig opposition, led by the *Examiner*, were far more sympathetic, and she took the trouble to write a letter of thanks to the editor. A petition for royal clemency was addressed to the prince regent, and letters went to both the lord chancellor and the home secretary, the two political figures who might allow her to escape the hangman. That to the former drew his attention to the dubious evidence on which she had been convicted. It noted the "mistakes" of Charlotte Turner in respect to the cook's isolation in the kitchen and the failure to call Thomas King, who had been in the front kitchen while she was in a back room, to the witness box. The convicted had herself been seriously ill, which apothecary Ogilvy would have corroborated. What is more, he had treated the ill long before Marshall arrived on the scene and might have raised other "favorable circumstances, yet he was not examined on the Trial."

At the eleventh hour there were two dramatic developments. A young chemist, Thomas Wansbrough, had with experiments proved that arsenic did not prevent dumplings from rising or make them dark and heavy and did not blacken cutlery. He brought these discoveries to the attention of the Turners, for they were prosecuting Eliza, in the hope of securing their support for a respite of the execution while his findings were further investigated. Hope was dashed by Marshall and Silvester, who dismissed them as worthless. Another chemist, Gibson, employed by a firm of chemists and druggists, remembered Robert Turner declaring the previous October that he ought to be securely confined lest he destroy himself and his wife. This suggestion of the junior partner's fragile mental stability did not have the desired effect on the family or the relevant authorities. The Turners agreed to visit the condemned cook, perhaps in response to the mounting public hostility towards them, but it did not go well. Orlibar and Robert did contemplate lending their names to another plea for clemency until the recorder warned them that it might divert attention from the doomed Eliza and excite suspicion of themselves. She went to her death attired in virginal white; refused to confess as the rubicund chaplain hoped, for she did not trust him at all; and again protested her entire innocence. Her father found the fee to reclaim her body from dissection, as the law allowed, and she was buried in the churchyard of St. George the Martyr, Bloomsbury. At the funeral mourners were numbered in the thousands, and afterward the Turners' place of business was besieged by angry demonstrators.[18]

Against the background of the widespread popular belief that Eliza had been the victim of judicial murder, John Marshall made an ill-advised and unwise attempt to prove her guilt. He gave a more detailed account of the treatment and convalescence of the victims and cautioned, now aware of Wansbrough findings, that the blackened knife had not been "complete" proof of arsenic. Of course, he had identified it as such in court, and it was a factor in the cook's conviction and execution. He cited her cautioning Gadsen against the dumplings and then eating them herself. "This deliberate action carries the strongest proof [of the justice] of her conviction," he argued. Realizing she would be identified as the "cause of the mischief," Marshall continued, she was determined "to destroy herself to evade justice." Her resistance of all remedy, such as the milk and water he prescribed, was for him additional proof of her guilt. She would have gone to the assistance of the pregnant Mrs. Turner had she been innocent. To this he attached a misquote of the trial evidence, asserting that she had been heard in the kitchen to say that she would have her "spite" on her mistress. In short, she had the "idea of premeditated revenge." In her book collection had been found one whose passages concerning methods of procuring an abortion had clearly been consulted. Although Marshall did not name arsenic, it was a known and dangerous means to that end, and Charlotte Turner was heavily pregnant. For the surgeon this was one way the cook could have revenge on her young mistress. His final proof was the cook's efforts, as he interpreted them, to incriminate the maid and the elder apprentice.[19]

A counterblast to Marshall was published in November. A witheringly harsh commentary on the trial sought to demonstrate "that the law has been converted into an engine of oppression, and an instrument of vengeance." The authors were William Hone, a radical journalist and thus an inviting target of the Tory government, and John Watkins. Behind the latter's less notorious name the charges of gross injustice might be published with greater safety. Titled *Important Results of an Elaborate Investigation into the Mysterious Case of Elizabeth Fenning*, it pulled no punches on the trial. In the nation's capital and with the lives of a respectable middle class family thought imperiled from taking poison, surely the best in medical aid would have been engaged. This should have been no problem in the metropolis. "No apology could be made for so strange a neglect, and instead of a regular physician two apothecaries were summoned in succession on the same day." And one of these was Marshall, a friend of the family, who did not see the patients for several hours, by which time they had somewhat recovered. Yet, he alone was examined as to the symptoms and their cause. Essential to justice was the examination of the first apothecary on the scene, Ogilvy, and he should have stated to the court all that he observed. Marshall did not contradict the testimony that arsenic would not prevent dough from rising, and he was so ignorant of the poison that he swore it would blacken a knife.

Similarly, "unfortunate in the extreme" for the accused was the fact that the clerk to the magistrates who took the depositions against her was yet another Turner family friend. He was then employed against her as the solicitor of the prosecuting Turners. Contradictory evidence was deposed against the prisoner at the trial. Charlotte Turner, a prosecutrix, swore coal was not delivered on the day of the poisoning, and this the maid corroborated, but both were in error. They could not have missed the delivery. Added to this was the influence of class. The prosecutors by their silence encouraged the circulation of aspersions upon Eliza while she lived, and they even entertained them after she had been executed. One such example was the baseless story that she had twice attempted to poison a family for whom she worked before joining the Turner household. Masters and mistresses "were incessantly devoted to the vociferous execration of the wickedness of servants, who poison those who give them bread and work." The presumption was of the servants' "murderous inclinations." Of course, the trial had been decided by the judge in his summary, and its absence from the Old Bailey reports raised grave doubts of the verdict. Silvester had overlooked anything favorable to Fenning and had assailed her with "almost unbelievable ferocity."[20]

The sensational findings of the *Elaborate Investigation* and the questions asked of the "probity of English justice [were] wholly unprecedented." Hone's modern biographer argues that "there had never been a comparable exposé of injustice." Beyond that, his "demolition of the Crown's evidence against Fenning, and his revelations of the subsequent efforts to alter the judicial record, coupled with a poignant tale of human suffering, was one of the first detailed criminal investigations conducted by a journalist." This was a wretched and audacious attempt "to shake the confidence of the people in the administration of public justice," as organs supportive of the government put it. But the Fenning case did not slowly fade away. Among the lower order, rumors circulated of deathbed confessions to the crime, among them that of Robert Turner, who had died in the hospital after reportedly confessing that he had mixed the poison in the food prepared by Eliza Fenning and was, consequently, guilty of the offences for which she was executed. The *Examiner* reported the story on June 14, 1829, and while it acknowledged that it did not know if the tale was correct, it did think it was very likely. Robert Turner had on one occasion betrayed symptoms of insanity while seeking to purchase arsenic, only to be refused by the gentleman of the store. Indeed, that gentleman carried this information to the recorder, the *Examiner* claimed, but Mr. Justice Silvester refused to act upon it. This episode confirmed that newspaper's conviction that there was "not sufficient evidence to convict" Eliza Fenning.

The middle classes read in 1857 the widely reported closing address of the defense counsel of Madeleine Smith. This upper middle class young woman was accused of poisoning with arsenic her lower middle class lover, who obstructed her path to a very desirable marriage. Her counsel reminded the Scottish jury of the tragic case of Eliza Fenning, who had been hanged asserting her complete innocence only for her death to be followed by confessions by other persons. He implored the jury not to add this case to the existing catalogue of injustice. They returned a verdict of "Not Proven," a Scottish oddity that amounted to an acquittal. Reporting on this, the *Leicester Chronicle* declared that Eliza had been executed for a crime she never committed. A decade later, on July 13,1867, Charles Dickens published in his journal *All the Year Round* a long article by a contributor under the title "Eliza Fenning (The Danger of Condemning to Death on Circumstantial Evidence Alone)."[21]

Eliza was but another victim of the "Bloody [criminal] Code." Not until 1861 was the penalty of death removed from her alleged crime of attempted murder and confined to murder, espionage, treason, arson in royal dockyards, and piracy with violence. There was, however, a slowly mounting public unease over the excessive number of executions that found expression in such national newspapers as the *Morning Post*. Clearly, the threat of the gallows was no longer the deterrent the lawmakers had imagined. Hence the search commenced for punishments that would deter criminals without a "profligacy with human life." Penal transportation to the other side of the world for life was one, for in the opinion of prominent counsels the dispatch of a convict to Australia had a sobering effect on his or her family and friends. Eliza would have preferred death. The construction of modern penitentiaries and additional houses of correction promised to be of help, as would the creation of efficient police forces to prevent crime. Robert Peel, the home secretary during the 1820s, followed a dual strategy of securing the deletion of minor crimes from the "Bloody Code" and creating London's unified Metropolitan Police. Three thousand men—all at least five feet, seven inches tall and dressed in instantly recognizable uniforms—patrolled the streets of the metropolis.[22]

Those members of society most likely to find themselves in conflict with the law belonged to that vast section of it, the lower orders. Hone and Watkins, in commenting on the Turners, stated that the plaintiffs' "opulence was pitted against the Humble Poverty of their servant maid." Defendants occupying the bottom rungs of the social ladder were cynical about ever receiving justice. The high speed, even of capital trials—Eliza's was completed in a day—and the rapid return of verdicts, usually in no more than a few minutes, did not inspire confidence in the law. Although counsel might be retained, the cost was normally beyond the means of the poor and the investment often of dubious value. Eliza's parents somehow scratched together the two guineas needed for Alley, but he could do no more than cross-examine the prosecution's witnesses and did not do that particularly well. Not for a number of years were such counsels permitted to sum up the defense for juries. Fairness for female defendants was particularly problematic, the world of the law being exclusively male. "There were no women coroners to inquire into suspicious deaths," no women inquest jurors, no women magistrates at committal hearings, no women judges presiding over trial, no women solicitors or barristers, and no women jurors sitting in judgment on the accused. Women were denied the franchise throughout the century and, not sitting in Parliament, had little direct influence on the legislation that governed their lives.

The enduring controversy following the execution of the unfortunate Eliza served as an unintentional advertisement for the poison she allegedly used. Arsenic, " the poison of poisons" , cost next to nothing and was readily available, for its numerous domestic uses provided potential poisoners with ample reasons for its possession. What is more, it was relatively easy to administer in food without immediately alarming the victim, who soon suffered intense pain in the stomach and bowels, violent retching and vomiting, and acute diarrhea. Death usually occurred between 12 and 36 hours. In little more than a half decade following Eliza's controversial execution, there was a sudden and startling spurt in arsenical poisonings by women.[23]

CHAPTER TWO

A Rising Tide of Arsenic

MARY THORPE, MARY VOCE, AND Mary Bateman had proved that among the gentler sex were women capable of committing the worst of crimes: murder. All three of them, and Eliza Fenning, were rooted in that class of society whose members were engaged in a daily struggle simply to survive. Their sorry plight did not benefit greatly from the Evangelical Revival of the late 18th century that carried over into the 19th and grew steadily stronger. The assumption was that the inculcation of true religion was essential for a society both moral and virtuous, but the expanding middle class was convinced that the drunkenness rife among the lower orders curbed their moral education. What could be expected of children raised in families and in neighborhoods "without any conception of purity"? Another impediment was the "religious justification of the subjection of women." St. Peter and St. Paul referred to women in their Epistles as the weaker vessel, for which scientists later provided biological confirmation. Men, went the argument, were in possession of reason, faculties, and muscular power that made them the natural governors of society whom women should obey. How much of the male middle class doctrine of patriarchy penetrated down to the lowest rungs of the social ladder may be difficult to assess correctly. In his epochal *Commentaries on the Laws of England*, however, Sir William Blackstone commented in the mid–18th century that the "lower rank of people" were ever fond of the old Common Law. Husbands who were laborers understood it to grant them the right to inflict domestic chastisement so long as the stick they used was "no thicker than one's thumb." Rarely were struggling poor families blessed with great domestic harmony, hence violence was all too common. Gruesome cases of marital conflict attracted the attention of the press, such as the desperate and battered wife who stabbed her drunken husband and fled when he unexpectedly regained consciousness. She assured the policeman she bumped into on the street that she would commit murder if forced to return to the man who had for years subjected her to unbearable physical abuse.[1]

Two. A Rising Tide of Arsenic

The execution of Eliza Fenning was followed by two decades during which the murder of husbands by wives naturally caught the attention of the media. This was a crime of "petty treason" under the law, and the guilty spouses were subjected to an especially demeaning passage to the gallows. They were drawn through the assembled crowd on a hurdle, a makeshift sleigh to which they were harnessed. Susannah Holroyd purchased arsenic in April 1816 and gave as her reason the suppression of rodents. Her true motive may have been her "connexion to another man." The following morning, she added the poison to her spouse's coffee and to his gruel. This less than appetizing dish was no more than a quart of water in which oats or barley had been mixed. Her husband refused to consume more of the gruel because of its peculiar taste. Their hungry son, aged eight, was less discriminating. Both were soon dead, as was the infant daughter of the couple's lodger. Gossips soon murmured that this baby was not Susannah's first infanticide. The discovery of arsenic in the husband's stomach, though the validity of the analysis was still questionable given the lack of a truly convincing scientific test of its presence, saw her indicted for willful murder. It was the number of her alleged victims that distinguished her crime. Her defense was that she had been dispatched for the poison by her husband and knew nothing of what he did with it after she handed it to him. She was not believed, and on the gallows she confessed to his murder, asserted that he had passed the gruel innocently to their son, and claimed that their infant had died of natural causes. At the baby's tender age of eight weeks nothing was more common. She was hanged on September 16, 1816.[2]

Infidelity was often the motive for killing one's own husband, mariticide, and arsenic was the preferred weapon of choice among wives of the lower orders. Not only was it simple to obtain for next to no cost and relatively easy to administer successfully, but also its posthumous identification was rarely if ever genuinely convincing. Nevertheless it was all too common for symptoms neither exclusively nor definitively arsenical to be accepted as proof. Rebecca Worlock was infuriated by her husband's jealousy and his use of opprobrious epithets. She unwisely persuaded a stranger to accompany her to a druggist's on her quest for arsenic and foolishly declared that she intended "to do for" the "hell of a fellow at home." Circumstantial as this evidence was, three medical men conducted the autopsy on the deceased and then disagreed on the cause of death. After a trial of eight hours, the jury took a mere seven minutes to find her guilty of murder. She was hanged.

Mary Woodman's motive was more complex. She was accused of murdering her "mild mannered" husband with a concoction of lead oxide, laudanum, and arsenic while engaged in an extramarital relationship with an itinerant fiddler. What is more, she stood to collect £20 from burial clubs on the death, so there was a financial inducement for homicide. Life insurance initially had the middle class as its target, but the 19th century saw the establishment of a wide variety of associations to serve the poor who for a few pennies a week in premiums sought a private funeral for a dead family member and avoidance of the shame of a burial in an unmarked collective grave. Mary Woodman was hanged.[3]

Earlier convictions of women for poisoning, especially with arsenic, had often seemed questionable. In the absence of a confession, where was the reliable proof that the poison had been the cause of death? This concern rose again when Mary Wittenback went to trial at the Old Bailey in the summer of 1827. The Grand Jury had returned an indictment for the willful murder of her chronically unfaithful husband, Frederick. They had been wed 20 years, and of their seven children only three, all girls, had survived to adulthood. With Frederick about to go off yet again on an amatory adventure, Mary made a suet pudding for his midday meal. He was soon vomiting and complaining of intense pain in his legs and blindness. "I think I am poisoned," he told one concerned neighbor, and "thought he was done for." Charlotte, one of the three daughters, was sent to fetch Dr. Dillon, the surgeon of St. Pancras parish. His delay in arriving led a neighbor to recommend another surgeon, Mr. Jackson. Mary objected to him on the grounds he would be "too dear." Another neighbor then called at Jackson's "shop," and he sent an emetic to the house that "operated considerably." The house-surgeon of St. Pancras Workhouse, Charles William Wright, who boasted 10 years' experience, next appeared on the scene. The ill man was still vomiting "considerably" and complaining "of a great and burning [pain] at the pit of his stomach." Convinced that the patient had taken "something of a poisonous nature" but uncertain what it was, Wright resorted to a stomach pump. By this time the wife was also sick, and so in pumping everything out of her stomach he was confident he had saved her life. When the husband died, Wright opened his stomach and from its inflammation deduced "some mineral poison was the cause." On testing the little that remained of its contents he was unable to find either arsenic or "any other poison." That did not dissuade him from offering an opinion that the stomach had been "so completely washed out, as to have no trace of poison." He declined to swear that the deceased "did die of poison, or that he did not." Nonetheless, it was his belief "from all the symptoms" that the patient had been poisoned. What was still lacking was supporting scientific evidence.

When Garrett Dillon finally reached the house in the early hours of the morning, having been summoned again, this time by Mary, he found her husband "almost in a dying state." He agreed with Wright that "the symptoms were produced by mineral poison being taken into the stomach," every one of the medical men being "conformable" to that "idea." In preparation for court, Mary Wittenback had acquired by whatever means a defense counsel, Clarkson. Under cross-examination Dillon denied that a stomach pump, even if in inexperienced hands, was "a violent means to have recourse to." He confessed his own lack of experience with the instrument and admitted that "it might produce inflammation [of the stomach] if used roughly, and in an injudicious way." Presumably, Wright had been far more careful. Similarly, he granted that a strong emetic might cause inflammation "but in the majority of cases it would not." There had been no conclusive identification of arsenic, however. Yet the widow was convicted of poisoning her husband and immediately collapsed into hysterical screaming. Her crime being "petty treason," she was dragged to the gallows on a "hurdle" and hanged at Newgate on September 17, 1827.[4]

Yet another poor and desperate young woman was Jane Scott, who, at the age of 15, resorted to prostitution. A son was born, and she neither abandoned him nor effected his death. An opportunity opened to improve her wretched lot when George Richardson desired to marry her once he could afford to do so. He set about acquiring the required means, and she quickly followed suit. Having long stolen from her parents, she cold-bloodedly resolved to kill them. She assumed she would share in what remained of their means, and what she had her eye on was their furniture. For her parents she prepared a bowl of porridge into which in all likelihood she mixed arsenic, and a day later both were dead. An inquest was held, and the coroner's jury convicted her of poisoning them. At her trial she was acquitted of murdering her father but found guilty of killing her mother. She then made a full confession in which she listed her victims: her mother; her son, perhaps to open the bridal path; and her niece, in an especially cruel act of revenge on her sister following a dispute between them. She qualified as a serial killer and went to the gallows at Lancaster Castle on March 22, 1828. There she suffered the terrifying torment of a bungled execution, much to the horror of the spectators. In her case, there was no lingering doubt about her conviction, and that could also be said of Kezia Westcombe and her lover, Richard Quaintance. They entered into a murderous conspiracy, resolving to poison their current spouses with arsenic he acquired. But there was a slip between cup and lip when Quaintance's wife declined to drink the tea he had laced with the poison. The pair's plot was exposed, and they went to the gallows in August 1829, each holding the other responsible for the conspiracy yet each admitting individual guilt.[5]

One more hard-hearted young poisoner was Mary Ann Higgins, who murdered the uncle who had raised her from childhood when the death of his brother (another of her uncles) left her, she assumed, the sole beneficiary. To hasten the passing of the man who had been like a father to her, she served him pea soup laced with arsenic and told the coroner at the inquest on this sudden death that she had been goaded to act by her boyfriend, who backed his words with physical violence. Both were sent to trial. He was acquitted for want of sufficient evidence, while she was convicted. Reportedly, 15,000 turned out to watch her execution. Public executions were becoming "a species of festive comedy or light entertainment." The list of arsenic poisoners continued to lengthen, but science was about to prove that definitive evidence of arsenical poisoning could be found in a corpse.

Robert Christison, a Scot, had studied analytical chemistry in France under the noted European scientist Mathieu J.B. Orfila. He returned home to Edinburgh, took the chair in Medical Jurisprudence at the university there, and in 1829 published his *Treatise on Poisons*. This was "the first comprehensive nineteenth-century treatise on forensic toxicology originally published in English." Criminal poisoning depended for its success, he wrote, on its "imitating the effects of natural disease." This made arsenic peculiarly dangerous, not least because of its ready availability in lethal doses for no more than a penny or two. Practically tasteless, odorless, and moderately soluble, it was simple to administer. Moreover, a doctor attending a violently ill patient would often ascribe the death to one of the common complaints and diseases whose symptoms bore a similarity to those of the poison. Nevertheless, Christison assured his readers that the detection of arsenic in a body remained possible if the analyst were truly skilled. Consequently, he stressed the necessity of both exhaustive autopsies and complete searches throughout the entire body for traces of the poison.[6]

A poisoning trial in Bristol in 1835 could claim to be the first to capture the attention of the entire nation, reported as it was by the provincial as well as the national press. One reason for such "unprecedented" interest was the lengthy delay between the crime and its investigation. The absence of any indisputable evidence of arsenical poisoning allowed the death to be considered natural. The judge, in his opening remarks when a trial was eventually held, was unable to recall a similar one in which there was such an extraordinary interval between the death and its investigation. He thanked "the wonderful ways of Providence in bringing every particular of the mysterious tragedy to light." Was not the accused a woman of apparent "respectability," although her reputation would not have survived a thorough examination? Mary Ann

Burdock, as she was known, owned and operated a successful lodging house, which enabled her to afford full legal representation in court. The trial was one at which the recorder of Bristol, Sir Charles Wetherell, was to preside. He was obliged to sneak into the city. A committed Conservative, he had opposed the Parliamentary Reform Bill of 1832 and was despised to the point of violence by its more liberal population.[7]

The accused, Mary Ann Williams, was equally repugnant to the general public. Born in 1805, she had been raised in a family of agricultural laborers. As was customary for daughters of her class, she was expected to support herself and contribute to the family income by finding employment as a domestic servant. At the age of 19 she arrived in Bristol and found employment, although, like many others in her situation, she succumbed to the temptation to compensate herself more adequately for long days of ill-paid drudgery. That path led to dismissal, so she sought a supportive male and found him, she thought, in Charles Agar, a tailor. They married in 1819, but it was not long before he left her on discovering she was unfaithful. A dalliance or two later she was running a respectable lodging house with Charley Wade, a ship's steward, whose name she took. The mother of two children, one of each sex, whose paternity was uncertain, she supported the chronically unwell Wade. He needed investment to go into business, and Mary's avaricious eyes fell upon a recent lodger, Clara Ann Smith. An elderly widow of 60, she was believed to be in possession of considerable wealth. She had married a successful ironmonger, John Smith, from whom she inherited "ample" property on his death in 1828. Her habit was to move from one lodging to another, and there were signs in 1835 that she was planning to quit that of Mrs. Wade, which probably induced the landlady to act swiftly. Mrs. Smith kept a strongbox beneath her bed in which it was believed she guarded her wealth. The rumor was that the box held hundreds of pounds in gold coins; £100 in bank notes; and a collection of valuable jewelry, trinkets, and gold watches. Suddenly, Mrs. Smith died after several hours of severe stomach cramps and vomiting and was hastily laid to rest in the cemetery of the local church. To anyone who made inquiries about her end, Mrs. Wade remarked somewhat unnecessarily that she had died poor. What did not go unnoticed was the lodging house keeper's ability soon afterwards to deposit £500 in a bank and loan another £400 to Wade to start a trade venture. When he too succumbed to illness, she inherited his business and swiftly married bigamously, for legally she was still the wife of Agar. The new husband was another tailor, Paul Burdock.[8]

Mrs. Burdock had every reason to be content with her life. She had relative youth, being no more than 30, was physically attractive, and owned a highly respectable lodging house whose furnishings she intended to improve. She alone knew that her comfort resulted primarily from the successful poisoning of Mrs. Smith a year earlier, a death ascribed to natural causes. After so many months buried in the churchyard of St. Augustine's Church, her remains seemed unlikely to reveal traces of poison if disinterred. Mrs. Burdock's personal satisfaction proved short-lived, however. A persistent and inquiring nephew of the late Mrs. Smith appeared on the scene and refused to believe that she had died poor. He had expected to benefit handsomely from his aunt's passing and industriously nourished a suspicion about her sudden death and swift burial. Why, he asked, had Mrs. Burdock's situation improved so dramatically soon after the death? Then there was the statement by Mary Allen, the young servant assigned by her mistress to Mrs. Smith. She informed the investigators who interviewed her that she had seen Mrs. Burdock administer a yellow powder to the elderly lodger. This was enough for the coroner to order an exhumation—the first to take place in England "for the purpose of chemical analysis."[9]

Three days before Christmas, a postmortem was conducted before several surgeons at the Bristol Royal Infirmary. The examiners were struck by the well-preserved condition of the body, and with such discoveries many undertakers were quick to employ arsenic as an embalming fluid. The surgeons, noting a "large quantity of viscid yellow matter," removed the internal organs and forwarded them to the Bristol Medical School for analysis. This was undertaken by William Herapath, a founder of the school and its first lecturer in chemistry and toxicology. Born and raised in a successful brewing family, control of which he assumed on his father's death, he studied chemistry to advance his career as a maltster. He liked this science so much that he soon made it his career. Skillfully conducting innovative, delicate tests, he converted the yellow matter into yellow arsenic, proving that the dead woman's stomach had contained a considerable quantity of that poison. On the penultimate day of the year, the inquest "found that Mrs. Smith had died from arsenic administered by Mrs. Burdock." Arrested, she awaited trial at the next assizes on the charge of willful murder. Had she been indicted and tried for theft, she later remarked, the hundreds of stolen pounds would have been seized. Instead, the £500 would now go to her children.[10]

The inquest unleashed the public's intense hostility towards the accused. Whenever seen she was verbally assailed with "execrations and groans" and "frightful and discordant yells." Her legal advisers made an application for the trial to be moved out of Bristol, for it was plain that a fair trial there was unlikely. The jury would be drawn from a populace "who exhibited a strong feeling against the prisoner." Should she somehow be acquitted, it was feared that serious disturbances would ensue "from the fury of the lower orders." Not until 1856, in the sensational case of William Palmer, was an application for the removal of a trial granted.[11]

Heavily escorted into the city, the recorder took his seat at nine o'clock in a court "filled almost to suffocation." The streets leading to it were choked with people throughout the day. Mrs. Burdock maintained her composure all through an extraordinarily long day of evidence, and the court did not rise until close to midnight. Saturday was to prove equally exhausting, but she exhibited little sign of tiring. Her countenance remained "altogether of a pleasing description." She paid close attention to what was said and from time to time spoke to her solicitor when she wished a question put to a witness. The prosecution called 19 of them over the two days and reminded the jury of the presumption of innocence until the contrary was proved. The prosecutor presented evidence of the prisoner's less than good circumstances when known as Mrs. Wade and told of her securing £700 soon after Clara Smith's demise. The two decisive witnesses were Mary Anne Allen, hired at the age of 14 for three shillings a week to wait upon Mrs. Smith, and William Herapath. A lodger, Evans, testified that the prisoner had requested he purchase arsenic for her, and a second witness swore it was yellow arsenic. Evans handed it to Mrs. Burdock in a small paper parcel. The very young Miss Allen remembered her employer making a basin of gruel for Mrs. Smith and adding two pinches of the yellow powder from the packet Evans had described. She inquired what it was for and was told it was simply something to ease Mrs. Smith as she was so "griped." Allen had noted both the care with which her mistress washed and cleaned her hands after handling the yellow powder and the strange reddish color of the gruel following its addition. She had also been cautioned by the prisoner not to eat anything Mrs. Smith left, explaining that the lodger spat in it. She suggested the summoning of a doctor when Mrs. Smith was very ill, but Mrs. Burdock rejected the idea even though the lodger became extremely ill after 30 minutes and died in dreadful agony no more than two hours later. Allen also watched the prisoner take a variety of valuable adornments and items from the corpse before it was laid out within 48 hours for burial in a "very common way." When paid, Allen continued, she was instructed not to mention the circumstances to anyone—least of all the addition of the yellow powder to the gruel.[12]

Herapath was the decisive witness. He explained more than a year after the death how he had found yellow arsenic in the yellow powder seen in the stomach of the corpse. Realizing how difficult the science would be for the jurors to understand, he brought to court the metallic arsenic he had obtained by his innovative steps. Clara Smith's body had contained enough poison to cause her death, he emphasized. In cross-examining Herapath, the defense strove to show that the color could have been caused by something other than arsenic, possibly cadmium. This Herapath rejected outright, for he was the "English discoverer of cadmium." Here at last was a genuine expert giving authoritative evidence. Herapath's reputation was made, and eight years later he was still being hailed as the "celebrated analytical chemist of Bristol, by whose skill the poison was detected in the stomach of Mrs. Smith."[13]

The defense called six witnesses to attest to the prisoner's character. The first of them, Charlotte Thomas, had lived with Mrs. Smith in October 1833. Mrs. Burdock, she swore, had been very kind to the very ill elderly lady and had inquired if she should send for a doctor. Mrs. Smith had snapped that she did not want a doctor to murder her. The likelihood of the affluent widow's departure probably prompted Burdock to dispense a far larger dose of arsenic than she had previously administered. This was revealed a day after the trial in a confession of sorts the prisoner made to a female acquaintance. Charlotte Thomas, on taking the stand, endorsed Mary Ann Burdock's opinion of the widow as practically penniless and an alcoholic. She used to fetch brandy and rum for her every day or night, she told the court, wine three times a week, and medicine every other day. The money to pay for them came from the prisoner. Nor had she seen "money, watches, trinkets or parchments" in the possession of the deceased.[14]

After two exceedingly long and tiring days of evidence the recorder delivered on the third day his summing up, which took him nine hours to read. The members of the jury would decide whether the prisoner lived or died, he stated, and there were three points on which they must make up their minds. Had poison been the cause of death, had the poisoning been carried into effect by the prisoner, and had she known she was poisoning the deceased? If they had conscientious and rational doubts, they must acquit her. He took particular care, however, to remind them of the evidence of Herapath. The chemist "had manifested great nicety in making his experiments, which were not only satisfactory to himself, but also to every competent judge who had witnessed them."[15]

The jury deliberated for no longer than 15 minutes before reaching a verdict. With their return imminent there was brief chaos in the court as those present struggled to secure the best view of the prisoner. Eventually order was established and the foreman in the "most solemn manner, and evidently with a great degree of feeling, returned the verdict of Guilty." After the sentence of death, Mary Ann Burdock was taken to the prisoner's room beneath the court, where she exhibited the "most perfect indifference to the awfulness of her situation." She sat on a stool and immediately requested a glass of beer; a second helping was refused her. On Tuesday she saw her relatives, among them her children and her brother, all of whom were greatly distressed "by the hardihood of her demeanour." She was hanged on Wednesday before a crowd that, according to some estimates, numbered 50,000.[16]

What then was the significance of Mary Ann Burdock's conviction and execution? The recorder, as he had informed the jury, knew of no other case where so long a passage of time had elapsed between a poison death and its successful investigation. The "idea of scientific analysis was new," and its usefulness to the law had at last clearly been shown. This case was "the first in a rapidly increasing series of prosecutions facilitated by the legal system's mounting reliance on improved methods of chemical analysis." Three years after Burdock was hanged, the Medical Witnesses Act enabled coroners to have doctors attend inquests and carry out necessary autopsies and toxicological analyses. Fortunately, there was a "ready supply of skilled medical men due to the establishment during the previous decade of medical schools and laboratories, such as that in Bristol of which Herapath was one of the founders." Not that all doctors responded willingly to the call for which their recompense was far from generous. Meanwhile, printers of broadsides, usually single sheets of paper, directed at the lower orders, were given fresh encouragement. One large sheet usually provided an account of the crime, the trial, the confessions of guilt, the dying speeches, and graphically depicted the hangings. Indeed, fresh broadsheets were frequently printed each day of a long trial. During and in the aftermath of the Burdock trial, newspapers, national and provincial, greatly expanded their coverage of criminal dramas. Mary Ann Burdock was for a while the "most notorious nineteenth-century poisoner," her name a "household word," and she contributed to a growing popular unease over the "possibility of poisoning by the preparers of food and drink in a household."[17]

More eye-catching was the means of willful murder of illegitimate children by desperate unmarried women, who were undoubtedly ignorant of Mary Voce's employment decades earlier of arsenic. Ann Sherrington and Thomas Smith were tried in the spring of 1836 for the willful murder of their illegitimate infant, whom they had thrown into the stream that ran through Cheltenham. Although Sherrington could not afford a defense counsel, she had one appointed and was fortunate in his selection. "Interesting Trial for Murder" was the heading of the account in London's *Morning Post*. The evidence plainly proved that Sherrington had no intention of concealing the birth and made clear the terrible conditions under which she strove to raise the child. The father, Smith, "would not allow her anything." Somehow, she managed to put aside enough in November to secure the assistance of a midwife, who, much to her credit, refused to take payment when a fine boy was delivered in December. Sherrington's collection of bed linen indicated her intention to keep the infant. Destitute, she lived on dry bread for three days, pawned her own clothes to pay for the room in which she and the child existed, and did not deny any clothing for the baby. She consulted the midwife about whether the clothing was sufficient for the winter. The surgeon who gave evidence expressed the opinion that Sherrington suffered from milk suppression and had, going out in the cold until the day of delivery, contracted milk fever. This would deprive her at intervals of her reason. Hence, she threw the child into the stream. It was evident upon the body's recovery that the baby had been first strangled with a handkerchief. The defense then called a succession of respectable citizens with whom Sherrington had lived as a domestic servant, and all attested to her kindness when dealing with their children. In summing up, the judge was another who put three questions to the jury. Was the infant killed by strangulation, was the mother the strangler, and did she know right from wrong at the time? He pointed out that the jury must say "whether the kind, the loving, the affectionate mother, did all at once, with a loss of reason kill the child"? The 12 male jurors found her not guilty on the grounds of "insanity at the time." The father, who had his own counsel, escaped with an upbraiding by the judge for his failure to show kindness to the mother of his child.[18]

Later that same year, in November, Jane Hale went to trial at the Old Bailey for the willful murder of her illegitimate infant. Aged 18, employed as a "servant of all work," suspected of being pregnant, she was given a notice to quit. This expired on November 19, and on that very day she gave birth. When the doctor summoned by her concerned mistress, Sarah Jeffreys, examined Hale, he determined she had given delivery to an infant. This she at first repeatedly denied, finally admitting that the infant was hidden in the bed's quilt and blankets. The police, on being summoned, recovered a knife stained with blood. At the inquest the coroner asked one of the policemen if he noticed "any aberration of the intellect." Not any, he replied. In response to a juror he denied that there had been any threat or intimidation to induce her to confess, and Jane Hale was committed to trial.

At the Old Bailey she was represented by a counsel probably paid out of a fund created by the London sheriffs for the defense of persons indicted in capital cases about whose guilt there was some doubt. Two surgeons gave evidence, George Ford Dayton and William Bernard Robinson, the latter fully endorsing his colleague's testimony. They had jointly made a detailed examination of the dead child. Under cross-examination Dayton had considered the marks on the infant's face unimportant. They had in his opinion been inflicted while Hale made the delivery herself. If she had been standing up and if the baby fell to the floor, this would explain the bruise on the back of its head. He found no evidence that the bruise had injured the brain. Addressing the possibility that the infant had been born alive, Robinson was of the opinion that it would have been "a very small degree of life" and that the infant might have died immediately after its birth. Indeed, it may have died before separating completely from the mother. The attending nurse contradicted the policeman, who testified that Hale had said that she deserved punishment. The nurse was even more emphatic on the state of Hale's mental health. Asked by the defense counsel if on Saturday and Sunday the prisoner had appeared in an insensible state, she replied, "Quite so." Nor could she remember ever telling Hale that she had murdered the child. Found guilty only of concealing the birth, Jane Hale was sentenced under the changes to the law in 1803 and confined for two years. It was plain that the "gravity of murder—both the crime and the penal consequences—attracted attention to the possibility of insanity." Indeed, a leading member of the Royal College of Surgeons commented: "There is no crime that meets with such sympathy, and often of the most ill-judged kind, and an almost partisan feeling has frequently been evinced, not only by the legal, but even by the medical profession." This came to the aid of those unmarried mothers who resorted to poison to solve the problem of an unwanted illegitimate child.[19]

The temporary insanity defense of milk fever had failed to save Mary Thorpe from the gallows in March 1800, but the plea of insanity was entered as the defense two months later of a man charged with treason. He had attempted to kill the king. James Hadfield was a grievously wounded veteran of the French wars. His severe injuries had threatened to sever his head from his body and had "cut across all the nerves which gave sensibility and animation" to it. Discharged, he became a family man with a wife, children, and employment and attended the Drury Lane Theatre on May 15, 1800. A popular comedy was being staged and George III, in recovery from an illness which the public believed was insanity, intended to grace the performance. His royal party included the Queen, their four daughters, and the Duke of York, the commander of the British army whose orderly Hadfield had once been. When the monarch leaned over the balcony of the royal box to show himself to the patriotic audience below, Hadfield rose in the nearby stalls and fired at him. He missed his target and was rapidly subdued. Hustled into a room beneath the stage, he was questioned by the Duke of York, among others. He expressed a natural concern for his wife and announced that it had not been his desire to kill the king. He improvised a credible defense. Unwilling to take his own life, he thought merely an attempt to assassinate the monarch would serve him as well.[20]

Because his offense was high treason, he was guaranteed a defense counsel, and it was his good fortune to have assigned to him one of the stars of the bar. Though small in stature, Thomas Erskine was a legal giant. Fearless, fanatical in his devotion to personal freedom, insanity was his only available defense strategy. As then written, the law only exempted a culprit from the severest punishment if he had suffered a "total deprivation of memory and understanding," and if he did not regard the "atrocious act" as contrary to "the laws of God and nature" and was unable to distinguish right from wrong. Yet Hadfield's attempt to shorten the king's life had clearly been premeditated, while his alleged motive was the severity of the punishment he anticipated. The trial witnesses testified that he had behaved throughout as if sane. Erskine countered that the law required an accused, if he or she was to be exempt of punishment, to be in a "state of prostrated intellect," without knowledge of his name, his condition, his relation to others, or the location of his property. This definition of madness amounted to nothing short of idiocy, Erskine continued, and the prisoner would need to be so helpless and delusional that his mental faculties were overpowered and his reason usurped. Erskine drew attention to Hadfield's earlier acts of insanity, such as his intention, until neighbors intervened, to dash out the brains of his infant child on a wall. In the words of his counsel, he regarded "as realities the most impossible phantoms of the mind which compelled him to act as motives irresistible." Erskine revealed he was preparing to call a score of medical witnesses who would testify to the accused's madness. Delusion with neither frenzy nor raving madness was the true character of insanity Erskine asserted. The judge and the attorney general, the lead prosecutor, agreed to halt the proceedings. They accepted that at the time of the attempted assassination the prisoner had been deranged. The jury returned a verdict of not guilty "by reason of insanity." This ground of acquittal aroused political uneasiness. Would the verdict become a precedent that would permit other criminals to go free? Parliament hurriedly enacted the Criminal Lunatics Act. Those so acquitted were to receive a verdict of not guilty on the grounds of insanity and be remanded in an asylum during the monarch's pleasure. Hadfield would not be released into society. He went to the capital's Bedlam asylum, which professionals in mental health—then called alienists—decried as no more than a receptacle of "waifs of criminal law" where they were kept out of sight and mind.[21]

That delusion with neither frenzy nor raving madness was, as Erskine had argued, "the true character of insanity proved [a] short lived hope." The root of the difficulty was a culprit's derangement at the time of his or her action. Any consciousness that it was wrong invalidated the plea of insanity. John Bellingham, who, in May 1812, assassinated Prime Minister Spencer Perceval in the lobby of the House of Commons, was insane, his counsels contended. However, the judge instructed the jury that the defense had failed to prove that at the time of the act the prisoner did not consider it against the laws of God and nature, and he was swiftly executed without a proper trial. Thirty years later, a young London barman shot twice at Queen Victoria and Prince Albert as they passed him in a carriage. Neither of them was injured but he was indicted, as Hadfield had been, for high treason. His counsels entered a plea of insanity based on Erskine's epic performance, and there was evidence of mental instability in his family. When the jury nevertheless convicted him, the three presiding judges sent the case back to them for reconsideration. At the second time of asking they found him not guilty on grounds of insanity, and he entered an asylum, where he had a long and peaceful life.[22]

Three years later the nation was again stunned by the fatal and mistaken shooting of the prime minister's private secretary. The killer, Daniel M'Naghten, was a sober and prudent Glaswegian with a sharp mind who had amassed a fortune that was imperiled by the failure of his latest "get rich quick" scheme. He succumbed to a paranoid delusion that he was a victim of Tory persecution by the government. The prime minister was his target, but he mistakenly shot instead Edward Drummond, Robert Peel's civil servant. Here, it seemed, was another opportunity to clarify the legal definition of insanity, for the Scot had undoubtedly lost his reason. He retained a defense counsel of high repute, Alexander Cockburn, who went on to become the lord chief justice. He announced his intention to call a succession of qualified witnesses whose evidence would be "beyond the reach of all suspicion or dispute." They would testify that the accused was a victim of such uncontrollable impulses that he was simply unable to behave as a "reasonable and responsible being." The right and wrong test was inapplicable in cases of delusion, Cockburn asserted, and his argument impressed a fellow barrister as "one of the most masterly ... ever heard at the English bar." The judge advised the jury of the attorney general's inability to counter the medical evidence of the defense, and M'Naghten became another assassin acquitted on the grounds of insanity. He was dispatched to Bethlem Asylum, and there he remained until his death in 1865.[23]

Clearly, the verdict had not clarified the law on insanity, so the House of Lords formulated a series of questions for submission to the nation's judges. They were more on the effect on the law of alleging an accused suffered from insane delusions. But now called upon "to found abstract opinions with no facts to go upon," the judges did not assist greatly the administration of justice. The only ground on which an alleged lunatic was entitled to an acquittal, all but one of them concluded, was positive proof that at the time of the act the accused was laboring under such a defect of reason from mental disease that he did not know "the nature and quality of the act he was doing." If he was so aware, was he unaware it was wrong? These were the M'Naghten rules, and the alienists, a group of emerging and influential professionals who studied the brain and considered themselves experts in the treatment of mental illness, were not satisfied with them. Mental incapacity following "intellectual, not emotional or volitional disorder" was acknowledged, but an insane person "might know the nature and quality of his act and that it was wrong and forbidden by law, yet commit it as a result of mental disease." Thus, the judges were restating more or less the test of right or wrong in reference to the "particular act" with which a person was charged at the time it was committed.

The judges were alive to the growing public fear, which the Hadfield decision had excited at the very beginning of the century, that the apparent grant of punishment immunity to the insane would in some way allow other great criminals to take advantage of it. Would this jeopardize the security of society for there was no recognition of "irresistible impulse" as the decisive factor in a person's commitment of a capital crime? What is more, the M'Naghten rules might mislead juries. An accused's general understanding of right and wrong might cause a jury "to misjudge wrongly concerning [his] knowledge of the particular act at the time." If in the act of committing the crime he knew right from wrong and that what he was doing was wrong, he should be found guilty whether insane or not. Therefore, although insane, he was "not necessarily exempted from the punishment of his crime." In the words of a noted barrister, "assuming one of the qualities of a sane human mind to be self-restraint, and supposing this barrier has been removed by insanity, ought the sufferer to be held criminally liable for his acts, although evidence existed that he was conscious of the difference between right and wrong"? Predictably, confusion continued. Happily, the rules did not inhibit juries in their use of common sense in deciding "whether the accused should be held criminally responsible for his [or her] actions."

Thankfully, juries had been liberated almost two centuries earlier from punishment for disagreeing with presiding judges. Until 1670 jurors had been liable to fines and imprisonment for their contrary decisions. From that date it was established that "the jury must be independently and indisputably responsible for its verdict free from any threats from the court."[24]

That so many women escaped conviction of willful murder having killed their infant or child, who were their principal victims, reflected a deepening belief that childbirth, and postnatal depression often extending well over a year after the delivery, brought on at least temporary insanity. In 1810 a London physician assessed the causes of insanity among the female patients of the Bethlem Asylum. He concluded that for a substantial number of women, insanity was "occasioned by childbirth." In short, a "woman's inferiority of intelligence and nervous frailty [were] all linked to the vagaries of her reproductive functions." Women were more vulnerable to insanity than men, went the argument, because the instability of their reproductive system interfered with their sexual, "emotional, and rational control." Puerperal and lactation insanity were in the process of definition. But juries were also moved to compassion by the brutal conditions under which pregnant women of the lower orders, especially those of them who were young and unmarried, lived. Distressful circumstances and distress of reason were linked, and the line between those who were sad and those who were mad remained blurred.[25]

Chapter Three

A Plague of Poisoners

Deaths from poison in the years 1837 and 1838 reportedly numbered 540, although there was no shortage of them in the two or three years prior to those dates. Almost one year to the day after Mary Ann Burdock's execution before a massive, celebratory crowd in Bristol, Betty Rowland was hanged at Kirkdale Gaol, Liverpool. On November 19, 1835, her third husband, William Rowland, had died after a very brief illness. A friend of many years had seen him a week earlier and thought him in perfect health. Meeting the widow a week later and both mindful of the rancorous gossip that she had poisoned her previous two husbands and suspecting her of repeating the offense, he resolved to advise the authorities. A policeman called at the house, where he found a wake in progress with the usual heavy drinking, and when those present joined the widow in declining to suspend the funeral to allow him to consult the local coroner, he took her into custody. For this he had no evidence, and she was immediately released. However, a senior policeman, Superintendent Thomas, heard her admit that she had mistakenly added arsenic to her husband's gruel believing it to be sugar. Such fatal errors were all too common in kitchens where both were kept. The funeral went ahead, but the body was quickly disinterred and the stomach examined by a surgeon, who detected a large quantity of white arsenic. The widow was unable to explain away her earlier "partial confession" of innocently adding arsenic to the gruel. A Manchester druggist from whom she obtained the poison testified that while it might be mistaken for flour, it could not be confused with sugar. Her acquisition of the poison appears to have been decisive for the trial jury, notwithstanding her insistence that she and her late husband had at times "lived happily and were very fond of each other." Indeed, she had realized soon after he died the terrible mistake she had made but had been too frightened to admit it for fear of finding herself in criminal difficulties. This was somewhat at odds with the confession heard by Superintendent Thomas, and she was convicted of willful murder. Her public death became a public free-for-all. The authorities indicated that the execution would take place at a morning hour whereas it was scheduled for the mid-afternoon. The vast crowd of disappointed morning spectators who filled the fields and roads around the County House of Correction, Kirkdale, quickly became unruly. The police, on restoring a semblance of order, quit the scene only for further chaos to ensue. Ruffians set upon the "large sprinkling" of women, stealing their stoles, tippets, bonnets, and shawls. When her time came, Betty Rowland repeated to the chaplain present that she had mistaken arsenic for sugar. Rowland had just taken communion, and "it was not likely," a sympathetic *Kentish Gazette* observed, "that she would die with a lie on her mouth."[1]

On the day of Rowland's hanging, April 9, 1836, Harriet Tarver went to her public death in Gloucester, and less than a week later Sophia Edney was executed in Ilchester. Each was less than half the age of the middle-aged Rowland. Both trials fed the nagging doubt of convictions in which there had been no scientific proof of arsenic as the cause of death. This, in turn, helped account for the persistence with which resolute prison chaplains strove to secure confessions from the condemned women. This would enhance the assumption of divine forgiveness and prove the justice of the convictions. The Tarvers had appeared to live relatively comfortably, yet she bitterly resented his unfaithfulness. When, following her recent purchases of arsenic, he complained of acute stomach pain, raging thirst, and cold sweat, suspicious minds fastened on poisoning as the cause. The busybodies were confident the rice pudding he ate for breakfast had contained poison. He had started his day's labor in good health, a work colleague reported, but was heard to say an hour later that "he thought he must have taken poison." He returned home, and the surgeon who attended him, John Hiron, surprised by the patient's rapid death, conducted an autopsy. The condition of the stomach and his chemical tests on its contents gave him "every reason to suppose" that Tarver had "died of poison and that it was arsenic." Sensibly, Hiron sought a second opinion. He consulted Dr. Thompson of Stratford, who corroborated "in the most scientific and decisive manner" Hiron's opinion. His tests, he declared, had proved "incontrovertibly" death from arsenic poisoning. The widow's subsequent confession was but a confirmation.[2]

John and Sophia Edney had made an "ill-concerted match." When they first met, she was in "humble service" at the Bristol home to which he delivered eggs, butter, and poultry. Aged 16, she was naturally averse to marrying a man 45 years her senior. But wed they did, and, perhaps inevitably, she developed a strong interest in a much younger man. Their attachment became the motive for her actions. Her interest in the

Burdock case, for she was in Bristol at the time, may have influenced the choice of means. When her husband, now 68 and reduced to gathering watercress as a means of income, suddenly fell ill, she turned for advice and assistance to a friendly neighbor, Elizabeth Dunn. For three days John constantly vomited, suffered severe pain in his belly and bowels, and was always thirsty. Her neighbor urged the calling of a doctor, and one came on the second day, Thursday, March 3. He had no knowledge of the patient and with a handful of thoughtful questions excluded food poisoning as the cause of the illness. Sophia told Dunn the doctor had diagnosed an inflammation of the kidneys, but his prescriptions of a powder and a "mixture" were instantly hated by the patient. The "stuff," he complained bitterly, "had burnt his inside out," and "all the way up to his throat was raw and on fire." He grumbled repeatedly that the tea and gruel prepared by his wife did not taste the same as that Dunn made for him. When Sophia brought him a teacup of milk, he asked if she had added the unpleasant "stuff" to it, and when she denied it, he put his finger to the bottom of the cup and contradicted her. And after the small sip he was persuaded to swallow, he vomited. She had assured the druggist from whom she acquired arsenic, and with whom she had discussed the Burdock case, that it was required to suppress rats. This was a vermin problem of which the ever-present, helpful, and observant Elizabeth Dunn was entirely ignorant.

The swift passing of the elderly man saw a second attending surgeon, Edward Wade, make an examination of the body over the young widow's objection. Her opposition naturally gave rise to talk when the surgeon denied ever diagnosing inflammation of the kidneys. Instead, he suggested that a mineral poison of variable effectiveness had been introduced into the deceased's stomach. The variability was in the vomiting. One victim might vomit immediately, whereas the poison might linger in the stomach of another for "some hours." Seeking confirmation of his diagnosis he forwarded the stomach and its contents to William Herapath, who employed six tests. He declared any one of them "infallible." Consequently, the very small quantity of poison detected did not dissuade him from confirming its lethal presence. The jury at her trial convicted Sophia Edney of willful murder, and shortly before her hanging she "acknowledged the justice of her [death] sentence and confessed the time and manner of administering the poison." Of her guilt there could, therefore, be no doubt.[3]

Scientific proof that arsenic was a cause of death suddenly became available. James Marsh, a chemist, published it in the *Edinburgh Philosophical Journal*, which excitedly declared that it could identify one-fiftieth of a milligram of the poison. The prosecutorial worth of the

Marsh test was swiftly established, even though it was not entirely foolproof, for it could not measure precisely the amount detected and was unable always to distinguish arsenic from antimony or tartar emetic. Marsh soon solved this problem, but another remained. The "reagents essential to the test, the substances known to react characteristically when [placed] in contact with another designated substance," had impurities that threatened the positive findings. Moreover, not only did the analyst require a very high level of skill but also a laboratory in which to perform the complicated analysis. Hence the importance of the speedier and simpler process published five years later by Hugo Reinsch, a German chemist. His test and analysis could be made on the spot, thereby delivering the results in minutes. Not surprisingly, it became the preferred choice of a great many investigators. Yet the "reagents" remained a problem, and this fallibility created opportunities for able defense counsels to exploit during the adversarial poison trials.[4]

Herapath, Marsh, and Reinsch were making it more difficult for successful prosecutions for poisoning to be based almost exclusively on circumstantial evidence. Something in addition to an accused's possession of arsenic, ample opportunities to administer it, and possible motive now seemed necessary for a sure conviction. Not that the scientific advances deterred murderers. Crimes in general, and poisonings in particular, were known to be rising. The state of the economy was a factor. Good harvests and the boom in trade came to an abrupt halt in 1837, and the country descended into a prolonged depression, with unemployment reaching "hitherto unknown proportions." Already hard, the lives of the poor became far harder. Squeezed between high food prices and the lack of work and thus of income, they were driven to desperate measures. This the Constabulary Commissioners failed to recognize. The poor, in their opinion, had simply succumbed to the "temptation of obtaining property with a lesser degree of labor than by regular industry." A more profound thinker, Thomas Carlyle, the author of three volumes on the violent French Revolution of little more than a generation earlier, warned in 1839 "that the condition and disposition of the Working Classes is a rather ominous matter at the present, that something ought to be said, something ought to be done, in regard to it."[5]

Here was an environment in which the public became fascinated by cases of brutal murder. The crimes of Burdock and Edney were but two examples coinciding as they did with the gradual emergence of the press as the "predominant instrument of news distribution." The violent and radical French Revolution had a telling impact on British politics. Lord Ellenborough announced in 1803 the British government's opposition to the emergence of a "pauper press." There was to be no place in

Britain for a popular press that might seek to organize the lower orders into a formidable force for political change. Taxes and duties imposed on newspapers discouraged the establishment of a press that elements of the lower orders might have been able to afford. Only very slowly did newspapers become a major if not a sole source of information for the increasingly literate working classes. By mid-century it is estimated that possibly 60 percent of the population could read. For the literate and the illiterate poor there were clubs and groups that could be joined for a very small fee to hear a newspaper read aloud. The brief time they had for this measure of relaxation and information usually meant it was a Sunday weekly to which they listened. Another option for the literate poor was to call at a pub that subscribed to a newspaper, much to the distress of early temperance campaigners. A reduction in the 1830s of several of the taxes on the press did open the door to somewhat less expensive newspapers, such as *Lloyd's Weekly*. In 1846 the proprietor of the *Newspaper Press Directory* boasted that it had a great and extensive influence on public opinion. The eradication of the remaining "taxes on knowledge" in the 1850s, culminating with the removal of the paper duty in 1861, finally brought the founding of a penny press. Technological developments—first the steam press and then its rotary version—made possible the swift mass production of copies whose countrywide distribution the railway mania made possible. Not that the journalists who sought recognition of their professional status were accepted as gentlemen. They excited distrust and distaste for their exposure of "unpalatable and often embarrassing facts." Irritated magistrates took steps to keep them away from their hearings, while some coroners excluded them from inquests. This impaired the reporting of suspicious deaths. A marked increase in poisonings, a capital crime with which women were increasingly identified because they outnumbered male poisoners, could in the opinion of London's more liberal *Daily News* "be traced to the national character of the lower class, with its 'coarse and animal brutality, unchecked by religion, uninformed by intelligence, uncontrolled by virtuous activity, unsupported by self-respect.'"[6]

At mid-century the House of Commons released statistics on criminal poisonings during the previous decade. Eighty-seven women had been tried for murder or attempted murder in England and Wales. Seventeen wives were hanged for the murder of their husbands. Mariticide, it seemed, was nothing short of an epidemic, but those who committed it were greatly outnumbered by the men who killed their wives. What the laboring classes learned from sensationalist "broadsides" and weekly newspapers was the apparent presence everywhere of homicide. Especially notable and disturbing remained infanticide, and there was a suspicion that the alarming official figures had been carefully underestimated. During the four-year period of 1852 to 1856, "over six hundred mothers were charged with having suffocated, poisoned, starved, drowned or even decapitated their babies."

There were indications of a significant moderation of public opinion on this crime, and the case of Mary Furley illustrated this. The press, London and provincial, was appalled by her conviction and sentence to death for drowning her baby while attempting to commit suicide. She was but another mother tortured "'into an act of insanity by the cruelty of fortune.'" She lived without any means of support and feared her child would starve to death. Her case was sympathetically portrayed as a crime "not of malice prepense, but of excess of affection." How could she leave her child to the mercy of a world that drove her to "seek shelter in the grave"? Who could conceive that "such an offence as hers could be regarded as Murder?" Happily, after an agonizing and terrifying wait before the date of her execution, her sentence was commuted. The judge was harshly criticized for leaving the jury "without any palliating circumstance." Why, critics asked, did sentences of death depend so often upon "biliary secretions of the judge who dooms?" Why, in trials concerning property disputes, did the losing party have a right of appeal? Why did the criminal law fail to make "human character and human freedom merely as valuable as chattles and money?" Why was Mary Furley treated as a convict and eventually sentenced to the punishment thought to be almost as severe as death, that is transportation, instead of a brief term of imprisonment? Sarah Dickenson, that same year, was found not guilty of the murder of her son "being at the time in a state of insanity." Julia Eliza Scales, Martha Brixey, and Elizabeth Huntsmen were also acquitted on the grounds of an "unsound mind." Mary Ann Hunt was found guilty and sentenced to death and her plea of the belly—that is, that she was pregnant—was rejected by an improvised jury of matrons. The evidence that she suffered bouts of hysterical violence saw the government pressed to consider whether at the time of the crime she had experienced another fit of temporary insanity. The home secretary, Sir George Grey, directed three eminent medical men to examine her state of mind only to be advised that the matrons had made a clinical error. She was "quick with child." Grey announced her respite for several months until the end of her confinement. At that point the nature of her commuted punishment would be revealed. She was transported to Australia.

A truly exceptional case was that of Rebecca Smith, one of the four daughters and two sons of a small farmer and landowner William Pryor. On his death in 1830, Pryor sought to protect the women in his family, not one of whom was fully literate. He bequeathed his small estate to his wife on the understanding that on her death the monies raised by the sale of goods and possessions would be evenly divided among the daughters. Shortly after her father's demise, an impetuous Rebecca married a wastrel over the opposition of her family. Philip Smith was a known drunkard and a physical abuser. The couple had 11 children, of whom only the very first, Jane, lived to maturity. The second child, a boy, died after 14 weeks of a bowel complaint, and another quickly passed away from natural causes. Infant mortality was common, so the children's deaths initially aroused little suspicion. On her mother's death Rebecca received her quarter share of the £400 raised. Her family moved to a nearby depressed town, Westbury, and rented 10 acres of land. Philip legally controlled his wife's inheritance and frittered it away. While Rebecca labored in the farm fields daily to earn a pittance for the family's upkeep, he drank away most of what little he earned. She took in a lodger for additional income and on May 16, 1849, gave birth to a son, Richard. She anticipated fatalistically his early death and refused to summon a doctor when he fell ill with pain and vomiting. He died not long after she was reported to have acquired poison, and the suddenness of his passing persuaded the coroner to have an inquest and order a medical exhumation. The local doctors who conducted the postmortem reached the conclusion that a metallic poison had proven fatal, and they recommended a second opinion. The stomach and its contents were dispatched to William Herapath, who found arsenic, which had in his opinion been administered through the mouth. She, as had mothers before and after her, dipped a finger in the poison and then allowed the infant to suck it. The coroner's jury found her guilty of willful murder, and she was committed for trial at the next assizes. Influenced by the popular tittle-tattle concerning the earlier deaths of the Smiths' many infants, the coroner opened a second inquest and ordered the exhumation of two of the long-dead children. Herapath once again investigated and found arsenic in both corpses. "This is I believe," he reported with understandable pride, "the first incidence on record of arsenic being discovered after an interment of eight years and I therefore wish it to be circulated that the years have no effect on removing traces of arsenic." The odds of the poison escaping detection had suddenly shortened. "However, in the absence of any clear evidence of who had administered it in the earlier deaths, Rebecca Smith was indicted only for the murder of her recent child."[7]

Her trial opened at the Wiltshire Assizes, Devizes, on August 9, 1849. The jury's composition was a little unusual. Several members were prominent local figures: one was a former judge, another was a magistrate landowner, and a third eventually became the county's sheriff. They were not run-of-the-mill jurors and likely had a powerful influence on the verdict. None of their colleagues could have been ignorant of the case, a popular weekly headlining its account of the inquest "Supposed Murder of Eleven Children by Their Mother." Although Rebecca had legal representation, the medical evidence and that of a line of witnesses told heavily against her. One of the latter was her sister Sarah, whom the prosecution compelled to testify, but she strove to minimize the harm. The defense counsel contended that the evidence was circumstantial, that there was no proof Rebecca had administered poison, that during her puerperal illness she may have inadvertently given it to the child. What, the defense asked, was her motive to kill? In summing up, the judge instructed the jury to reach a verdict on the evidence they had heard in court and not on what may have happened in the past. They returned after less than an hour with a conviction and a recommendation for mercy. The judge, convinced of Rebecca's guilt, sentenced her to death and told her not to hope to escape the law's punishment of her crime.[8]

The following day, now condemned, Rebecca made a truly shocking admission to the prison chaplain. She had killed, in addition to Richard, seven of her earlier infants shortly after their births. If this qualified her as a serial killer, there was a surprisingly compassionate tone to the press commentary. Her husband's behavior was dwelt upon. He brought home little of his insignificant earnings as a laborer, whereas she had toiled in the fields for four shillings a week and then did all the housework. There was a measure of credibility to her claim that he had driven her with violence to commit her crime, and her "fear that the children would come to want operated so powerfully upon her that she destroyed them in the way stated." There was even a measure of respect for her conduct while awaiting death. "Free from guile or hypocrisy, she unhesitatingly confessed her crime, and acknowledged the justice of the punishment that awaited her, and frequently expressed a hope that others would take a warning by her fate." Petitions for clemency were delivered to the Home Office, where Sir George Grey rejected them. He was later to explain that the evidence of "pre-planning and deliberate poisoning" of so many deaths made a commutation impossible. However, Rebecca Smith's execution proved to be the last of mothers who murdered their own infants. The crowd that witnessed her death was huge. "People were there from every part of the country—old, young and infants and chiefly of the laboring classes," but women vastly outnumbered men.[9]

A close reader of the press during the 1840s might have supposed that the murder of husbands had achieved the proportions of a biblical plague. Executions of murderous wives were reportedly to be seen almost everywhere, being published and republished extensively and prominently in London and provincial newspapers. The *Banbury Guardian* fancied that "every class of society contributes its recruits to the trade of murder," but the apprehensive middle classes may have taken some comfort from the assurance of the *Daily News* that this, the most serious crime, was rooted in the lower classes. "Deplorable as it is," *Bell's New Weekly Messenger* commented, "we cannot gainsay the fact, that among English women of the humbler classes the settlement of conjugal and pecuniary difficulties by the summary help of arsenic is already a habit, and one that is increasing." The stability of working class marriages was compromised chronically by poverty, domestic violence, and sexual promiscuity. The married women who murdered rarely chose strangers as their victims. They concentrated almost exclusively on parents, husbands, siblings, and children, committing covert crimes of comparative ease with poison. A number of the guilty parties qualified as serial killers.[10]

This terrifying label was usually applied to triple murderers who had a "cooling off period" between the deaths. That women were capable of calculated and ruthless violence was a truth to which most middle-class men shut their eyes, preferring the patronizing and patriarchal assumption that the domestic angel was emotionally passive, submissive, and maternal. But women bent on murder had in poison a solution for their physical inability to overpower a grown male, and among them were psychopaths. As such, they disregarded the law and the rights of others. They lacked the ability to empathize or fear punishment yet successfully pretended to love others. A German researcher created the word *psychopathy* in 1888, but this mental illness had long been recognized under different terminologies. A French physician who studied mental health, Philippe Pinel, had at the opening of the century spoken of "mania without delusion," and of "impulsive insanity and moral idiocy." Eventually it was assumed that evolution had built into the human brain a central core of moral reasoning that was more or less universal. This religion reinforced. The central core was missing in the serial killer, who was devoid of moral but not intellectual judgment. She or he sought social dominance and was aggressive in the pursuit of benefits unhindered by the slightest concern for those who were harmed.[11]

Part and parcel of a serial killer's makeup was a traumatic and abusive childhood, an inability to establish a strong emotional attachment with parents and siblings, a hot temper, the prospect of material gain far outweighing the cost of human life, cold-bloodedness in dealings with partners and children, and the pleasure and excitement of wielding power over victims. The attire was not perfectly tailored for Sarah Dazley. The "enormity of her wickedness" gained her a reputation as Bedfordshire's "Female Blue Beard." Her father, a barber and a rat catcher, having squandered his comfortable inheritance, was imprisoned for debt and died of consumption. Her mother's promiscuity surely influenced Sarah's own choice of "extreme profligacy," and allegedly she boasted of having had seven husbands in seven years. The two marriages that she most certainly did have were marred by intense friction and frequent threats of fatal terminations. Her first husband was Simeon Mead, by whom she had a child, Jonas, and both father and son conveniently died at a time when she desired to move on to William Dazley. His death and her clear intent to hasten on to George Waldock set tongues wagging. The local Anglican priest brought this to the attention of a county magistrate, and he passed it on to the coroner, along with sufficient evidence to warrant an inquest. Dazley's corpse was exhumed, and an examination of the lining of his stomach suggested that an irritant poison had been administered. For a more decisive analysis the remains were dispatched to the Bedford Infirmary. Next the coroner ordered the disinterment of Mead and the child. All that remained of the father was a skeleton, but metallic arsenic was detected in the child's remains. Accused of all three deaths, Sarah Dazley was committed for trial at the Bedford Assizes only for the Grand Jury to exclude Mead from the indictment, and she was charged with the death of Dazley alone. The judge in his summation emphasized her "hard and impenitent heart," and the jury sprinted to a conviction. Perhaps 10,000 spectators watched her die, few of them respectfully solemn and quiet. The *Bedford Mercury*, noting the carnival atmosphere, questioned what use ministers of religion were to society when the "most immoral of sights draw their congregations to the town which is the place of the most revolting exhibition that can be exposed to public view."[12]

A notoriously immoral figure was Sarah Westwood, the daughter of a laboring man. She was rejected by her parents, whom she had shamed by being a loose woman and the mother of an illegitimate child. She removed her husband with a massive dose of arsenic, their relationship already poisoned by her "criminal intercourse" with a lodger, Samuel Phillips. Tried and convicted of willful murder, she went to her public death at Stafford on January 13, 1844. By contrast, Eliza Joyce was considered a "mild and not uninteresting woman." In 1840 she wed a widower, William Joyce, and became the stepmother of his several offspring by his first marriage. The couple added another to the family, Ann, but Ann and her stepsister Emma Joyce died in 1843. Soon the eldest of the stepchildren, William, fell ill with stomach pains and vomiting. On investigating, his father came to the conclusion that his spouse was administering arsenic to his son and so informed the authorities. Committed for trial on an indictment of attempted murder, she was acquitted by the jury, which had been unable to discern a motive for the crime. Evicted from the home by her hostile husband, she entered the local workhouse, where, on falling ill with what she imagined was a fatal sickness, she confessed to killing the two girls with laudanum and of attempting to remove young William with arsenic. She had the dubious distinction of being the "last woman to be executed in England for a murder to which she had pleaded guilt."

Three months later, Mary Gallop committed parricide. She was the child of devout Wesleyan Methodist parents, although her mentally unstable mother eventually took her own life. Her father, stern and pious, was nevertheless a good man in her opinion. While she was still a young girl, he had escorted her to both Sunday school and day school. During their residence in Liverpool, she became attached to the young apprentice who was their next-door neighbor. When the Gallops moved on to Crewe, she and the young man corresponded, and she showed the letters to her mother but not to her father. Twenty years old, "short of stature, of a florid complexion, with a somewhat heavy countenance," she desired to marry the apprentice and profoundly resented her father's obstructionism. Her first thought was to leave home and seek employment in Liverpool as a domestic servant. However, on overhearing a conversation concerning a wife who had rid herself of an unwanted husband with a dose of arsenic, she calculated that there would be little likelihood of detection if she resorted to poison. Her father's arsenic symptoms, she assumed, would almost certainly be attributed to his chronic bowel complaint. This proved to be her fatal miscalculation. Tried for her father's willful murder and convicted, she kept her appointment with the hangman three days before the end of the year.

On almost the same day in 1844, Mary Sheming, another wife of another "poor hard working laborer," found herself at the age of 51 responsible for the raising and care of six children. Two of them were illegitimate products of the "abandoned course of life" of one of her daughters. The number of mouths to feed "lay heavy on her hands," she complained, and if no allowance was made, she was convinced that something would have to be done. She advised a coffin maker that his services would soon be needed, and on the day she purchased arsenic she prematurely registered the death from convulsions of one of the illegitimate infants. That he did not die for another two weeks did not escape local notice. The body was exhumed, arsenic was present in it, and she was convicted and executed of willful murder having unsuccessfully striven to blame two of her older daughters for the crime. A petition was submitted in relation to her case by the "competent [municipal] authorities." There was no appeal for the commutation of the death sentence. Instead, it sought a postponement of the execution in order to spare the town two executions on the same day.[13]

The unmasking of Sarah Freeman as a multiple murderess raises the possibility if not probability that she was a psychopath. Born in 1817, Sarah Dimond was the daughter of a "decent man." Her hot and violent temper and promiscuity alienated her entire family as she grew older. Functionally literate, five feet tall, yet vain, her small features and protuberant eyes gave her a "most malignity" of expression. She worked as a prostitute, gave birth to two illegitimate children, and while pregnant with a third married Henry Freeman. Possibly, he was induced to enter into matrimony by the clergyman whom she named as the father of the expected infant. The villagers of Shapwick, Somerset, drove her out of the community, and she moved no great distance to Bridgewater. The third illegitimate infant, John, died in November 1843, and not long afterwards husband Henry followed him to the grave. Neither sudden death was investigated. The magistrates who held the purse strings were committed to economy, and inquests were expensive. Such "criminal parsimony" was roundly condemned by *The Times*. Sarah's collection of £20 from a burial club escaped comment, and she frittered it away in the capital before returning to Bridgewater with every intention of rejoining the family she had alienated.

There was no warm welcome from her parents or her two brothers, Charles and John, whom she appears to have hated. In Bridgewater she acquired arsenic before journeying on to Shapwick, where three days after her arrival her frail mother began to vomit and be cursed with diarrhea. She died so swiftly that the attending doctor, Phillips, gave "break-up of nature" as the cause on the death certificate. The most hostile and determined of the brothers, Charles, then fell ill. He vomited and complained of stomach pain, a sore throat, and neuralgia. Sarah's verbal response to his persistent efforts to drive her out of the family and village was, in the recollection of a neighbor, "I'll soon take care of that," and "If he doesn't look damned sharp, I'll take damned good care he'll not be here long himself." The doctor, noticing the strong similarity of Charles's symptoms with those of his late mother, concluded that he was being poisoned. Hearing this, Sarah prudently quit the village for Bridgewater, only to be arrested there the very next day.

There was an inquest on Charles's death, and the coroner, probably influenced by the now raging local gossip, ordered the exhumation of the bodies of the mother, Henry Freeman, and the infant John. The stomach and intestines of each were dispatched to William Herapath for analysis. He detected arsenic, and on the strength of this the coroner's inquest concluded that Sarah was guilty of murder and committed her to trial at the assizes. She was charged with administering arsenic to her husband, her illegitimate son, her mother, and her brother. The Grand Jury lay aside the cases of husband and son, "the evidence being considered incomplete, although of a very suspicious character." Tried for the willful murder of Charles alone there was after 12 full hours of evidence a conviction on the "clearest testimony" of guilt. The decisive evidence was yet again that of the famed Herapath. Sarah strongly protested her innocence to the governor of the prison following the verdict, accused her brother John, a prosecution witness, of the deaths of his mother and his brother, claiming he had stolen from her bag the poison she had purchased in order to take her own life. The governor and an undersheriff did make a brief investigation and concluded that the whole of her statements "were a tissue of falsehoods." She walked to the scaffold without the "slightest assistance," and her last words were, "I am as innocent as a lamb."[14]

Sarah Freeman's widely reported public death did not deter Catherine Foster from disposing of her husband. She had been pressed into marriage with a close childhood friend, John Foster, a Suffolk farm laborer for whom she had a high opinion but no affection. He stood in the way of her return to the life of a domestic servant, which she had enjoyed. So, after three weeks of marriage, she rid herself of him with arsenic. With its discovery, her fate was sealed, and she made a frank confession of her guilt yet "studiously avoided attending to any circumstance which might explain the horrid deed." The "carelessness and brutality" of her hanging drew national attention to her case. A well-known supporter of public executions raised it in Parliament. He conceded that her death before a huge audience ought not to have been as protracted as it was lest it arouse popular opposition to this form of capital punishment. After all, it was the first female hanging in Bury St. Edmunds for 47 years. Even more shocking was the case in 1847 of Mary Ann Milner. She was accused of poisoning with arsenic her mother-in-law, her brother's wife, and the latter's child. She gave her reasons in a written confession to the chaplain of Lincoln jail, but at her request they were considered almost too insignificant to be taken seriously. Her husband's parents had not treated her well, entering her house as if it were their own and taking away whatever they liked without any discussion with her. Equally vexing was her husband's gifts of "money and things" to his parents. Her brother's wife was another vexation, behaving towards her so unpleasantly that she poisoned her and also her daughter in an especially spiteful act of revenge. Was her violent response to such minor personal irritants evidence of psychopathy? Her "only imaginable motive," according to the press, was her collection of burial club payments, consequently "more deliberate murders probably could not be found in the annals of English law." She escaped the hangman by privately strangling herself in her cell some hours before she was scheduled to meet him on the scaffold. Her cheating of a public death, and the disorder amounting almost to a riot among the disappointed spectators, gave her end a measure of unexpected celebrity. She was the last condemned female prisoner who did not spend her final hours of life under the close watchful eyes of two members of the prison staff.[15]

Murders were being committed, it seemed, for payments made to the families of deceased persons who had invested in burial insurance. Sarah Freeman had quietly collected £20 on the deaths of her husband and infant, and it was surprising that this revelation did not lead to sinister talk sooner. Four years earlier the connection of burial insurance and unexpected deaths had attracted considerable attention. Two closely related Irish immigrant families lived side by side in rat-infested Stockport cellars, where it was prudent to have arsenic on hand. George and Honor and then Robert and Anne had five children, twin boys and three girls. Of the latter, Maryanne was the eldest, aged four; Jane was a little younger; and Elizabeth was an infant. Catherine, the daughter of Robert's brother George and his wife, had died earlier. The infant Elizabeth's death was followed a month later by that of Maryanne, and one of the medical men who attended them diagnosed arsenic as the cause. Before long there was gossip about poisonings with a financial motive. "Suspected Cases of Poisoning Children to obtain their burial money" was how the *Morning Herald* headed its account of the inquest. Recent evidence had come to light, the coroner announced, "which would probably tend to show" that the mother of Maryanne was the guilty person. He was referring to the finding of the surgeon, John Rayner, who on discovering one grain of arsenic in the girl's body concluded that there "could be no doubt of the cause of death." He then went to the Catholic cemetery for the disinterment and examination of Elizabeth's body, buried a month earlier. He again found arsenic in a quantity that, in his opinion, was sufficient to kill. The coroner commented on the mother's apparent lack of concern over the deaths, her thorough cleaning of the cellar to ensure there was no vomit for testing, and her washing of Maryanne's pinafore on which there would have been vomit stains. Both mothers had a motive to kill, he continued. Maryanne had been a member of the Benevolent Society, a burial club, since June; Elizabeth had been enrolled in it for the few months of her life; and Catherine's parents had made the required payments for a far longer period. The collector of the society's dues remembered Robert Sandys repeatedly inquiring how soon Maryanne would be a full member. The club would then pay out on her death three pounds, eight shillings and sixpence, with an additional two shillings for drink. Since the cost of a child's funeral was at most 15 shillings, the balance was profit. The coroner's jury after two and a half hours of deliberation convicted all four adults, Anne for the willful murder of Maryanne and Elizabeth, and Robert for aiding and abetting her. That same charge of aiding and abetting was brought against Charles and Honor, although only Honor was charged with the willful murder of Catherine.[16]

Two London dailies, the *Morning Herald* and the *Morning Post*, whose target readership was the metropolitan middle classes and which normally restricted coverage to politics, the theater, and society, reported at some length on the criminal trial for the murder of Maryanne. That the attorney general conducted the prosecution was another indicator of its perceived importance. The accused had a defense counsel who argued eloquently and at length that the evidence was insufficient to warrant convictions. The jury agreed within 15 minutes and acquitted all four. The attorney general then decided to prosecute Robert and Anne for the murder of Elizabeth on essentially the same body of evidence, but Robert's repeated inquiries about the infant's full membership of the Benevolent Society saw him alone convicted. His counsel sought and secured a delay of the execution until the next assizes, at which his sentence was commuted to transportation for life. Although the prosecutions of the Irish immigrants had been less than successful, they went far to convince "much of the population that scores—hundreds—thousands—of the poor routinely murdered their children for cash." From this date the burial clubs began to proliferate and the laws intended "to break the connection between child life insurance and murder" proved "mostly ineffective."[17]

As it happened, burial payments were made by some mill owners to the families of employees who died, and this knowledge proved an irresistible temptation for Betty Haslam. A widow with a single surviving child, Alice, she married a widower, Henry Eccles, in 1842, who had three children. He worked in a Manchester mill during the week, returning home to neighboring Bolton each Saturday evening and retracing his steps on Sunday evenings. Consequently, he was only briefly in the children's lives. His two young sons worked in a Bolton mill whose owners made modest burial payments. They would pay 50 shillings on the death of one of the Eccles' boys, a sum that would have taken him 17 weeks to earn. Betty poisoned stepson William with an arsenic-laced damson pie and lost no time collecting the 50 shillings. Avarice was her downfall. She sought the same allowance on the death of her own daughter. Alice was ineligible for the payment, not having been a mill employee, and the claim excited the suspicion of Mrs. Eccles. The mill's bookkeeper sent a doctor to examine the body of the dead boy, remembering that the mother had refused to permit an autopsy at the time of his passing. He found white powder adhering to the lining of the stomach from which he concluded that an irritant poison had been the cause of death. This a chemist confirmed following his employment of "all the various tests which science suggested." At the criminal trial, evidence was introduced of her purchase of an ounce of arsenic, while her defense counsel argued that the evidence was too doubtful for a verdict that carried the death penalty. After a brief retirement the jury returned with a conviction. Betty Eccles was hanged at Kirkdale Gaol, Liverpool, in May 1843, having confessed to the murder of William. She "would not say but hardly denied" killing Alice.[18]

Three years later in the summer of 1848 the trial of Mary May concentrated minds on the connection of burial clubs and willful murder. A growing number of the truly poor were enrolling husbands and children in the ever-expanding insurance business. Often the modest dues of membership were paid just long enough to collect the insurance, and death then followed. Mary had given birth to 16 children, 14 of whom had not survived. In the age of arsenic so high a rate of loss inevitably gave rise to gossip, for it far exceeded that which was usual from the manifold natural perils to the very young. The unexpected death of her first husband was another topic of gossip, and she was later to imply that it had not been natural. Her second husband was Robert May, a laborer, and one of their two children was the sole survivor of her first family. She kept a small shop and took in lodgers to increase the family's income, and one of them was her half brother. Unbeknownst to him, she enrolled him in a burial club, the New Mourners Society of Harwich. To ensure he was accepted, she declared him both younger and physically sturdier than in truth he was. The death benefit would be £10, and she approached the local Anglican priest, the Reverend Wilkins, for a supportive certificate about his passing. That she desired him to bend the truth caused him to alert the authorities. An inquest was called, the body was exhumed, and her purchase of "brown powder" shortly before her half brother's death told heavily against her with the discovery of arsenic in the corpse. England's noted toxicologist, Alfred Swaine Taylor, found sufficient poison to kill two adults. Committed to trial, the Reverend Wilkins paid for May's counsel even though he did not doubt her guilt. "The Crown's case was circumstantial yet compelling," the press commented. Her counsel delivered a powerful address, stressing her reputation as a caring mother and attentive nurse of her ill stepbrother and her lack of a credible motive to kill him. Who could believe she would murder him for a paltry £10? Unfortunately, her counsel had been denied enough time to prepare the defense properly, which was not unusual, and his several errors were corrected by the judge and prosecutor. This undoubtedly influenced the jury, who convicted her. In donning the ceremonial black cap and sentencing her to death, the presiding Lord Chief Baron expressed strong disapproval of the "evil tendence" of death societies. He considered "exceedingly mischievous any association that could give you an interest in death, without the person insured knowing anything about it, and furnish you with a wicked and base means of getting rid of him, that you might obtain a small sum."[19]

A burial club was at the center of the Geering case, which was tried at Lewes, Sussex, in early August 1849. Richard and Mary Ann Geering had been wed for 30 years, and three of their sons—James, George, and Benjamin—lived with them. The father and two of the sons were members of burial clubs, and Mary Ann's hasty collection of the insurance following Richard's death inevitably gave rise to village scandalmongering. When over the next seven months two of the sons died, and Benjamin fell seriously ill with symptoms all too familiar as those of arsenic poisoning, popular suspicion of the bereaved wife and mother deepened. John Pocock, surgeon and apothecary, had attended all of the men thanks to a charitable bequest. He had found nothing suspicious about the deaths of the husband and two sons, but when the third became ill with essentially the same symptoms, he turned for advice to surgeon Ticehurst in the nearby town of Hastings. The coroner ordered the exhumation of the bodies, and in that of the father the inflammation of the intestines convinced Ticehurst that arsenic was the cause of death. Being nothing if not thorough, he placed the contents of the abdomen together with the stomach, heart, pericardium, and liver in a jar and delivered it to Alfred Swaine Taylor on May 1. While that analysis was underway, Ticehurst turned his attention to the bodies of the deceased sons. On finding them much the same as the father's, he sent their relevant organs also to the industrious Taylor. The professor had just published *On Poisons in Relation to Medical Jurisprudence and Medicine*, a text for "medical men, who in the course of their professional work, might be called upon to testify in a case of suspected poisoning." In it as in his leading articles in the *London Medical Gazette*, of which he was the editor, he identified the "rise of public, 'scientific' poisoning as the new threat facing society and its defenders." In the surviving son's vomit he found two grains of arsenic, and another seven in a metallic and crystalized form in the dead pair's organs. Their bodies were impregnated with it. He drew the conclusion that, although he could not state the exact quantity administered, it must have been "very large." This was an early example of Taylor's willingness often to say more than his scientific findings warranted, and it was reflected in the press. "Wholesale Poisoning" was the headlined account in the *Yorkshire Post*. Mary Ann Geering's seven purchases of the poison were documented at the trial, as were her quarrels with her husband over money. She had imprudently complained to neighbors that he was a great trouble to her and she wished him dead. Her defense counsel, who was appointed by the judge when her daughter admitted she had not the money to retain one, sought to ridicule the burial club motive. Who could believe, he asked the jurors, that she would kill her husband and two sons and attempt to murder the third for so pathetic a sum? The total that could be claimed was estimated at between £15 and £30. The 12 men of the jury did so believe, and they found her guilty in barely 10 minutes. While awaiting execution Mary Ann confessed to all three murders and was hanged at Lewes, as the press put it, "for the lucre of burial fees." The obvious solution was the abolition of burial societies, *Bell's New Weekly Messenger* argued, and for the state to "grant burial as a right of all."[20]

"Is the poisoning mania, after more than two centuries of sleep, revived among us?" elements of the press asked. Readers of newspapers, or those who for whatever reason listened to them being read aloud, came to believe that there was indeed an alarming escalation of homicide and serial killing by women of the lower orders. Poisoning trials at the Old Bailey, when compared with the preceding 10 years, had increased almost fourfold between 1839 and 1848, and in that decade's final year, 1849, there were three notorious cases, those of Geering, Ball, and Smith. Mary Ball murdered her husband, Thomas, who was three or four years younger than she was. The union had been very painful for her. Only one of their six children survived, and Thomas was physically abusive, drank far too much, and was chronically unfaithful. She in turn engaged in a sexual relationship with his employer's young son and was denounced by her husband as a whore. He administered a sound thrashing to her and left for a few days. She threatened to poison him if he returned, and in apparent preparation for it purchased a pennyworth of arsenic ostensibly to suppress bedbugs. His sudden death soon after his reappearance resulted in an autopsy, although the attending doctor had attributed it to natural causes. When he saw white powder, he sent the organs off to the University of Birmingham for analysis, and in them was more than enough arsenic to kill. The Crown's case was that Mary murdered her husband to enable her to be with her much younger lover, while her defense counsel strove manfully without success to establish that there was too much reasonable doubt for the jury to find her guilty. Several petitions seeking clemency were sent to the Home Office, and one of them drew attention to the division of the jury on the conviction. Unanimity was only secured on the understanding that the verdict would be accompanied by a strong recommendation for mercy. This the judge challenged, which led the jury to return a unanimous verdict minus the recommendation. In considering the appeals for mercy, the home secretary's mind appears to have been made up to reject them by the Rev. Henry Bellairs, a stipendiary magistrate at the prison, who in a private letter opposed compassion. While awaiting her trip to the gallows, the prison chaplain took advantage of the governor's brief absence to subject Ball to a form of torture. Determined to extract a confession and repentance, he forcefully held her hand over a lit candle until it blistered, all the while assuring her that otherwise her entire body would burn in hell for a hundred years. This gruesome incident was reported to the magistrates by an assistant matron who witnessed it, and the chaplain was suspended. The governor on his return was informed by Ball that she had put arsenic on a mantel shelf behind and above the table at which her husband ate and told him that, if he wanted to add salt to his meal, he would find it there. She may have assumed that, if he mistakenly took the poison, she could not be held responsible for the accidental death. When the governor inquired what had made her commit the crime, she replied that he had a habit of going with other women and had used her ill. She was the first woman in 18 years to be put to death publicly in Coventry.[21]

The century's second half did not begin reassuringly for a public unnerved by newspaper reports of multiple female poisonings during the previous decade. They could not have been unaware of the emotional aftermath of the trial of Charlotte Harris, which in the hands of the press became a saga. She, her slightly younger husband Henry Marchant, and their two children lived in Bath in "pretty good circumstances." He was a stonemason with a very good wage, while she sold oranges as a supplementary income. Both were in the prime of life, their age difference a mere four years, and they appeared to get on well together. Yet she purchased arsenic from a Bath chemist and Marchant fell ill on April Fool's Day, 1849. His symptoms were "usually observable in a case of poisoning." Initially, she resisted summoning medical aid but later called in a surgeon, Lloyd, who treated it as a natural illness. His patient died thirteen days later, and when he recommended a postmortem, the widow objected to the body being cut open, and Henry Marchant was speedily buried. To this point Charlotte had committed a perfect murder only for her motive to be suddenly revealed. She was "infatuated" with William Harris, an elderly man of perhaps 70 who lived nearby and possessed property. He had offered her marriage more than a month earlier and she had told acquaintances that it would be a good thing if she were a widow. On the day her husband became ill, she was seen going to Harris's house, and two days after Henry's death she was again seen with the elderly man of property. A week later she wed him. Such unseemly haste nourished unseemly talk. The body was disinterred, and the viscera were sent off to William Herapath for analysis. In his words, the presence of arsenic was "indisputably proved." She was sent for trial on the charge of willful murder.

After two full days of evidence the jury deliberated far longer than usual before finding her guilty. Mr. Justice Cresswell was in full agreement and sentenced her to death only for her counsel to enter a plea in arrest of execution on the grounds of her pregnancy. Confusion ensued once the judge ordered the doors of the court to be closed and instructed the high sheriff to impanel a jury of matrons. Twelve of those who had not escaped were chosen and instructed to retire to a convenient place and have if they so desired a medical adviser. They confirmed that she was quick with child. Her life was therefore spared during her confinement, but Home Secretary Sir George Grey made it clear that, once she was able to walk, she would be making her way to the public gallows. This extended delay gave the many opponents of capital punishment, and especially the capital punishment of women, ample time in which to mount a campaign for the commutation of her death sentence. One contention was that, "socially, the execution of it would do harm" and would be an outrage on the public good. Another petition—one "largely supported by the women of England," or so the *Daily News* asserted—was a protest "against the outrage of humanity contemplated in the execution of this wretched woman." Her sentence of death should be reduced to a "fitter and more efficient punishment." The more liberal well-known political figures, such as Richard Cobden and Henry Labouchère, aligned themselves with the appeals. "The scenes of public terror and death gratify the depraved appetite of the uneducated masses for violence and blood," they argued, "and, instead of being salutary warnings, become stimulants to further crime." Charlotte Harris was being transformed from a murderess who could not excite public sympathy into a devout and caring mother fully worthy of compassion. Under the weight of this pressure, Sir George Grey compromised. In November, he respited the death sentence during Her Majesty's pleasure, and, finally, in the spring of 1850 Harris was sentenced to two years of solitary confinement followed by transportation "beyond the seas for life." The Harris case, *The Times* commented, "transcends anything we have yet reported." In response, Grey assured the House of Commons that few poisoners escaped justice because the "'detection of murder by poison was so easy.'"[22]

Before the public had time to digest this sentence of a female poisoner who had cold-bloodedly killed her husband in order to free herself to wed a gentleman of property, there was a report of yet another wife who allegedly poisoned her husband and escaped the gallows. Anne and James Merritt had been married for almost nine years and were poor. James was a turncock for the East London Waterworks Company and earned 30 shillings a week. They occupied three rooms and had five children, and she had a sterling reputation both as mother and spouse. Three of their offspring had succumbed to childhood illnesses, and she probably suffered a depression, which deepened with her husband's extended bouts of drunkenness and their consequent bitter quarreling. A week before he became seriously ill, she purchased twopence worth of arsenic, one pennyworth for her sister and the other, she later explained, to put an end to her own desperate life. She changed her mind about suicide when, surprisingly, James started coming home sober. Her first choice of medical attention for her husband was Francis Toulmin, a surgeon, who had known her before her marriage and was no stranger to her husband. Toulmin was temporarily unavailable, as was Mr. Brooks, her next choice. Her third selection—another surgeon, Welch—declined to call at the home but sent two pills, which she administered to James. Much later that evening, January 24, Toulmin did arrive and treated the patient for his vomiting, intense stomach pain, and leg cramps. On returning home he sent pills containing calomel and opium to the Merritt household and made a call there the following morning, Friday, only to be told that James was dead. The cause became an instant topic of malicious gossip, for he was known to have been a member of a burial club, the Clapton Benefit. Anne Merritt quickly pointed out to those around her that if the burial insurance, seven pounds 10 shillings, was her motive she would surely have kept James alive for eight days longer in order to collect the full amount of £10. Toulmin, who considered the death somewhat unusual, "proposed a post-mortem." He did not insist upon it when the wife made no personal objection and explained that her husband had "great [religious] objection" to the cutting open of his body after death. Later that morning the coroner's constable called on the widow and mentioned the likelihood of an inquest. She saw no such need, as her "husband died a natural death." The authorities, on the other hand, were in earnest about an investigation of possible poisoning, so they even exhumed the body of the deceased's father and examined it for arsenic. None detected, the cause of death remained as the doctor had diagnosed, cholera.

That did not dissuade the coroner from instructing Toulmin to conduct a postmortem on James Merritt. He was assisted by his medical partner, while Welch sat in as the observer. The removal of the entire stomach and its contents revealed a number of red spots, which were often "observed in persons who have died of an irritant poison." So, stomach, intestines, and a portion of the liver were placed in an earthen jar and in a bottle, and Toulmin personally delivered them to the London Hospital, where they were analyzed by Henry Letheby, professor of chemistry. His reputation had been tarnished several years earlier during a trial in which prussic acid was the alleged poison. Letheby persuaded the defense counsel, Sir Fitzroy Kelly, who was later to become chief baron of the Court of the Exchequer, that the distinctive odor of bitter almonds coming from the deceased's stomach "might have been caused by her eating apple-pits." She would have needed to consume an unimaginable quantity to produce that odor. In Merritt's remains he detected more than enough arsenic to prove fatal, adding that much of that administered would have been lost during the intense vomiting. In his opinion it had been administered "not more than two or three hours before death." The coroner committed Anne Merritt for trial at the next assizes on the charge of willful murder. The inquest evidence was largely repeated, and her defense counsel, his fee financed by the sheriffs' special fund, read her statement to the magistrates. She had acquired the arsenic for her own use, being unable to live any longer with her drunken husband, but she changed her mind when he finally came home sober. She first placed the arsenic in a cupboard to which her husband was known to go for powders, so she destroyed the poison in the fire for fear he would think it was soda. The jury, impressed with Letheby's evidence, convicted her with a strong recommendation for mercy on account of her excellent character. Not that this excluded a sentence of death.

She attracted considerable public sympathy. A bullying police investigator was reprimanded by the judge for endeavoring to entrap her "in a most unmanly and unjustifiable manner." A number of newspapers did not find the medical evidence convincing. In a widely circulated letter to the editor of the *Daily News*, a member of the Royal College of Surgeons disputed Letheby's opinion on the length of time arsenic would be held in the stomach. Digestion, he emphasized, was far slower in the stomach of a drunken man. Merritt had a history of drunkenness. The *News of the World* likened the case to that of Eliza Fenning, which after 35 years was still believed to have been a travesty of English justice. Could the press, both metropolitan and provincial, "passively allow a fellow creature's life to be forfeited to confirm the fallible opinion and (it may be erroneous) judgment of a medical professor?" Were the prosecution's professional witnesses found to be in error, this case would stand as yet another landmark warning on the peril of circumstantial evidence. Absent any evidence of the condemned woman's administration of arsenic, could the public permit the execution to go ahead on the "mere humbug opinion of a doctor?" "Will it look either gracious or graceful," the *Bucks Advertiser* inquired, "to strangle this woman upon circumstantial evidence the most trifling?" That she was scheduled to hang on Easter Monday raised the question of her execution blighting a religious festivity. Once again, the home secretary compromised with the mounting press pressure. He selected three distinguished medical experts, one of them Sir Benjamin Brodie, the royal physician, to re-examine Letheby's apparently decisive opinion on the length of time the poison was retained in the stomach. One of the three confidentially advised Letheby of their opinion that it might have been longer. He responded with a letter for submission to Sir George Grey in which he insisted that for longer than four hours was improbable but not impossible. Anne Merritt's death sentence was another commuted to transportation for life.[23]

The trial judge, in his summation, had drawn attention to the horrible frequency of such crimes, as did *The Times*. That they cropped up almost every month was indicative, the leading newspaper worried, of "some signal depravity in the social institutions of the age." The press, not fully liberated of the "taxes on knowledge," reported in abundant detail criminal trials, especially those for murder. This, as the Harris and Merritt cases demonstrated, was giving newspapers a growing role "in the decision whether to hang or reprieve condemned murderers," particularly women. There were exceptions to this trend, and Mary Reeder was one. She was executed alongside her brother-in-law for the murder of her sister, who was his wife. He supplied the arsenic, and his wife's removal would allow them to continue their immoral relationship. They were not a couple to generate public sympathy. The *Daily News* remarked that the estimated 30,000 spectators who thronged the streets of Cambridge to watch their public deaths evidently did so "to gratify curiosity, and departed from the 'lesson of the gallows' no better than they came to it." The following spring there was another sensational poisoning case on trial, and it naturally engendered massive public interest. The accused was another female for whom the press did not attempt to generate popular sympathy on account of her "terrible celebrity" and her reputation as a "professional poisoner."[24]

The woman in question had, in 1828, at the age of 17, married Richard Chesham, an agricultural laborer in the Essex village of Clavering. They had six children, a daughter and five sons, and family life was a grim struggle. His wages were low and the cost of food was high. Four of the undernourished boys fell ill in January 1845, and their heavy vomit seeped through the floor of their room and the ceiling of the neighbors' room below and collected on the breakfast table. Two of the four, Joseph and James, died within days of each other. The attending doctor diagnosed English cholera, improbable as this was in the depths of winter. Sarah opposed a postmortem, declaring unbearable the thought of the boys being cut open. Some time later she was accused of poisoning the illegitimate infant of an unwed mother, Lydia Taylor, who had been dismissed as a domestic servant in the house of a farmer, Thomas Newton, the father. The severe illness and then demise of young Solomon Taylor became a topic of tittle-tattle. Lydia maintained that Sarah, already the focus of talk over the deaths of two of her sons, had acted at the prompting or inducement of Newton, who had no desire to be burdened with maintenance payments in support of mother and illegitimate child. Sarah's infrequent intimate contact with the child gave the mother's accusation an element of credibility and spurred on the sinister gossip. When a witness came forward with compromising if somewhat suspect information incriminating Sarah, she was arrested on August 11, 1846, and detained in custody. The exhumation of the bodies of her two sons quickly followed. The stomachs and contents were removed and forwarded to Guy's Hospital, London. There they were analyzed by Alfred Swaine Taylor.[25]

He fed the mounting poison hysteria. Secret poisoning was an escalating moral evil, he wrote, one which required the attention of professional toxicologists. The detailed reporting by the press of inquests and trials helped to explain in his opinion the relentless increase in the covert crime. Poisoners were taught how homicide was detected and what steps to take to avoid that inconvenience. "A large proportion of modern novels," he went on, "may be regarded as convenient handbooks of poisoning." Taylor was one of those who described Edward Bulwer-Lytton's *Lucretia* as a "most complete revelation of the art of murder by poison." The author quickly replied that he had carefully omitted details that "might lead to mischief." If administered in small doses at long intervals, Taylor contended, the symptoms occasionally resembled those of common afflictions such as severe dyspepsia. Nor did barristers escape his censure. He was following a well-trodden path. In his *An Analysis of Medical Science*, published more than two decades earlier, John Gordon Smith had warned "would-be experts" of the peril of the law courts. There they would face "dextrous" advocates whose principal aim was to "trick" and "deceive." Taylor looked to inquests, if conducted properly, to remove "unfounded suspicions, which often arise in cases of sudden death." Regrettably, not every coroner was "sufficiently aware of the importance of the chemical branch of evidence in cases of suspicious deaths." He informed the inquests on the two boys and young Solomon Taylor that in the former he had found more than enough arsenic to cause death but none at all in the body of the infant. Ignoring this, the coroner cavalierly added the child's death to Sarah Chesham's charge sheet, with the result that three rapid trials were held over the course of two days at the Shire Hall, Chelmsford, Essex, in March 1847. She was acquitted in each of them thanks largely to the skill of her defense counsel, Charles Chadwick Jones, who had presumably been appointed by the presiding lord chief justice. Jones had 20 years of experience and had been admitted to the select ranks of the serjeants-at-law. Unless it was "proved clearly and conclusively" that someone administered the poison, a charge of murder cannot be sustained, Professor Taylor acknowledged. An accused should be acquitted notwithstanding suspicious circumstances if there was a variance of medical evidence and an absence of positive proof of arsenic in the body. In the second and revised edition of *On Poisons*, the toxicologist was severely critical of Letheby's "purely speculative and wholly indefensible" opinion in the Merritt case. He had brought "disgrace on legal medicine leading to acquittal of the guilty and conviction of the innocent."[26]

Sarah Chesham quit the docks with her freedom intact. An intelligent woman, she had understood a lesson of Mary May's conviction and execution. Massive doses of poison led to sudden death, which excited dark suspicion, but administered in small doses a death might be attributed to natural disease. Yet influential organs of the press remained convinced of her guilt. *The Times* was in the vanguard. Prior to her three acquittals it had depicted her as a "reputed poisoner" who for a price willingly "put any expensive or disagreeable object out of the way." Richard Chesham fell into this category of unfortunates in 1850. He had a persistent cough, chest pains, and severe stomach pain and consistently vomited. The doctor who had identified English cholera as the cause of his sons' deaths now attended him, and when he expired in mid–May 1851, a postmortem was held and severe tuberculosis was named the cause. Nevertheless, a number of "suspicious circumstances," and the widow's evil reputation, sufficed for the coroner. He sent the stomach and intestines to the ever-ready Alfred Swaine Taylor for a thorough analysis. Finding no more than a very small quantity of arsenic, he could not state positively that it was the cause of death. However, in the bag of rice removed from the Chesham home he detected enough arsenic to kill six adults, for each grain was coated with it. Sarah had sworn that she had not fed any of her father's rice to her husband, a denial contradicted by other witnesses. Had he eaten the rice, a larger quantity of arsenic ought to have been detected in his body. Since so little was found, how could she have murdered him? Taylor offered a simple solution to the puzzle. She had killed by administering it in small, regular doses, he suggested, thereby accelerating her already ill husband's passing. Not that he convinced the jurors, who settled on consumption as the fatal illness. Although Sarah was again at liberty, the coroner, who four years earlier had added the alleged murder of Solomon Taylor to her charge sheet, now referred the case to the magistrates.[27]

The magistrates' clerk queried whether the evidence was strong enough to secure a conviction for administering poison with the intent to commit murder. Professor Taylor thought there would be little chance. He was sure that arsenic had been the cause of the husband's intermittent attacks, but for a safe conviction "strong medical proof" was necessary, and this the Crown did not have. Undismayed, the magistrates committed her for trial at the next assizes. *The Times* welcomed the decision, speculating, "What havoc may not have been wrought by a murderess in the full swing of her profession for four years together?" Sarah Chesham approached her fourth trial for willful murder at a distinct disadvantage. Her rescuer in the trials four years earlier, Sergeant Jones, was too ill to act once again as her defense counsel. The only legal assistance she received came from a "gentleman of the bar" who expressed a willingness to "put such questions to the witnesses" that were in her opinion material. There would be no thorough cross-examination of damaging witnesses, and one was produced by the magistrates' industrious clerk. She was Hannah Phillips. A former close neighbor and friend of Sarah, the pair had recently fallen out. The press was quick to note how "conclusively" Phillips testified on her revealing conversations with the prisoner, and many a newspaper crowned her as the trial's most important witness. Sarah, she stated, had admitted poisoning the child of Lydia Taylor, and had said there was no sin in killing ill husbands who were a household burden. An unhappy wife should simply bake and poison a pie. Sarah had not been happy with Richard, and Phillips implied that she had already initiated a relationship with his intended replacement. The report in local newspapers that Sarah had told Phillips she had indeed murdered her sons was instantly republished in the London dailies. To its credit, the *Morning Chronicle* dismissed the story as "altogether false." There had been no such confession, it announced.

The *Morning Herald*, on the other hand, found "contemptibly laughable" the evidence of medical men since they themselves daily prescribed the "self same poisons" as medicines. The medicinal use of poisons dated from the ancient world. More recently, Thomas Fowler had in 1786 published a *Medical Report of the Effects of Arsenic, in the Cure of Agues, Remitting Fevers, and Periodic Headaches*. His "Solution" became a popular and widely used therapy in the 19th century for a variety of ailments, from asthma to syphilis. The poison's medical benefits were promoted by the circulation of Jakob von Tschudi's report in 1851 on the arsenic-eating peasants of mountainous Styria. His claim that it benefited their physical appearance and robust health did not go unchallenged. Alfred Swaine Taylor was one of several experts who dismissed the story of arsenic eaters as a fable. W.B. Estevan, a physician, in a lengthy article in the journal of the British Medical Association criticized Tschudi's article as unscientific. He had accepted hearsay evidence and had failed to prove that what the peasants actually consumed was arsenic by analyzing it chemically. That did not discourage many a doctor and chemist from accepting as valid Tschudi's findings. Critics asserted, however, that "Orthodox medicine was literally poisoning its patients" and that poisonous medicines were the cause of "increased sickness amongst the populace."[28]

In summing up, the judge was less than judicial. He warned that the safety of mankind would be at risk if in this case there was no conviction. He appeared to accept at face value the statement attributed to Phillips that the prisoner had confessed to the murder of her two sons. Yet there was a measure of press uneasiness, not least the unwillingness of the medical men to swear positively that the arsenic detected in the deceased's stomach was sufficient to cause death. Bearing this in mind, the Crown had amended the indictment. Willful murder was replaced with the administration of poison with intent to murder, another capital crime. Sarah Chesham had the doubtful distinction of being the last woman to go to the gallows for that crime. Then there was the credibility of Phillips's recollection of her conversations with the prisoner, which had gone largely unchallenged. Not that this discouraged the bulk of the press from convincing itself, and as it hoped its readers, of the justice of Chesham's conviction. *The Times* once again took the lead. It reported that the executed Mary May had blamed Sarah Chesham for her crime, that twice before, in her trials for the deaths of her sons, "although her guilt was said to be clear," Chesham had escaped justice. What is more, she had learned from the medical evidence against her on both earlier occasions how to poison without risking identification as the culprit. She had killed her husband with repeated small doses of arsenic, and the evidence of this, the press assured its readers, was "too clear to admit of any doubt." Frighteningly, the Fourth Estate added, there was "too much reason to fear that many others had also fallen victims to evil designs of [that] wicked wretch."[29]

Sarah's continuous assertions of her innocence, her "profane" declaration that she had no need of repentance, and her constant refusal to make a confession became fresh sources of uneasiness about her guilt. The newspaper that described itself as a voice of the working classes, *Reynolds's*, offered some comfort with its report that the jail's chaplain, who had ample opportunity to observe the condemned woman, believed she had been justly convicted. Chilling aspects of her behavior were allegedly documented—and four decades later were defined as the indicators of a psychopathic personality: callousness, an utter absence of remorse, and a habit of poisoning for the "mere love of slaying." But the plain determination of the authorities to convict her of a capital crime, even amending the indictment to circumvent the lack of sufficient arsenic to account for her husband's death on the original charge, inspired multiple posthumous challenges to her conviction and execution. The policeman who led the investigation, Superintendent Clarke, being convinced of her guilt, came under heavy criticism for her acquittals in the earlier three trials. Hence a suggestion that, determined to convict her at the fourth opportunity, the police improved the evidence of arsenic in the rice after its seizure from her home. Others place her alongside unfortunate Eliza Fenning as another martyr of criminal injustice. Not one of Fenning's alleged victims died, whereas all of Chesham's did. The latter's ardent defenders have been less successful in accounting for the willingness of so many of her contemporaries to step forward with damning evidence against her. A possible explanation of their conduct has been the malign influence on them of a press-inspired poisoning panic.[30]

Aware of the widespread public belief that Sarah Chesham was a professional poisoner, agents of Madame Tussauds "Chamber of Horrors" requested permission to take casts of her head. This the authorities refused. Her execution outside Springfield Prison, Chelmsford, on March 23, 1851, was watched by another immense gathering of spectators. They came from the neighboring counties, and while the great majority hiked, others chose the less tiring alternative of the railways. Sporting members of the capital's "swell mob" came down by train from London, often alighting at a station stop before Chelmsford in an effort to escape police vigilance. The extraordinary extent of the public's interest in this woman's end was the report of it in the local newspaper, which catered to the needs of the residents of the tiny village of

John O' Groats on the northeastern tip of mainland Scotland. Sarah Chesham was another who suffered an unnecessarily long and excruciatingly painful public strangulation at the hands of the incompetent and nervous public executioner, William Calcraft. Another topic of press discussion was the question too important to be overlooked. Should not Parliament limit the ease with which poisons, especially arsenic, could be obtained? Rigid controls needed to be placed on the sale of poison in every form. When required, other than for medicine, the application ought to be endorsed by a magistrate, or a church or chapel minister, or some other well-known local figure. The bill already before Parliament, introduced by the Earl of Carlisle, was considered defective in these respects.[31]

A clause to exclude women from the purchase of arsenic, given their prominence in poisoning deaths, was withdrawn in the face of vehement female protests. Under the act, particulars of every sale were to be entered in the vendor's "poison" book: the date of the sale, the name and surname of the purchaser and that person's abode and occupation, the quantity sold, and the purpose for which it was required. There were to be no sales to persons unknown to the vendor unless in the presence of a witness, and the purchaser must be of full age. When less than 10 lbs. was sought, the white arsenic was to be colored with soot or indigo in the hope of avoiding the numerous fatal kitchen mishaps where arsenic was mistaken for flour. Vendors who violated the act's provisions were liable to fines of £20, but they were often lax in their respect of the provisions, and a free trade in poison quickly appeared to be as robust as ever. Before long the press was in full cry for restrictions on the sale of other dangerous materials, such as strychnine, for there was little evidence of a slackening in the high incidence of murder by poisoning. The *Illustrated London News*, which began publication in 1842, had the middle class as its market, but the *Penny Illustrated Newspaper* was a weekly that from 1861 catered to the working classes on the social ladder. So did the *Illustrated Police News*, which had a circulation of 150,000 in 1872 and 300,00 in 1877. Both weeklies were accused of encouraging crime with their "detailed illustrations."[32]

Historian Jan Bondeson has examined 56 cases of murder committed during the second half of the 19h century. Twelve were unsolved. Of the remainder, only three were the crimes of women equipped with poison. Many victims were shot, revealing the ease with which revolvers were obtained. Equally striking was the frequency with which killers' counsels sought to advance the insanity defense.[33]

CHAPTER FOUR

A Form of Clemency

THE ARSENIC ACT RECEIVED ROYAL ASSENT in mid–June 1851, and the regulations for the safe sale of the poison were widely circulated by the press. Of course, the lower orders, among whom the vast majority of poisoners were believed exclusively to be found, were probably less aware immediately of the measures designed to keep it out of their hands. Another reason why the act was bound to be limited was the widespread use of doses of the poison to kill rats as well as humans. On the other hand, an improvement in the quality of policing merited the attention of the general public and of poisoners. London's Metropolitan Police, established in 1829, was a new police force under the supervision of the home secretary, but there was public resistance to a national police force out of fear it would jeopardize British liberties. Nor did the new police immediately inspire public confidence as skillful gatherers of evidence with which to convict criminals. But starting in 1856 new police forces were organized in municipal boroughs, rural counties, and large provincial cities and towns. Against a background of deepening public uneasiness as demobilized veterans of the Crimean War against Russia became restless given their difficulty finding employment, there was at least greater interest in a national regularization of policing. There were signs that the transportation of criminals to the other side of the world, Australia, was nearing its end, and a realization that if "the country must for the future learn to live with its criminals, it must pay the price of protection against them." The funding of the provincial police—and by the end of the 1850s there were 259 separate local forces—remained in the hands of tightfisted magistrates. An innovation was the creation of a national inspectorate of constabulary to promote Home Office standards of policing. The Treasury granted subsidies to those forces judged efficient by the inspectorate, thereby indirectly acknowledging that crime was a national problem. Perhaps it was not a surprise that the working classes, who made up a large proportion of the population, suspected the new police of being agents of those occupying the higher rungs of the social ladder.

Rate-payers whose taxes financed the police sought a less costly alternative to these uniformed instruments of crime prevention. They believed that detection would be a less expensive means of crime solution. Press sensationalism of violent crimes, such as murder, and the attempted assassination of the Queen, reinforced arguments for detective departments. The middle classes saw in social discipline, and the swift solving of crimes, an essential ingredient of their civilized and sophisticated society. Charles Dickens was among those popular authors who nourished the belief that plainclothes policemen would protect them from the "dangerous classes." Such assurances did little to diminish the suspicion of the lower orders that policemen in plain clothes would be agents of class espionage. Even among the middle classes the close dealings of detectives with criminals led to a nagging fear of police corruption. Several senior detectives of the Metropolitan Police were suspected in 1877 of fraud, forgery, the acceptance of bribes, and of "tipping-off" criminals of intended police action. Three of them were jailed for two years. Then there was always the danger that the detectives would become, as some of them did, a political police with the eventual creation of a "Special Branch." As a result, in many police divisions, detective investigations were conducted by uniformed senior police officers. Inspector Coward had led the investigation of Ann Merritt, Superintendent Flanagan conducted that of Sarah Ann French, and while Mary Ball was investigated by Constable Vernon, Sarah Chambers was relentlessly pursued to the very end by Superintendent Clarke. His personal conviction of her guilt may have caused him to cross the line by "improving" the evidence against her.[1]

Not that the law was always enforced. Quickly exposed for failing to abide by the terms of the Arsenic Act were druggists who continued to sell fatal doses of the poison without coloring it with indigo or soot. This was the instrument of death acquired by Mary Emily Cage. She and her husband had been married for 20 years of "continual strife," during which she had given birth to 17 children, not all of whom were fathered by James Cage. She was promiscuous, formed liaisons, and from time to time quit the cottage. On this latest occasion she returned after six weeks with one of her daughters, Sibella, who—pregnant—had left with her and soon gave birth to an illegitimate infant. James, who had served a brief term of imprisonment for assaulting his unfaithful wife, decided to repeat this form of chastisement. Soon afterwards he fell seriously ill. Mary sought medical advice, and the doctor diagnosed rheumatism. His medicines proving ineffectual, she persuaded a neighbor to purchase a pennyworth of arsenic, declaring that it was needed by another of her daughters to suppress the mice that were pestering her. From this moment James's condition continued to deteriorate. He complained of pain in his throat, stomach, and bowels before sinking into delirium and dying. Mary Emily lost no time organizing the funeral, only for the rector to intervene. As the church bells tolled and bearers lifted the coffin from the bier outside the cottage, he requested that it be returned to the cottage. He appears to have been surprised at the absence of opposition to the immediate interment and the lack of any inquiry into the death. The coroner announced an inquest, during which the discovery in the cottage of powder similar to that obtained for Mary by a neighbor saw her sent for trial at the Ipswich Assizes. The jury convicted her of willful murder by the administration of poison in small doses, and the judge sentenced her to death.

Her execution was delayed because the hangman, Calcraft, was already busy in Norwich and the "Warwick hangman" also had his hands full. Mary Emily admitted being a sinner but told the chaplain, "I am innocent of the murder of my husband." To reassure those members of the public who might have had reasonable doubt that justice had been done, for the evidence had been circumstantial not scientific, the press portrayed her as a spouse whose gross immorality merited the severest punishment. She spent nights with other men, bringing them into the cottage, where she locked her husband in another room or sent him to the local public house with one of their sons. Nor were the deaths of five of her children six years earlier forgotten. Had she murdered them? The body of one of the children was exhumed, but, there being no chemical analysis of the stomach and its contents, the jury returned a verdict of natural death. After all, one of the infectious diseases might have been the cause of the tragedies. A crowd of eight thousand, composed of young men and women of the lower orders, witnessed her gruesome death on the scaffold erected in front of the Shire Hall, Ipswich. The pharmacist who had sold the colorless poison to her escaped the fine of £20 that the Arsenic Act imposed.[2]

That same year, 1851, proved to be a difficult one for Sarah Ann French and her husband William, a farm laborer. Their infant was exceedingly sickly, and her sister, Jane Piper, lodged with them and her presence brought to the cottage daily her young man, James Hickman. When his sweetheart moved on, his calls continued, and he read to the ailing young boy the "nice books" supplied by the parson. Over time intimacy deepened between Sarah and Hickman, and he may have assured her of his desire to marry her if she were a widow. William fell ill over Christmas and died on January 8, 1852. The suddenness of the death of the "hale well-conditioned young fellow" stirred the coroner into action, but there being no clear evidence of a crime, the inquest concluded that the death had been natural. This verdict did not satisfy the senior local policeman, Superintendent Flanagan of the Sussex Constabulary. He pursued an investigation, which revealed the widow's "circumstances," one of which was her purchase of arsenic. Another was her exceedingly close relationship with Hickman. His presence during William's last days and final hours of life naturally gave rise to scurrilous talk about their intimacy, which intensified when he replaced the deceased in house and bed. Jane Piper returned and became the third occupant of the bed, and the ménage à trois sparked even more sinister talk of a "dreadful crime" committed "entirely from the unrestrained indulgence of an impure desire."[3]

A second inquest was called, the body was exhumed, and the stomach and its contents were sent to Alfred Swaine Taylor, who found an adequate amount of arsenic to cause death. Impressed with the evidence of so renowned an expert, the inquest jury convicted the widow of murder. Did she wish to say anything, the coroner inquired. "I am not guilty: I am quite innocent, if it is the last word I had to speak; that was the last thing in my thoughts." Hickman was the guilty party, she announced, but on the coroner's warrant she alone went for trial at the next assizes.[4]

The two questions the trial jurors were required to answer were did she administer the poison, or did she know of and sanction the act? The judge had at the last minute provided her with legal representation, and her counsel argued that Hickman might have been the murderer. That she suffered fits and during the trial fell into a stupor for which a doctor applied "restoratives" might have been advanced as another line of argument, but it was not made. A plea of insanity often amounted to a plea for clemency. The judge in his summation was content to clarify the law for the jurors. It made no difference whatever, he told them, if they thought the prisoner administered the poison by her own hand or if she knew it was administered by another person or whether she had counseled that person to supply it. Even if Hickman had some hand in the death or in the administration of the poison, Mr. Justice Parke continued, she was guilty of murder in the eyes of the law if she had prior knowledge of it or in any manner counseled him to commit it. Having deliberated for two hours, which was somewhat longer than was usual even in capital cases, the jury returned with a verdict that the judge interpreted as a conviction. Sarah Ann French was sentenced to death.[5]

Once again, the press sought to nip in the bud any expression of public sympathy for this doomed woman, for appeals on behalf of condemned criminals were being made to the new Conservative home secretary, Spencer Walpole. Opponents of capital punishment were the vanguard of the appellants, but the press dwelt upon the immoral character of Sarah French's conduct to prevent "any mercy being shown to her." Of those women who had recently been executed for poisoning their husbands, "perhaps none ever exhibited so revolting a want of feeling in carrying out her diabolical plan of murder as this wretched criminal." On the night of the very day, the Sabbath, on which her husband was buried, the *Oxford Journal* reported, "the depraved woman" gave license to her desires under circumstances so revolting that it declined to "recall them to recollection." Perceived violations of mid–Victorian morality told heavily against the lower orders. The prison chaplain thoughtfully authorized the press to reveal that she had fully acknowledged her guilt to him and "the justice of her sentence." What is more, he protested against "the public confidence in the verdicts of juries being at all suspended upon so uncertain a thing as a condemned criminal's confession." The justice of a conviction, he insisted, did not need to be vindicated by any such admission of guilt for its acceptance by the general public, because such confessions were often "most uncertain and shifting" in their details. Many spectators rented upstairs windows in neighboring houses to ensure a clear view of her "long and severe" strangling at the end of Calcraft's short rope.[6]

The talk that females convicted of murder were being treated with greater leniency than was customary by the current home secretary had clearly not proven true for Sarah Ann French. Nevertheless, the cases of Betsy McMullen and Celestina Sommer suggested that juries were increasingly reluctant to convict certain female poisoners of a crime that carried a death sentence and that the Home Office was disinclined to send a woman so condemned to her appointment with the inept hangman. The justification for clemency was frequently "extenuating circumstances," although they were rarely clearly defined. Daniel McMullen was a flour dealer in the mill town of Bolton, and his tempestuous and violent relationship with his wife, Betsy, was fueled by their common addiction to drink. She, according to their domestic servant Mary Hatton, seldom went to bed sober. When they fought, she used the kitchen weapons at hand—knives, basins, and the rolling pin—while he kicked her violently and "ill-used" her. On June 21, 1856, he became ill two weeks after his most recent bout of heavy drinking, and a surgeon, Dorrian, was called. To the inquest that followed her master's death the domestic servant gave damning evidence. She chronicled the suspicious conduct of the mistress. She often added a pinch of white powder to his food and tea, and eventually to the medicine prescribed by Dorrian. He was very sick and often vomited, and when, on one occasion, he drank only a little of the tea, the domestic servant emptied the remainder into a bottle and sent it to the doctor. Clearly suspicious of what was taking place, she took advantage of the mistress's drunken condition to remove from her pocket the paper containing the white powder and passed this also to the surgeon.[7]

Dorrian, on being called by the coroner, reported finding in the paper "tartarised antimony," which he had not prescribed but which was valued by medical men in the treatment of cholera and as an emetic. During his postmortem examination of the body there was no appearance of natural disease to explain the death, but it was similar to that caused by "excessive and improper use" of tartarised antimony. If it did not cause the death, it certainly accelerated it. An analytical chemist, H.H. Watson, then reported his discovery of traces of antimony in the bottles containing medicine and tea and its presence in the deceased's liver and kidneys. J. Rowland Simpson, a Bolton druggist, told the inquest of the widespread sales in the town of penny papers containing emetic powders of tartarised antimony and cream of tartar. He "usually" cautioned the purchaser to be careful in its use and to divide each paper into four doses, he testified. No less damning under the circumstances was the evidence that the couple had jointly insured their lives for £100 payable to the survivor. The coroner's jury concluded that the death had been accelerated by antimony willfully administered by the wife and expressed stern disapprobation of the indiscriminate dispensing of such medicines. Betsy McMullen was committed for trial at the next assizes. The inquest had exposed the "most extraordinary practice" among Bolton's druggists of selling powders, known locally as "quietness," to women whose husbands drank heavily. The division of the papers containing the powders into four or five doses corresponded with the strength of four or five grains. This powerful medicine was wholly unfit to be dealt with by ignorant persons, and if administered carelessly or wickedly was an "exceedingly dangerous poison." Consequently, as the *Dublin Medical Press* commented, the powders were not inappropriately named "quietness," for if taken they were likely "to terminate in the grave."

"I have merely to say that it is a case in which I fear it will be your duty to bring in a bill for willful murder," Mr. Justice Willis advised the grand jury at the assizes. The trial did not want for medical evidence attributing the death to the administration of long continued doses of antimony. Betsy McMullen had the good fortune to be represented by a highly skilled counsel, Mr. Sergeant Wilkins, who declared that, happily, such cases were "very unfrequent." Moreover, there was no proof of what would be a poisonous dose, or that such a dose could be swiftly countered by antidotes. The truth was that antimony's toxicity was comparable to that of arsenic yet was often less than fatal because it caused violent vomiting that expelled "most of the toxin from the body before it [could] be absorbed." This discouraged its "misuse as a murder weapon." Mr. Justice Willis, a stalwart of the patriarchy, was appalled by the evidence of this woman "lying in a man's bosom, and almost breathing his breath, should be administering to him, unknown to him, a medical drug for the purpose of sickening him, with whatever effect." This was a "most horrible thing." The jurors, however, in the words of their foreman, took a "merciful view" of the case and, after deliberating for no more than 30 minutes, acquitted Betsy McMullen of willful murder and convicted her of manslaughter. The verdict did not please the judge. They had gone out of their province, he reproved the occupants of the jury box, and for reasons not strictly connected with the proven facts had set aside capital punishment by convicting her of a secondary offense. However, her conduct had been "utterly inconsistent with her duty as a wife," so he would make an example of her in light of the apparent practice in Bolton of selling "quietness." He sentenced her to transportation for the term of her natural life.[8]

The case attracted national attention, and not just because the jury had treated with clemency this woman charged with murder. This had not been particularly unusual during the Bloody Code and its 200 capital crimes. What caught the attention of the press and thus of the public was the jury's stern criticism of the vast number of Bolton vendors who sold a dangerous drug so recklessly. Trained chemists had long argued that those who dispensed drugs should not be entirely ignorant of them, and that sellers of arsenic, in particular, should be licensed. But it was not until 1868 that chemists and druggists whose names were not to be found on the Register of Pharmaceutical Chemists were disqualified from "trafficking in drugs and poisons."[9]

The Sommer case, on the other hand, excited public interest and considerable controversy because it fortified the suspicion of a gender change in the enforcement of the criminal law. Celestina Christmas was one of eight children of a respectable silversmith. As such she was raised in relative comfort, had the benefit of an education, and qualified as a member of the lower middle class. Perhaps seduced, she gave birth to an illegitimate daughter, to whom she gave her own surname since the father was never identified. From birth the child was sent to a minder, Julia Harrington, who was paid a half crown, eight of which made a pound, each week. Occasionally, Celestina increased the payment to five shillings and financed it out of her earnings as a music teacher. Some time after her marriage to Charles Sommer, a stern Prussian engraver, she collected her daughter from the minder, brought the child back to her home, took it into the cellar, and cut its throat. The Sommers' maid,

Rachel Munt, aged 16, heard the tragedy taking place and the following morning brought the body to the attention of her sister, who happened to be making a flying visit to see her. Her sister reported what she had seen to the authorities, and on confirming the information the police arrested Celestina.

The trial on an indictment of willful murder opened at the Old Bailey on April 7, 1856. Her good fortune equaled that of Betsy McMullen, for she had in Sergeant Ballantine a defense counsel of great ability. In his cross-examination of Rachel Munt he dwelt upon her inactivity, remaining in bed while overhearing what was happening in the cellar and not giving a thought to drawing it to the master's attention when he returned home. She could not have been frightened about approaching him for she admitted that he was always good to her. On the other hand, she may have been discouraged from so acting by the master's physical mistreatment of his wife, whom he beat. Indeed, her mistress appeared chronically unhappy and tearful. A policeman, Joseph Howe, overheard the conversation between the prisoner and a visitor, the former minder Harrington, when the latter sought to comfort her. The mother's behavior in his opinion was not that of a woman in her right mind. She talked to herself, frequently about the plays *Hamlet* and *Richard III*, declared that the child had been her dead brother's, and admitted that she had killed it not knowing what to do for the best. Under cross-examination, something of a Ballantine specialty, the policeman confirmed that the prisoner talked aloud to herself and said that her very first words were the identity of the actor who ought in her opinion to have played the lead roles in the two plays. She may have talked for as long as three quarters of an hour, the policeman estimated, but he did not think she was rambling. Ballantine failed to convince the jury that the accused had been out of her mind when examined by the police and thus deserved to be treated with a measure of clemency. Instead, after a brief recess, the jurors found her guilty of willful murder, and she was sentenced to death.[10]

Petitions for clemency, at least the commutation of the death sentence, were delivered to the Home Office. A month earlier, Mary Weeks and Emma Mussett, who had been convicted of murdering their children and sentenced to death, had escaped the gallows. Their sentences had been commuted to transportation for life. The home secretary's decision to save this later woman from a public hanging by ordering her imprisonment for life was vehemently protested. Elements of the press considered Celestina Sommer an exceptional case. No earthly reason could be assigned to this crime, they contended, apart from a miserly desire to save the cost of the child's weekly maintenance. What is more, she stood convicted of "one of the most diabolically cruel murders that ever brought a human being to a level with demons." If ever a woman deserved to be hanged, it was Celestina Sommer. Newspapers argued that a capital crime, willful murder, administered so partially and capriciously should either be abolished or restored to its original strictness. *The Queen*, which was usually concerned with the fashion and culture of the upper classes, wanted the prerogative of mercy removed from the hands of the secretary of state at the Home Office. He expressed the hope "that no erroneous opinion will get abroad that women may commit murder with impunity." In Parliament, Lord St. Leonards inquired if it was the intention of the government to introduce a bill and to advise "the Crown to exercise the prerogative of mercy to all cases in which women were the offenders." Lord Granville replied that the recent commutations had arisen "from special circumstances of an exceptional character." In a clear attempt to quiet the mounting uneasiness, however, he gave an assurance that the government had "no intention of altering either the tenor or execution of the law with regard to female criminals." This statement was welcomed by the *Carlisle Journal*, an advocate of the abolition of capital punishment. It predicted that after the commutation of Celestina's death sentence the "Executive" would not be permitted by public sentiment to execute women. The *Journal* would have been more accurate had it limited the women saved from the gallows to mothers who murdered their young children. Temporary insanity and depressed circumstances had long led juries to treat such women with a measure of clemency. Celestina Sommer was shipped first to Millbank Prison, then to Brixton, and finally to Fisherton House, an asylum near Salisbury, which took private and pauper patients. There she died at the age of 31 in 1859.[11]

Government assurances of gender equality in punishment failed to extinguish the deepening suspicion that in some way or by some means women who committed murder were escaping the punishment set by the law for that crime. Also, uneasiness deepened over the crucial importance of expert medical opinion in poisoning trials. No longer were the doctors content to be "indifferent auxiliaries of justice," *Dublin University Magazine* carped, and were now seeking to "'direct and administer it.'" What is more, they were permitted to testify "on the basis of opinion—and even opinion not derived from their own first-hand observation." There was controversy over the expert evidence during the trial of William Palmer, for famed toxicologist Alfred Swaine Taylor had failed to find the alleged poison in those body portions he examined. That, according to the experts for the defense, William Herapath and Henry Letheby, should not have been a problem had strychnine been present. A truly skilled expert, they testified, could detect that poison with ease "regardless of dose and its material contamination." And on the steps to the gallows Palmer made the enigmatic statement that he was innocent of poisoning by strychnine. This raised fresh concerns about the justice of his conviction, and one London newspaper, the *Examiner*, expressed grave doubt, as had a chaplain in an earlier case, of the wisdom of the attempts to extract a confession from him. This implied a want of credible evidence in support of the verdict. Palmer's defiant last-minute utterance would damage science, the *Association Medical Journal* feared. What then was the public to make of the evidence of alienists? What trust could they place in this class of medical men later known as psychiatrists? Their testimony appeared to have proven decisive in the trials of two women charged with the willful murder of their children.[12]

Alienists knew that the M'Naghten rules had not clarified the critical point at which the person who committed a violent crime should be judged insane. As the law was currently understood, if at the time of the offense the accused "knew right from wrong, and that he was doing wrong, he must be brought in guilty, whether insane or not." Yet clemency did on occasion move juries and judges "to repudiate this dogma in particular cases." Consequently, whether or not a prisoner for whom insanity was alleged was convicted or acquitted remained "a matter of chance." Alienists were in no doubt that the nature of insanity as a physical disease "must be guided by the knowledge of those," that is themselves, who had made it their study. They alone were the experts, for barristers were unable to appreciate the symptoms of the disease and believed that the medical men who perceived and recognized the "serious meaning" of the symptoms made the crime the proof of insanity. They might quite properly assert that there were two elements to the nature of the crime. The first was the knowledge that it was contrary to law. The second was "the will to do or to forbear doing it." The task of alienists, however, was to demonstrate that some insane have the former but are deprived by disease of the latter. "They may know an act to be unlawful but may be imputed to do it by a conviction or an impulse which they have not the will or the power to resist." Students of insanity agree that an "irresistible homicidal impulse" does occur, but when used to excuse a crime prosecuting counsels and public writers assail it as a "dangerous and absurd medical crotchet." They contend that the impulse can be resisted and that it makes no difference whether it is the result of disease, for the object of the law is to "make people control their evil impulses." A mother "worn down by anxiety and ill-health" falls into a depression, and "one day, in a paroxysm of despair, kills her children in order to save them from misery on earth, or because she is so miserable that she knows not what she does." Was this a valid medical diagnosis of Mary Ann Brough?[13]

On June 9, 1854, the throats of her six children were cut, and, having all but confessed to the crimes, she was found guilty of six willful murders by the coroner's jury and committed for trial at the Surrey Assizes. Proceedings opened at Guildford at the early hour of nine o'clock on the morning of August 9. Presiding was Sir William Erle, who had been elevated to the bench nine years earlier. His duty as a judge, opined a barrister of large reputation, was "by his technical knowledge and experience [to] bring the facts clearly before the jury." He was, of course, aware of the judges' response to the request by the House of Lords for their opinion of the law applicable to insanity in criminal cases. All but one of them had declared "that although a person may in a particular manner act under an insane delusion, and act in consequence thereof, he is equally liable with a person of a sane mind." Erle, since his elevation to the bench, had acquired a high reputation. He had a "very judicial manner," was thoroughly independent, exhibited an "earnest desire to secure justice in the cases he tried," swiftly grasped the material facts of a case, and reached a decided conclusion upon their legal effects. Not that he was entirely without fault. He had a habit of "looking into the air instead of into the face of his audience," which may have been due to his slight speech impediment, and he could be remarkably obstinate once he reached an opinion. Beneath him in the court sat the competitive counsels. The chief prosecutor was the "acute and clearheaded" William Henry Bodkin. In the words of one envious contemporary, he would have "attained a very high position" had his "education been equal to his natural ability." Edwin James, QC, led the defense. His first ambition had been to achieve stardom on the stage, but his acting career had been blighted, or so it was believed, by his far from handsome face. Called to the bar in 1836, he was made a Queen's Counsel in 1850 and developed an immensely profitable practice. Highly successful in court, he was appointed recorder of Brighton, which placed him on the bench temporarily to settle minor cases. His advocacy of political reforms, among them democracy, alienated the establishment, while his financial extravagance emptied his coffers and his monetary carelessness ultimately ruined his legal career in Britain. The first QC ever to be disbarred, he emigrated to the United States.[14]

Bodkin anticipated a defense claim that at the time she killed the children the prisoner was not mentally responsible. He fastened on circumstances that exhibited her "self-possession," and the senior police officer, a chief superintendent, testified that Mary Ann Brough was composed when she told him that she had been "all bad" on the day in question and had wanted the medicine prescribed by her surgeon, Izod. She put the children to bed, went for a walk, and on her return took to bed herself only for the children to keep calling out until midnight. She went downstairs to get a knife to cut her own throat but was unable to see because of "something like a cloud" and came across instead her husband's razor. With it she went back upstairs and severed the throats of the children before attempting to do away with herself in the same way. There could be no doubt, then, of the propriety of the verdict reached by the coroner's jury. However, the "great point for the consideration of the moralist, and even the jurist, [was] how far the woman [was] responsible for her own actions."[15]

James in addressing the jury complimented the prosecutor on the "fair, considerate, and impartial manner" in which he laid out the Crown's case. Speaking with "great eloquence and power" himself, he did not argue that this mother had been under any delusions and conceded that currently she was in all probability "perfectly sane." Instead, she committed the "dreadful deed" while under the influence of a "temporary frenzy and an impulse it was impossible for her to control." Using Alfred Swaine Taylor's book as his reference, he asserted that her "sudden frenzy" had been relieved by the blood that flowed from her self-inflicted wound. Hence the "dark cloud" of which she had spoken passed away and she became aware of what she had done. For this explanation to be accepted legally it required that there be independent proof that her state of mind at the time of the crime destroyed her knowledge of right and wrong. To this end James selected with considerable care several medical experts.[16]

Surgeon Izod, who had attended Mrs. Brough for several years, was the first of them to testify. He reported her severe bleeding from the nose in 1852 and her very difficult pregnancy of that same year. Then, eight days after the infant's delivery, she had suffered a paralysis that caused her to lose completely the use of her left side. She had lost her speech, and her face had become distorted. This may have called to the minds of a number of listeners "puerperal and lactation insanity." The latter, once known as "milk fever," had at the beginning of the century failed as a defense of temporary insanity. Brough gradually recovered, Izod went on, without ever entirely regaining her power, and he had noted symptoms of a disordered brain. Because of this he had instructed her to avoid excitement of any description for it would be dangerous and had repeated this caution just days before the crime.[17]

Next called was Forbes Winslow, already well known as an authority on insanity. He had financed his medical education by working as

The Times's journalist in the gallery of the House of Commons. He owned two private asylums in the capital and had established his discipline's first specialized journal. Health, he held, "was that state in which the mind was receptive to moral truths." The law "should adopt a simple test for [mental] responsibility, which was had the accused '*lost all power of control over his actions*'"? In his private opinion, Mary Ann Brough's crime bore "insanity stamped on its very face." Who could believe that a mother who cut the throats of her six children was sane? Winslow carefully assured judge and jury that murderers who escaped the extreme penalty of the law with the plea of insanity suffered severe punishment. The clemency was limited. Pay a visit to Bethlem Royal Hospital, he told critics; there they would find criminal lunatics confined "like wild beasts in an iron cage."[18]

Referring to Izod's evidence, Winslow declared that while paralysis might exist in some cases without insanity, it was always symptomatic of a disease of the brain. Heavy bleeding from the nose was "a symptom of a congested brain" and was considered "an effort of the brain to relieve itself." He had spent a decade and a half studying the brain, he informed the jury, had "carefully attended" the violence in this case, and had conducted a long interview with the accused. Under cross-examination by Bodkin, Winslow was of the opinion that the accused's brain was structurally disorganized and that this would make it far more disposed to be affected by a moral shock. Her husband's dramatic and far-reaching response to her adultery was certainly just such a great moral shock and would have created the dangerous excitement that Izod had repeatedly urged her to avoid. Re-examined by James, he remained convinced that at the time of the crime she had been suffering from a disease of the brain. Both of the other medical witnesses called by the defense, Daniel and Ingledew, corroborated Winslow's medical opinion that the prisoner's brain was diseased. All three were "medical gentlemen of extensive reputation," the press assured the public.

Mr. Justice Erle opened his summing up with a caution to the jury. The argument that the prisoner had acted under an uncontrollable impulse was a "most dangerous doctrine, for undoubtedly every crime was committed under some impulse, and the object of the law was to control impulses of that description and thus prevent crime." If there were grounds for supposing that, at the time the killings were committed, she was not in a sane state of mind, that would be a justifiable ground on which to acquit her. On the other hand, should the jury conclude that as a result of her unfortunate relationship with her husband she pondered violence to herself and others, which operating on her diseased brain made her temporarily insane during the act of violence, it was his duty to inform them that this would not excuse her from the legal consequences. It would be their duty to convict her of willful murder. After two hours of deliberation the jurors took refuge, the *Daily News* commented, in a most lenient interpretation of the law. The enormity of her crime had probably convinced them that she had acted under an insane impulse. She was acquitted on the grounds of insanity and ordered to be "detained in safe custody during her Majesty's pleasure."[19]

The verdict raised yet again "the extent to which an allegation of 'monomania' should be held valid as an excuse for the guilt of murder, and the kind of evidence to be received in proof of such an allegation." There was a belief that the plea of insanity had secured clemency for many a deliberate criminal who deserved stern punishment. Yet there was little doubt that persons who were victims of a "deficiency or malformation of intellect" had unjustly suffered the full pains and penalties of the law. One suggested solution to the puzzle of insanity was the "common-sense principle." It should regulate all such acquittals, and the "authority of medical opinion ought not to be accepted as all in all." Whenever the disease was apparent to all eyes, common sense would then be "of as much avail as medical theorizing."[20]

Mary Ann Brough was held in what was then called the Bethlehem Hospital Asylum, and there she died on March 18, 1861. An inquest was necessarily held on this "criminal lunatic," and the *Morning Chronicle* headed its account with the eye-catching "Inquest on Mary Ann Brough, the Esher Murderess, and Nurse to the Prince of Wales." She had breastfed him as an infant. At the time of her admission to the asylum her general health had been "apparently good," but it was not long before she exhibited "peculiar symptoms of mental derangement." In 1856 it was another paralysis of her left side, in 1858 apoplexy and paralysis of mouth and tongue. In 1859 further paralysis caused her almost to lose the use of her legs, and her mind became weaker. In 1861 she was so weak she was unable to sit up and was provided with a waterbed; and on March 17 she lost consciousness and died the following day. The coroner doubted that insanity had anything to do with her death, an embarrassing statement, only to be immediately contradicted by Dr. William Charles Wood, a senior member of the asylum's medical staff. He was convinced that an organic disease had been going on in her brain for some time and cited as evidence the paralysis of one half of the hemisphere of the brain soon after her admission. He did inconveniently admit that there had been considerable doubt of the insanity verdict seven years earlier, there not being at the time "much evidence to prove her insanity." This comment did not receive widespread circulation, and the coroner's jury made its contribution to the quiet passing of Brough's life with the verdict of natural death.[21]

Two months after Brough's acquittal of multiple murders a retired seafaring man died some 140 miles to the north in Boston, Lincolnshire. His death saw the emergence of a serial killer. Captain Peter Mawer had been ill for about two weeks with sickness, vomiting, and intense thirst. He had suffered similar symptoms in the past, but never before had they been so violent. His doctor, Thomas Small, did not suspect poisoning nor did the colleague, Young, from whom he sought a second opinion. When the patient died, both medical men were satisfied that the death was natural. They were to change their minds eight years later. Yet in 1854 the behavior of Mawer's housekeeper, Catherine Wilson, gave rise to suspicion and gossip. She had severely restricted access to the ill man, she alone administered all of his medicine, and to the one nurse who did gain entry he complained that he was always worse after drinking the tea Wilson made for him. On his death came the revelation that, just two days earlier, he had altered his will. His brother ceased to be the beneficiary, and everything was left instead to Wilson. The brother, John, a hefty bricklayer, did not take the news well and was not the only person who suspected that the housekeeper had exerted undue influence on the dying man and then poisoned him. Indeed, this tale of a poisoning was to become a recurrent topic of local gossip for the next eight years. A local solicitor advised John that the will was perfectly drawn up and attested and would be invulnerable to a challenge. There was a fear that the hefty bricklayer would resort to violence when the housekeeper would not even permit him to see his dead brother, so she secured police protection. The doctors were still seemingly satisfied that the death was natural, so there was no inquest. She did seek to ensure the body would not be easily exhumed in the event of an investigation. The undertaker was instructed to remove the coffin already in the chosen grave site at the Methodist burial ground, dig the grave deeper, and place the original coffin on top of that holding Mawer's remains. Mrs. Wilson quickly collected her interest in the Mawer estate, initially estimated at £50, and moved south to London.[22]

Under a slightly different first name she captured greater attention in the capital. She stood in the dock of the Old Bailey on June 16, 1862, charged with feloniously administering with intent to murder an ounce of sulfuric acid to Sarah Carnell. They had been friends for near on five years, having been introduced by Carnell's third husband. He was a friend of a man named Taylor with whom Wilson was living as man and wife. The women had met occasionally, but over the previous 11 months "Mrs. Taylor" had become a more frequent visitor. The

Carnells had a somewhat estranged marital relationship. An engineer, he lived away in Marylebone in order, ostensibly, to be closer to his place of work. In truth she had wanted him out of the home because, in her opinion, he drank too much liquor, and he generally annoyed her. Nevertheless, when he came to see her they cohabited, and she visited him from time to time at his lodgings. She became violently ill after taking tea. The vomiting and purging did not cause her to suspect that she had been poisoned, but she had been seriously ill during the three nights "Mrs. Taylor" slept at her lodging house. Wilson recommended a rhubarb draft, but on her return from the druggist she brought a "black draught." She poured the draft from a bottle into a glass, which became very hot, and on sipping it Carnell's mouth burned and she spat it out onto the bedclothes. Her son took it back to the druggist, who checked it and declared it "all right." She told him to throw away the contents of the glass and the bottle, and this he did. Therefore, there was none to be analyzed later. She had not drawn "Mrs. Taylor's" attention to the discolored bedclothes, but they were shown to the lodger who stopped in to see her and she believed he had taken them away. The druggist's highly qualified assistant later informed the court that when he tasted the returned draft it had not burned his mouth. A police inspector was summoned and saw the damaged sheet and the nightdress the lodger held, and they were handed to him by Sarah Carnell, who was prosecuting the case against her friend. "I did not know my husband was living with the prisoner when I gave the information to the police," she swore. The inspector, Burroughs, then escorted her to a surgeon, Thomas Kirkby, who examined her mouth and was shown the bed sheet, which appeared to have been burnt and smelled of acid. The police investigation was somewhat slapdash, but the officer who tracked down "Mrs. Taylor" discovered her walking arm in arm on the street with Mr. Carnell. The absence of definitive proof that sulfuric acid had been added to the black draft, and there being no evidence of the prisoner's purchase or possession of the acid led the jury to acquit her. That a woman as clever and intelligent as Catherine Wilson would have resorted to sulfuric acid as a fatal poison was difficult to believe, for it would be immediately detected by the victim and too painful to swallow. Moreover, she was already familiar with the nearly undetectable colchicum, which was medicinally prescribed despite its toxicity for acute gout and rheumatism. Easier to believe is that, infuriated by her husband's intimate relationship with Wilson, of which she repeatedly denied knowledge, Sarah Carnell manufactured a case against her. The presiding judge was satisfied that there was too much reason to believe the accused guilty and so summed up most unfavorably against her. Contrarily, the jury acquitted her. Wilson had scarcely escaped the dock when she was rearrested and charged with the murders of Maria Soames and Ann Atkinson.[23]

Maria Soames, like Sarah Carnell, kept a lodging house. She had two houses that faced each other on Alfred Street, Bedford Square, and rented rooms in both of them. Soames, a widow, and her two daughters, Ann Maria Soames, aged 20, the other slightly younger, lived in one of them, as did four lodgers, while another four had rooms across the street. The younger daughter had recognized Wilson during the Carnell case as the woman who had been a close friend of her mother at the time of her death six years earlier. Detectives made a "patient and protracted investigation" of Wilson's past, going back to her role as Peter Mawer's housekeeper and the sole beneficiary of his estate. While Wilson sat in prison for half a year, there was an exhumation in Boston of Mawer's remains and a belated inquest on his death. No evidence of poison was detected to support the still lingering suspicion concerning his demise, but, as the *Sun* remarked, there was no "moral doubt" that he had been poisoned. Cursed with rheumatism and gout, he had received the standard therapy, colchicum, more popularly known as "autumn crocus." Far stronger was the evidence against Wilson with respect to the sudden death of Maria Soames. Not long before Christmas, 1855, Wilson had taken an unfurnished room in the house in which the widow lived. Accompanying her was a much younger man, James Dixon, whom she described not entirely convincingly as her brother. He was soon ill and was treated by Dr. Whidborne, who had regularly attended the late Mr. Soames and other family members with the exception of Maria. He diagnosed rheumatic fever and became quite agitated on being informed by Wilson that she was administering colchicum. The drug was potentially dangerous, he warned, and ought not to be in the hands of someone who was not an expert in its use. Wilson confidently responded that she was well acquainted with it. On Dixon's death, she informed his family that he had died of galloping consumption, which the postmortem contradicted: his lungs had been perfectly healthy.[24]

On Wednesday, October 15, 1856, Maria Soames had called on her half brother Samuel Barnes, a draper, the executor of their father's will. Under it she received a legacy of £100, and he gave her nine pounds as a partial payment of it. Over the two following days, her health, which had appeared very good, deteriorated rapidly. Barnes, on calling to see her on Friday, did not think her dangerously ill, and Wilson was with her all of the time he was there. He was summoned by cab early on Saturday morning, and on arrival he found his half sister dead. Shocked by the suddenness of the death, he consulted his own doctor, who counseled him to insist on an inquest, which was held at the beginning of the following week. Wilson was questioned, as was Whidborne, but Barnes could not later recollect expressing his unease to the coroner. In his evidence at the criminal trial, he assessed his sister's annual income at between £80 and £100, although the elder of his nieces raised it significantly. She was now Anna Maria Naacke, the wife of a German watchmaker, and in her evidence stressed how friendly and physically close Wilson and her mother had been. They spent a great deal of time together in the kitchen, and her mother was frequently to be found in Wilson's room. The sisters had tea with their mother on her return from her Wednesday meeting with Barnes. Catherine Wilson came down and requested Maria Soames to come up to her room so they could speak privately without naming the topic. In the early hours of the following morning their mother came down to the girls' room to report a bilious attack and then went back to her bed. She was very ill, retching without throwing up, and complained of a pain in her chest. Anna Maria could not recollect how often Wilson was in her mother's room that day, which was not surprising since she was trying to recall conversations and actions of six years earlier. She was certain that she gave her something to drink. That evening her mother was no better, and a cousin, who had since emigrated to the United States, sat up with her overnight. On Friday Maria was still very ill, vomiting and retching, and Whidborne was sent for. This was the first time he had attended the widow. He diagnosed choleraic diarrhea, more commonly known as English cholera, and administered a mild preparation of opium. From his nearby home he sent additional medicine. Anna Maria remembered Wilson seizing control of it and alone administering it. The doctor had given to her the necessary "proper instructions," she explained to the questioning daughters, only for him to deny ever doing so. Anna Maria did not notice it improving her mother's condition; after one dose she "became immediately in violent pain."

Emma Rowe, a dressmaker, who occupied a room in both houses and from them plied her trade, confirmed the elder daughter's testimony. She had seen two medicine bottles, one larger than the other, which were always in the possession of Wilson and were kept by her in her locked room. When she asked her why, she was told it was "particular stuff and must be given by herself." For this she gave no reason. She then told Rowe that she had a secret to tell, which was that Mrs. Soames had done away with herself. In her presence, she had taken something in brandy and water that caused her death. Why had she not prevented it, Rowe asked, or not relayed the information to the step brother or to the daughters or to Whidborne? It was none of her business, Wilson replied. The doctor, on recalling the death of Dixon and Wilson's admission that she used colchicum as a therapy for his complaints, was asked whether it would produce the symptoms from which Mrs. Soames had suffered. "I feel perfectly convinced," he answered, "that overdoses of colchicum would do so." The medicine that he sent to her would not have produced them. During the postmortem he had examined the body for poison because of the surprising suddenness of her death and the talk of her possible suicide, but he had not entertained "any idea that poison had been taken." Nevertheless, the viscera were sent off to Alfred Swaine Taylor for analysis. The toxicologist came to the trial under something of a dark cloud. He had failed to find strychnine in the body of William Palmer's alleged victim in 1856, and his incorrect identification of arsenic had seen a Thomas Smethurst tried for murder three years later. In this case Taylor spoke of the impossibility of discovering a vegetable poison such as colchicum in a body after five years of interment. What is more, he doubted it would be possible after any more than five days. He had searched for poison in the viscera and had at the time concluded that "in all probability no vegetable poison would be discoverable in the body," for the excessive purging it caused "might remove any trace." But a single very large dose of colchicum would produce the deceased's symptoms. "Taking what I have heard of the incessant vomiting, retching, and purging, and assuming that it was taken in a fluid state, if taken at all," Taylor continued, "I do not believe any trace would have remained, even if the body had been examined at the time of death, or soon after."[25]

There was no definitive scientific proof of the cause of Maria Soames's death. Catherine Wilson's earlier profit from the passing of Peter Mawer had been alluded to, and the retired captain's afflictions, rheumatism and gout, were known. The prisoner's resort to colchicum as a therapy for these complaints—and in this she was not alone, for members of the medical profession so resorted—were briefly raised during the discussion of Dixon's death, when she alone had controlled the medicines and their administration. The two medical men, one of them the noted toxicologist, had identified the symptoms of the deceased as those associated with colchicum and English cholera or choleraic diarrhea. The jury, to no great surprise, rapidly reached a verdict of guilty. Mr. Justice Byles concurred. He had never heard of a case, he announced, where it was so clearly proved that murder was committed and where the excruciating pain and agony of the victim was watched with so much deliberation by the murderer. Recognizing the inconclusiveness of the scientific evidence, for no poison had been found, he went on to say that "it was not necessary in point of law, to show what was the nature of the poison of which the deceased died;

if that was so a person more advanced in medical skill and knowledge than the rest of mankind might go on poisoning with impunity."[26]

The general public might not be as certain as he was of Catherine Wilson's guilt, the judge surmised, so he set about ensuring that it knew what sort of person she was. This was not legal evidence, one newspaper was quick to comment, but in connection with other circumstances it was more than enough "to satisfy any reasonable being" of the justice of the conviction. To all intents and purposes, he accused and convicted her of multiple murders. He began with Peter Mawer. At the time he died it was quite clear that she was "perfectly well acquainted with the nature and effects of colchicum." In 1856 she was living with a man named Dixon who was attended when he fell ill by Whidborne. During the trial the doctor was not allowed to state the circumstances connected with Dixon's illness the judge informed those who either heard or read his summation, but he could now reveal that the symptoms were the same as those of Mrs. Soames. In 1859 the prisoner was in the habit of visiting a Mrs. Jackson in Boston, the judge continued, and was aware that she had withdrawn £120 from the bank and had it in her possession. Jackson died of the same symptoms after four days of suffering, and the money was nowhere to be found. A year later Wilson was connected with Mrs. Atkinson of Kirby Lonsdale, who came to live with her in Kennington, London, and was known by her to be in possession of a considerable sum of money. Taken ill with the now all too familiar symptoms of retching, violent purging, and vomiting, she died in great agony four days later. Had she been acquitted of the Soames murder, the judge observed, she would have been immediately put on trial for the murder of Mrs. Atkinson. Well before that she was tried for the murder of Mrs. Carnell with sulfuric acid, and although acquitted, there was too much reason to believe her guilty of this crime. So the trial judge had considered it his duty to sum up most unfavorably against her. This litany of "facts" rendered it extremely probable, Mr. Justice Byles concluded, that Dr. Taylor's startling statement was correct, that amidst apparent prosperity and obedience to the law "a dreadful crime and violence is rife in this metropolis, the destruction of life by secret poisoning." If anything was wanting to satisfy the jurors of the rectitude of their verdict it must have been fully satisfied by Justice Byles. Since 1853 four persons with whom Wilson lived on terms of friendship if not intimacy died exhibiting symptoms "precisely similar" to those of the unfortunate Maria Soames.[27]

The press made its contribution. The strong feeling of the public against her was illustrated by the absence of any effort to procure a remission of her death sentence. Even the Society for the Abolition of

Capital Punishment decided that this was a case that did not merit its intervention. Wilson was charged by the press not with one murder but a number. She was presented as a "systematic poisoner," whose acquittal of attempting to murder Sarah Carnell with sulfuric acid was delivered "in the teeth of the judge's summing up." At Mawer's inquest, held eight years after his death, Dr. Taylor had failed to find poison in his remains, so the coroner decided not to call those witnesses who could offer circumstantial evidence that would prove almost to a certainty that Mawer was poisoned. He therefore decided that there was little doubt of the nature of the poison she used. "It is vegetable and cannot be analyzed," and after a lapse of time is impossible to detect. "Justice is proverbial for the slowness of her march," the optimistic *British Standard* admitted, "but she is always advancing, and, tortoise-like, she never fails to reach the goal, and to inflict condign punishment on the perpetrators of wickedness." Wilson had paid the penalty of her "unparalleled offences." She maintained her innocence to the very end, and her final words were reminiscent of Palmer's six years earlier, "I am innocent." There was no doubt, the *British Standard* remarked, that she dropped into eternity with a lie on her lips. She had composed and written "in a firm legible hand" a statement to be laid before the Queen imploring clemency. She declared that her imprisonment for six months before her trial had prevented her from gathering evidence for her defense; that she had lacked the means to retain a defense counsel, although she was defended by the extremely able Montague Chambers; that her poor hearing left her unable to hear the evidence against her and therefore could not contradict it; that there was no proof of her possession of poison; that the witness to whom she allegedly revealed the secret of Soames's death had not mentioned it to anyone for six years. Nor had she a motive for taking the life, and no poison had been found in the exhumed bodies. Also widely published was her letter to her uncle and aunt, again a composition of an educated woman, in which she admitted to being a great sinner but said she was innocent of Soames's murder.[28]

The judge sent for defense counsel Chambers after the trial and congratulated him on his efforts but remarked that the evidence was too strong against his client. He then observed that of all the criminals he had himself defended and prosecuted as a barrister this woman was "the greatest criminal that ever lived." What made her crimes so shocking was the middle class respectability of her victims. Like Mary Bateman, she could not be fitted so conveniently into the ranks of the lower orders. She was an almost "entirely new profile of the female serial killer." She moved comfortably, as had Bateman years earlier, among members of the middle classes, gained their confidence, and was ever ready to serve and nurse them. She stole from them or convinced them to provide for her in their wills and did away with them not with arsenic but with overdoses of a medicine that was not easily identified more than a few days, if not hours, after a death. Yet she had been caught and punished not by science but by an accumulation of largely circumstantial evidence. Some 20,000 spectators watched her put to death on October 20, 1862.[29]

Nor was she quite so exceptional as she appeared to be in preying on members of the class above her. The middle classes had long believed that they would never find themselves in court accused of murder. But by the time Wilson was hanged there had been at least three sensational cases in which killer and alleged victim belonged to the middle classes. This raised in turn an important question. What impact would such cases have upon the lower orders who were constantly urged to be educated in "ascendant middle class morality [as] the best hope of vanquishing the contemporary domestic poisoner"?

CHAPTER FIVE

A Question of Class

BRITAIN'S EMERGENCE AS THE FIRST industrial nation—with its mills and factories, its deep coal mines, its steam railways and steam-powered seagoing vessels—saw the middle classes multiply in number and significance. They considered themselves the advance guard of the nation's progress. Socially, they strove to ape the nobility and gentry in manners and genteel behavior. Morality was cited as the guide of their private and public lives. Murders were committed by the lower orders, who were constantly told to emulate so far as was possible the middle class. But the trial of Dr. William Palmer in 1856 delivered a profound blow to the moral complacency of the middle classes, suggesting as it did that crime keeps pace with increases in refinement. As a leading legal scholar and future High Court judge commented sadly, Palmer was "'one of the proofs of a fact which many kind-hearted people seem to doubt, namely, the fact that such a thing as atrocious wickedness is consistent with good education, perfect sanity, and everything, in a word, that deprives men of all excuse for crime.'" In addition, the trial cast grave doubt on the infallibility of the experts who detected the poison in bodies. Alfred Swaine Taylor failed to find the strychnine that was supposed to have been the cause of death. What is more, the quality of his analysis and competence were disputed by two other noted experts, Herapath and Letheby. Yet it was possible for expert witnesses to testify on the basis of their opinion, which was not necessarily rooted in firsthand observation of the case. Robert Christison, considered "perhaps the greatest analytic chemist of the age," contended that the expert who derived facts and principles from the work of the hundreds of his predecessors "reasoned more soundly than those who boasted of their reliance only on direct experience." Then there was the suspicion that men of science when giving evidence acted as partisans of the prisoners whom they were defending, thereby abandoning objective scientific analysis in favor of financial gain or professional advancement.[1]

The prosecution of middle class poisoners, especially women, promised to be peculiarly difficult. They were hailed as the "symbolic keepers of society's values," the embodiment of a "greater, nurturing goodness, of purity and morality." There was skepticism of the ability of the new police to conduct successful investigations of such suspected murderers. The satirical *Punch* mocked the "defective detectives," while Mr. Justice Stephen was similarly scornful of their abilities. Recruited overwhelmingly from the laboring classes, they were in his opinion ill-equipped socially to solve crimes allegedly committed by the members of the superior classes. There followed a string of sensational cases, those of Christina Gilmour, Madeleine Smith, Ann Cornish Vyse, Constance Kent, Christiana Edmunds, Florence Bravo, Adelaide Bartlett, and Florence Maybrick. They were educated appropriate to their class and held respectable positions in society. Hence their alleged homicides stunned those standing on much the same step of the social ladder. After all, an "ascendant middle-class morality" had been seen as the model for the lower orders. But these women "revealed, in the most explicit manner, the hidden underbelly of 'respectable' Victorian domestic life," which not only astonished contemporaries but also fascinated them. One great advantage they had over the murderers of the lower orders was their financial ability to retain the very best available barristers to exploit the differences between expert witnesses, and with them confound the jurors. Not that the quality of juries inspired confidence. While the lowest of the low were excluded from them, those who did sit in the jury box were more often than not tradesmen and farmers. Their modest level of education made it unlikely, critics complained, that they would be able to follow and understand the evidence of eminent and argumentative medical scientists.[2]

A "combination of murder and [middle class] feminine sex appeal" captivated the general public. Christina Cochran was one of the four daughters and three sons of a very wealthy Scottish proprietor of a large estate, Alexander Cochran. He was understandably keen to ensure that Christina and her sisters enjoyed a life as comfortable as that in which they had been raised. Hence marriage was important, and the husband should be of "equal wealth or rank in life" as himself. For Christina he selected John Gilmour, the son of a "very respectable farmer." Unfortunately, her heart was set on John Anderson, a young man of excellent character and good moral conduct but of inferior class. He was the gardener of a local gentleman. Her parents did their best to keep them apart by isolating her and resorting to physical punishment. Eventually she was driven into a marriage with young Gilmour and immediately made plain her rejection of him. She spent her wedding night sitting in an upright chair and informed her husband that she would never enter his bed. He was chronically unwell, she later stated, vomiting almost every day until he died. His illness Gilmour attributed to Christina's breaking of his heart. She acquired some arsenic through her servant Mary Petersen, but on hearing from her the druggist's warning of the dangers of the poison, she threw all but one packet of it into the fire. This the servant witnessed. That packet, she told her mother, was to be used to end her life and thus the wretched marriage into which her father had compelled her to enter.[3]

That her husband became seriously ill, that she replenished her stock of the poison, that she twice refused to summon medical aid, and that Gilmour told a concerned farmhand who managed to sneak in and see him that, should he die, he wanted a postmortem to be held sparked sinister talk of foul play. As the gossip grew louder, the widow returned to her parents. The body was exhumed, and the liver and the contents of the stomach were sent to Edinburgh for analysis by the mighty Christison. He was in no doubt of the cause of the death. Employing the Marsh test as recently refined by a committee of the French Institute, he identified "properties peculiar to oxide of arsenic the substance in which [it was] usually administered as poison." This would account for the state of preservation of the area of the stomach he examined. Parts of the stomach had a peculiar yellowness, he added, not that this had been seen "in bodies in which arsenic was known to be the cause of death." The finding of arsenic in the liver proved "that it must have been administered in the living subject." The French had repeatedly found the poison in that organ, but this was only the second instance, he proudly boasted, of its discovery in Britain.[4]

Word of Christison's finding reached Alexander Cochran in his Renfrewshire home in November 1843. Uncertain of his daughter's complete innocence, he hurriedly ensured she was beyond the immediate reach of the law. Three men were hired to speed her safely to Liverpool, and a fourth who was emigrating escorted her across the Atlantic to New York. She traveled under his name, Spiers, and they had separate berths, but conscious of his far humbler station, she had "as little communication with him as possible." Meanwhile, the police questioned her parents, who denied all knowledge of her whereabouts, but the investigators swiftly realized what had taken place. Superintendent M'Kay of the former Renfrewshire Rural Police set off in pursuit. The vessel on which he took passage arrived in New York before that on which Christina Gilmour was traveling. Extracting her from the United States, and especially from the State of New York, took time. Her case captured transatlantic public interest, and she became the first alleged criminal surrendered by the United States government to that of the United

Kingdom under the terms of the previous year's Webster-Ashburton Treaty. By the time she stood trial in Edinburgh her late husband had been dead for over a year, and a largely sympathetic press lost no time preparing the ground for her acquittal. She had been goaded almost to "madness" by the compulsion to wed the deceased, the media reported, and there was insanity in her family. One if not two of her uncles were believed to be confirmed lunatics. Here, clearly, was the grounds for clemency. The prayers of all will be, the *Leeds Times* solemnized, "that God will permit her to pass through in safety the terrible ordeal that awaits her." This prayerful hope was reprinted in a host of newspapers, as was a warning to all middle class parents to beware "unrelenting opposition to an honorable attachment favored by a daughter" simply because the man she chose was of a somewhat inferior class. And there was a widely circulated report in the *Glasgow Courier* that it was confidently anticipated, from "well-informed quarters," that it would be impossible to prove the allegations against her and obtain a conviction.[5]

The Crown's case was strong but largely circumstantial. From the outset of the investigation the police were satisfied that arsenic would be found in the body. The doctor who conducted the postmortem was in no doubt of the cause of death, and this was true of the colleagues who dispatched the organs to Edinburgh for chemical analysis. Three parcels of arsenic had been traced to the prisoner, and for them she had given the dispensing druggist a false name. In short, she had obtained the poison secretly with a spurious statement. There was little reason to disbelieve, the prosecutor continued, that it was administered in small doses between December 29 and January 11. Nor could it be supposed that the deceased took the poison himself, whereas the prisoner had ample opportunity to administer it, although she had in her statement denied serving to him food and drink. What is more, she had a powerful motive. She had contacted Anderson soon after the death, a letter her father had destroyed. Could the jury "doubt the purpose for which the arsenic was obtained or the purpose to which it was applied"? There was, then, no reason "to relieve the law from awarding the full amount of the punishment."[6]

Her father ensured that she had the best possible defense counsel, a legal star. He was Thomas Maitland, recently the solicitor general of Scotland. His services cost approximately £900. At the opening of the trial's second day, which would see the presentation of the case for the defense, the three presiding judges, led by the lord justice clerk, were astonished to learn that public interest in the case was so great that the doorkeepers were charging for admission to the free court. In his closing address to the jury, which took four and a half hours to deliver,

Five. A Question of Class

Maitland acknowledged that the prisoner was covered by suspicion and that there was great skepticism about her innocence. But was there legal evidence, he asked, on which the jurors could find her guilty? Where, indeed, was the evidence that Gilmour had been killed, as the prosecutor asserted, with small doses of the poison? Where was the direct evidence of the accused's administration of arsenic to her husband? Where was her sufficient motive "in the proper sense of the word"? Had the jury heard any evidence of her alleged "remorseless hatred" for the victim? What they had heard was that she had behaved to her husband with "becoming attention" during his severe illness. If "there was wanting one link in the chain of evidence—if there was doubt, or at least obscurity of it—it was their duty," he concluded, "to give the prisoner the benefit of it, and return a verdict of not proven." In summing up, the lord justice clerk could find no "obvious motive for such a heinous crime" and repeated the defense counsel's assertion that if they had any doubt, the jurors could not find the prisoner guilty.[7]

Scotland had, under the terms of the union of the nations, retained its separate system of justice. In at least two striking particulars the Scottish jury in criminal trials differed from the English. Instead of 12 men unanimous in their verdict of guilt, there were 15 members and a majority verdict of eight sufficed for a conviction. Nor were they restricted to two verdicts, those of guilty or not guilty. As Maitland had reminded them, there was a third possibility. Without finding the prisoner innocent, they could find the Crown's evidence insufficient and thus the case "not proven." Critics of this "neutral" verdict considered it incompatible with the presumption of innocence, and in England there was a mistaken belief that following this verdict a retrial remained possible. Instead, the verdict was definitive and had the effect of an acquittal. Christina Gilmour escaped the consequences of her actions and lived for another 60 years in "singular piety."

News that another upper middle class Scottish young lady was accused of murder and that her victim was a handsome and socially inferior lover, for he belonged to that overlapping fringe of the upper working class and lower middle class, shocked newspaper readers. Here again was a case of sex and poison, and the coupling of Madeleine Smith and Pierre Emile L'Angelier created a far greater sensation than had the story of Christina Gilmour. On Saturday, June 13, 1857, she was served with an indictment to stand trial before the High Court of Justiciary in Edinburgh on the last day of the month. There were three counts, two of attempting to murder L'Angelier by administering arsenic to him on two separate occasions, and a third of murdering him with poison between Sunday night and the early hours of Monday morning. Eighty-nine witnesses were listed, among them medical gentlemen and chemists, and the "productions" included more than 200 letters that had passed between the couple and a private memorandum book or diary. As the *Berkshire Chronicle* reported, this case "has created an immense sensation in Scotland, and even in this country [England]."[8]

At the age of 21, Madeleine Smith had enjoyed a comfortable and easy life, although in the photograph probably to mark so important a birthday as her 21st she appeared more sullen than joyful. Her father and grandfather had constructed a number of Glasgow's modern buildings, and the son elevated himself professionally and socially by becoming an architect and marrying the daughter of the city's most distinguished architect and aesthete. Madeleine was born in March 1835 and grew up in a family exemplary in qualities their social inferiors were constantly urged to imitate: gentility, propriety, respectability, self-control, and morality. The Smiths lived in the "luxurious enjoyment of all that pertains, if not to great wealth, at least to the possession of a competence beyond the average of the prosperous commercial citizens of Glasgow." During the short winter months, James Smith rented suitable accommodation close to the city center, but from early spring until late fall the family resided in an ostentatiously impressive country retreat, 25 miles to the south, which he both designed and built. The staff of domestic servants were further proof of the Smiths' social status. He packed his eldest daughter off at the age of 16 to a London area finishing school in Clapton, once a rural retreat from the capital. She was to be instructed in the "Metropolitan graces," to soften her "Scotch accent by a due mixture of the more melodious English tongue." The town had become well known nationally a year earlier because of Anne Merritt's alleged murder by arsenic poisoning of her husband. No doubt the tale of the case was still a topic of excited discussion among the young ladies of the school. On the completion of her preparations for entrance into upper middle class social life at the marriageable age of 18, the school assessed her as intelligent and generally well behaved but with dangerous failings of temperament and character. All too often she responded to disappointments with sulks and temper tantrums and frequently was less than truthful.[9]

Pierre Emile L'Angelier's path in life had been far bumpier. He was born in the British Channel Island of Jersey just off the French coast, where his father, a French immigrant, had made a very good marriage and with his wife established a seed nursery. Pierre, their first child, was baptized in 1823 with an anglicized version of his name. On his father's early death, Pierre Emile Langelier went to Scotland to gain greater experience as a nurseryman. The death of his Scot patron obliged him to find other work, and in 1845 he returned to Jersey and from there moved on to Paris, where he lodged with relations, adopted the French spelling of his family name, and took work as a clerk. By 1851 he was back in Scotland and for a while subsisted on the charity of an Edinburgh publican and a kindly widow. He had always exploited his good looks and his attraction for women. Eventually he made his way to booming Glasgow, where his prospects promised to be greater. An elderly female acquaintance helped him secure a warehouse clerkship with W.B. Huggins & Co., and he carefully projected the image of a lower middle class male. He was better spoken, better mannered, and better dressed than the great majority of his fellow "shop lads," having taken to heart the medieval proverb "clothing oft maketh man." Another calculated decision was his forsaking of Roman Catholicism for Protestantism, the faith of the city's well-established citizens. A number of his work colleagues recognized him as an ambitious social climber, while the "better-sort" with whom he increasingly mixed thought him a little "forward" with ideas above his station in life. His mother described him far more gently as a "poor lad striving in a strange land to better his circumstances."[10]

A good marriage would open the doors of society, although his first attempt came to naught. His lengthy absence of more than five years from Scotland, and the warnings of the lady's close friends that her "French" beau lacked the resources necessary for marriage, allowed her relieved father to marry her off to a London "gentleman." L'Angelier spotted Madeleine Smith while she walked with her sister on Sauchiehall Street, the shopping center, and learned from his colleagues that she was the as yet unattached daughter of the prominent and wealthy architect. Here was a bright prospect. She was no startling beauty; the *Edinburgh Witness* observing unkindly that her slightly Norman nose and receding chin, which had undue prominence in profile, made her facial outline "disagreeable." Nevertheless, she offered a sure path to a world from which he was excluded. As one of his colleagues remarked, his relationship with her was from the outset one of "interest." He contrived a street introduction, which the rules of etiquette encouraged well-born young ladies and young gentlemen to decline. She had surely noticed him during her walks, although at the age of 32 his good looks were possibly fading a little, and in other respects he was a "small, insignificant creature," far beneath her socially. Yet a clandestine dalliance would inject excitement into her otherwise dull daily life, so she accepted the introduction and he responded with a flower on St. Valentine's Day. She ignored an important lesson of her finishing school, which had stressed the need for great caution when putting pen to paper. Before the end of the year, 1855, she was addressing him as "My Own Darling Husband" and signing her letters "thy ever fond wife, thy Mimi L'Angelier." Although her writing of such missives was virtually unstoppable, and their content "excessive dangerous" socially, she remained an intelligent young woman of 19 who was acutely aware of her social status and the luxuries and comfort her father's wealth made possible. Nor could she have been ignorant of his paternal resolve that her marriage would have to ensure their continuance. One reason her father moved the family to 7 Blythswood Square may have been the presence there of William Minnoch, a well-bred gentleman in every respect who was a junior partner of a well-established and successful merchant house whose senior partners were close friends of the Smiths.[11]

When L'Angelier indicated an intention to approach her father as a gentlemanly formal suitor for her hand, Mimi immediately excluded that course of action. Her father hated and despised him, she claimed, and her mother would rather see her dead than married to a mere clerk. Not that she had discussed the possibility with her parents. She was spending more time with the eminently eligible Minnoch. They attended a performance of Donizetti's *Lucretia Borgia*, who had gone into history falsely as a notorious poisoner. She named Edward Bulwer-Lytton as one of her favorite authors. His novel *Lucretia and the Children of the Night*, recently issued in a fresh edition, was condemned by the *London Medical Gazette* as the "most complete revelation of the art of murder by poison." She was, in short, well briefed on the use of arsenic. She expressed her surprise that L'Angelier's annual income was a paltry £50 and recommended he go to England to make his fortune. "Wealth," she lamented, was the "ruling passion" of the world, whereas love was no more than a "secondary consideration." They had in June 1856 consummated their relationship sexually in the woods behind the Smiths' summer retreat. A man of conventional morality, L'Angelier expressed his regret that this had happened, whereas Madeleine, more seducer than seduced, suffered few pangs of conscience. Hearing gossip of her ever-closer relationship with Minnoch, L'Angelier flattered himself that his own hand was far stronger. Under Scottish law, a couple who exchanged promises of marriage and then engaged in carnal intercourse in Scotland had entered into an "irregular" marriage. He demanded that in her increasingly active social life she behave as a married woman. Moreover, he held in his possession her voluminous and highly indiscreet correspondence, and this he would neither return nor destroy. Instead, he threatened to show it to her father or even make an approach to Minnoch. Desperately, she dissuaded him from either step with lavish promises of greater love and loyalty even as she quietly accepted Minnoch's proposal of marriage on January 28, 1857. But it would not be long before word of it circulated in local society and reached L'Angelier's ears.[12]

L'Angelier died in intense pain on the late morning of March 23. A French house friend and fellow clerk had noticed for some time a deterioration in his health and appearance. Pierre and Madeleine probably met at her bedroom window on February 19, and in the Blythswood house on February 20 and 22 after its other members had retired for the night. On the evening of March 22, he had left his lodgings with a pass key, which was for his landlady a clue of where he was going. After two of the February meetings, he had become extremely ill, suffering nausea, vomiting, and "purging" of the bowels. The surgeon who had been attending him for some time, Hugh Thomson, thought him one of those men who made much of minor afflictions. So, after a cursory examination, he diagnosed a "bilious derangement." Thomson again attended the patient on February 24, and although his symptoms were more severe, the possibility of poisoning did not cross the surgeon's mind. L'Angelier's symptoms did suggest progressive poisoning by arsenic, but, as Robert Christison had written, the success of criminal poisoning depended on its "imitating the effects of a natural disease." In this instance, "English" cholera and "Gastric or Bilious Fever" were the possible alternative causes of the illness, and gastritis was recorded as the cause of death.[13]

There were no coroners in Scotland, so an investigation into the death was launched by a handful of friends and his employer. Word of the death and the deceased's lengthy relationship with their daughter was carried to the Smiths by a female friend of L'Angelier. The parents were surprised since Madeleine had promised them 18 months earlier, when his name had arisen, to sever all connection with the mere clerk. The discovery of some of her letters confirmed that she had lied to them and revealed that she had planned a nocturnal conference with him at her bedroom window immediately before his fatal illness. The postmortem conducted by Thomson strongly indicated that arsenic was the cause of death. This directly involved the city's two procurators fiscal in the investigation, for they were public prosecutors charged to probe sudden and suspicious deaths. The stomach and several organs of the dead man were removed from the body, securely stored, and dispatched to Professor Frederick Penny for chemical analysis. The fiscals then obtained a warrant to exhume the reburied body and take possession of certain letters and documents of the deceased. The suspicion that the death had been neither natural nor accidental rapidly became a conviction. Madeleine Smith appeared before a magistrate and made a declaration undoubtedly prepared by the Smith family's solicitor. She admitted that she and the clerk had met at the barred window of her bedroom and had talked of marriage without taking any decisive steps. She described him as chronically unwell and denied any knowledge of the cause. She remembered giving him hot cocoa when they met one cold winter's night, although it was not at all certain that she was aware that "neither appearance, taste, nor smell [would betray] anything unusual." As for her three purchases of arsenic, they were for cosmetic use, and she emphatically denied having administered to him the poison or anything else injurious to him.[14]

The analysis of the organs provided evidence of arsenic sufficient to kill a small army of victims. Yet this suspect's status and respectability were cautions against a hasty prosecution. That she had a powerful motive to be rid of L'Angelier given her forthcoming marriage to Minnoch and the likelihood that the discarded lover might disclose the full extent of their intimacy could not be ignored. This would shame her family and exclude her from society. Nor could it be denied that she was in possession of the means—arsenic—having misled the druggists about its purpose, and hot cocoa would be a handy method of its administration. Her opportunities to deliver it were less clear cut. L'Angelier's first serious illness on February 19 led to the charge of attempted murder, but on that day there was no evidence that she was in possession of the poison. His fatal illness on March 22, which found her charged with aggravated murder, lacked secure evidence of them meeting that night. Then there was the question of whether the arsenic found in the body was that purchased from the druggists, for it had been colored as the recent law required, but that detected by the analysts had been white. Penny and Christison agreed that the druggist had been economical and careless in his use of the indigo prescribed for coloration by the Arsenic Act. He had mixed "exhausted indigo" with the poison, and as the name implied it lacked the bright, distinctive color. Instead, it was so poor and faint that violent vomiting might have weakened it to "some extent." Another possibility was that Madeleine Smith washed it in cold water to remove the coloring. Of course she might do this to use it as face wash, hence Christison recommended the Crown seek to discredit this specific cosmetic use of the poison. This was not done.

James Smith retained the best possible counsel for his daughter. Scotland's advocates were members of a faculty in the College of Justice, and at their head was the dean elected by the membership. He was the "premier of the professional men of his day." John Inglis was a Conservative, and a recent short-lived Tory government had appointed him solicitor general and then lord advocate, head of the system of prosecution.

As such he had then stood first in legal precedence and now as dean of the faculty stood second. In the opinion of a former adversary and admirer, Inglis was "probably as accomplished a man as the bar of Scotland ever produced." He was a counsel who would exploit to the full the weaknesses in the prosecution's case. His major problem was the love letters read into the evidence by the prosecution, which revealed in her own words that his client was an enthusiastic violator of Victorian sexual morality. His solution was to generate sympathy for her by concentrating on her alleged victim. He became more vehement in his language, more excited in manner, "more filled with loathing and horror at the wickedness of the man through whose vile agency a pure, affectionate girl, the pride of her father's family, had fallen so low as to be capable of writing those painful and disgusting letters. L'Angelier then threatened to use them against her as an engine of terror and oppression." In his concluding remarks to the jury, Inglis called to mind the case of poor Eliza Fenning, who had gone to the gallows pleading her entire innocence of attempted murder. Her execution had heightened popular concerns about convictions based exclusively on circumstantial evidence. "I pray God that neither you nor I may be implicated in the guilt of adding another to that black and bloody catalogue," Inglis declared, and there were signs his eloquence was having the desired effect. In his summing up, the lord justice clerk directed the jury to acquit her on the first and second counts, those of February 19 and February 22. On the third charge, that of aggravated murder, they might suspect that she was a person capable of harboring a "murderous impulse," and there was evidence that she had acquired poison shortly before she was to meet with the lover who threatened her with acute family and public embarrassment, but her alleged motive of revenge had been seriously compromised. So, he instructed them to separate mere suspicion from legal evidence. They followed his lead and found the capital case against her "not proven."[15]

The verdict was not given a universal welcome, and five members of the jury had voted her guilty. This trial had sent a thrill of horror into every home in Britain, the *Liverpool Albion* warned, "and filled the columns in the same week of the remotest provincial print at home, and the most popular Parisian newspapers." Never, in the opinion of the *Kentish Gazette*, had a "more dismal plot been conceived." The accused, who had been freed, was moved by a naked vengeance and the "solitary purpose to destroy an object of hatred." The *Morning Advertiser* regretted the public enthusiasm in favor of Smith and the fact that the exuberant joy of her acquittal was not confined to the court in which she was tried. In countless newspaper offices "clerks were driven to destruction by the turmoil while editors rushed madly about coatless, uttering profane oaths at those thought to be slowing production." One question that sprang to many minds was whether the case had exposed some broader and profoundly disturbing meaning for middle class society. After all, the personal conduct of the members of that class was forever being cited as the model that all other sectors of society would do well to emulate. Yet Smith and L'Angelier had conformed only to its "outward requirements and courtesies" while surreptitiously engaging in the most venal practices.[16]

The public had barely recovered from the drama and sensationalism of the trial of Madeleine Smith when a horrific murder within an apparently affluent middle class family resulted in the swift detention of one of its members, an adolescent female of 16, as the perpetrator. "There never was a case in the history of modern crime," one provincial paper commented, "which has excited more interest or which was more surrounded with mystery than the murder of Francis Saville Kent." Another reason for this crime's capture of intense popular interest was the police's circumspect handling of its middle class subjects, who included the child's father as well as one of his daughters. This reminded the lower orders of the social inequality of justice.[17]

The dead child was the favorite of the father's second marriage. Samuel Saville-Kent had made in 1829 a highly advantageous first marriage. His wife, Mary Ann Windrus, was the daughter of a wealthy and influential man. Samuel's social position improved, and his father-in-law's influence secured him a comfortable post in the public service. He became a sub-inspector of factories in the west of England and mixed with the "better sort" of society. His ambition was to secure promotion to the supervising inspectorate. The couple had a number of children, several of whom did not live beyond six months. A son and two daughters did survive, and two were added to the number in 1844 and 1845. They were Constance Emily Kent and William Saville-Kent. The declining health of his wife and her withdrawal from active family life had led Samuel to employ a governess, Mary Pratt, who devoted herself to the care of Constance. For a while she was little more than a nursemaid, but designation as a governess moved her into the lower middle class. When Mary Ann died in 1852 the family observed a customary period of mourning until in August 1853, when the governess became the second wife with Constance serving as one of her bridesmaids. The birth of the children of the second marriage gave rise, perhaps not surprisingly, to some resentment among those of the first. They believed they were not being treated as well as the new siblings.[18]

Tiring of an itinerant domestic life given the large area in which the factories requiring his inspection were located, Samuel Kent leased in the mid–1850s a house befitting his station in life. Road Hill House was listed as a handsome family residence, for it had 10 bedrooms, four dressing rooms, a nursery, a study, attached and detached offices, stables, and coach houses. Less than five miles from Trowbridge and nine miles from Bath, there was also a railroad station not four miles away where trains ran daily. This was important since Kent was frequently traveling for inspections.[19]

On the morning of Saturday, June 20, Francis Saville-Kent was approaching his fourth birthday. He was large for his age, weighing 35 pounds, lively, and something of a tattletale. He was found missing from his cot, from which he was not strong enough to escape unaided. Although his nurse, Elizabeth Gough, who slept only a few feet away from him, claimed to have noticed his absence as early as five o'clock in the morning, it was another two hours before she inquired if he was with his mother. The second Mrs. Kent ordered a search of house and grounds and for the summoning of the police. Her husband now stirred himself. He prepared to set off to Trowbridge to summon the police there, sent for the village constable, and gave orders that his heavily pregnant wife should not be disturbed. Two local men engaged in the search found the door to an outside privy open and, on entering, saw a modest pool of blood on the floor, and in the privy itself there was a small blanket and then the child's body trapped between the splashboard and the rear of the vault. On lifting the body out, they discovered that the head had almost been severed. The child had plainly been murdered, and the parish priest, whom Mrs. Kent had dispatched Constance to fetch, soon set off on a mission to recall the father, whom he encountered on his way back home.[20]

Before long Superintendent John Foley from the Trowbridge police station was on the scene along with two of his men. Also present was Joshua Parsons, the family's general practitioner, who young William Kent had summoned in his father's absence. Foley fished out from the privy a woman's "breast or bosom flannel," being a pad that cushioned the chest from the hard corsets. It was saturated with blood. Two other members of the crowd gathering at the house were Rowland Rodway, Kent's solicitor, and Joseph Stapleton, a surgeon who acted as the certifying surgeon at several of the factories inspected by his friend. He assisted Parsons at the postmortem. Among the investigating group was the wife of one of the policemen, who was employed as a female searcher. She strip-searched the servants, but Foley saved the middle class Kent females from this indignity. The bereaved father insisted that only an outsider could have committed this savage crime.

He had locked up the house himself the previous night, however, there was no sign of a burglary, and any murderer would have needed to be very familiar with the house. Present throughout the fatal night was a cast of 12: the Kent adults, the seven children of the two marriages, and three servants. Their intimate knowledge of the house would permit either one or two of them to take the child from the nursery without making a sound, and it was Joshua Parsons's opinion that the deceased had been first smothered, then carried to the outside privy, from which the murderer returned without awakening anyone.[21]

That there were no more than 12 persons present during the night of the murder meant that the police had a very limited number of suspects, for more than half that number were children. Not surprisingly, the attention first focused on the servants. Elizabeth Gough, the nursemaid, was the only female that the breast and bosom flannel fitted perfectly. How could the child have been taken without her knowledge, and why had she not awoken Mrs. Kent on first noticing the empty cot? A possible answer to these questions was that she had been consorting in bed with a man, and they had awakened the young boy whose silence had to be ensured. The rumor circulating among the locals was that Kent had been the man, his formidable sexual appetite severely limited by the fact that his wife was eight months pregnant. They might have used the spare bedroom that neighbored the nursery. Other rumormongers argued that he was in financial difficulties and to relieve them had murdered his son to collect burial club money. There was no such policy. Why, if he was the culprit had he on the day of the murder suggested, probably through his solicitor Rodway, that one of the members of London's detective department be acquired to solve the crime? To this Superintendent Foley vehemently objected, and it was not uncommon for provincial policemen to resist, and in this case obstruct imported professionals from the capital. On July 13, a personal request by one of the magistrates to the commissioner of the Metropolitan Police brought the desired action. A detective inspector and later a sergeant were sent to "dissipate the mystery." By the time Inspector Jonathan Whicher reached Road Hill House, some of the clues were no longer present. His relations with the county police could not have been improved by the magistrates' announcement that he was to be in control of the investigation, and that a reward of £200 would be paid for information leading to a conviction. Half was provided by the Treasury and the balance by Kent.[22]

Whicher's prime suspect was young Constance, and this suspicion of her was shared by the medical men who had been present following the discovery of the body. Two weeks earlier the coroner in opening the inquest had antagonized several members of the jury by declining to call members of the Kent family. This had the smell of special justice for the middle classes. The chief constable of Wiltshire had just announced that two persons had been involved in the crime, and this may have emboldened the disaffected jurors to demand the opportunity to examine Constance and William Kent. Both were briefly questioned, both denied all knowledge of the crime, and the unhappy jury concluded that the death was willful murder by persons unknown. A magistrate sought to appease the indignant public with an assurance that the house had been re-examined and re-searched and every occupant bar the infant, Evangeline, had been called upon to state what they knew. It also came to light that the two former servants whom Kent accused of hostility towards him had been tracked down and possessed solid alibis. Hence Constance remained the primary suspect. Parsons had told his handful of fellow mourners at the murdered child's funeral that Mrs. Kent had asked him to certify her stepdaughter as insane. Kent had added his voice to that of his wife. Of greater interest to Whicher was Constance's missing nightgown, which she insisted had been lost in the wash. He posted a reward of two pounds for its recovery. In early August the county police exhumed the child's body in the hope of finding the garment in the coffin. Whicher sensed a clue to the guilt of the girl of 16 in her "cold quiet." He interviewed her school friends, who thought her resentful of the better treatment accorded the second family and of the harsh attitude of her stepmother. Then there was Constance's fascination with the trial of Madeleine Smith, having followed newspaper coverage of it. Mrs. Kent had cut out from the daily newspaper articles on the subject and had hidden them only for them to disappear and reappear later during the thorough search of Constance's bedroom. Had Madeleine Smith shown that by cunning a middle class murderess "could become a figure of glamour and mystery"?[23]

Shortly before the magistrates met on July 20 to hear what progress had been made in the investigation, the rumor circulated that Kent and the nurse were "to be taken in." This explained the unusually large crowd of spectators outside the Temperance Hall. Six magistrates were present, as was the chief constable, four of his superintendents, and Inspector Whicher. From late morning until mid-afternoon, they met behind closed doors. The London detective informed them that from his inquiries, information received, and close examination of the scene of the murder, he believed the child had been thrown into the privy to drown in the excrement. The crime was the work of an inmate of the house, and Constance Kent was implicated. The magistrates issued a warrant for her arrest, which Whicher feared would worsen his relations with the uncooperative county police. They were more inclined to think Kent and the nurse were responsible. Whicher arrested Constance, though he quickly realized how unpopular this action was. Before the magistrates, he requested a remand of a week to continue his search for the missing nightgown and gather proof of the prisoner's animus to the deceased. Constance spent the week in Devizes Prison, which did not diminish popular sympathy for her though her social standing ensured greater comfort there than the lower orders received.[24]

She was brought back to the Temperance Hall a week later for a committal hearing. Her father equipped her with a highly qualified defense counsel who was both resolute and caustic. Peter Henry Edlin had been called to the bar at the Middle Temple in 1847 and for the next two years had a practice in India. He was a barrister of considerable ability who would soon become a Queen's Counsel and was to hold several judicial positions culminating in a knighthood in 1888. He outshone everyone at the committal hearing, especially the magistrates' clerk, Clark, who presented the evidence collected by Whicher. There was no prosecuting counsel to examine and cross-examine witnesses. Whicher had been unable to find the "least motive" for anyone other than Constance to commit the crime. She had, as she later admitted, come to hate her stepmother for usurping her biological mother's place while she lived and for disparaging her after her death. He asserted that Constance's mother, uncle, and grandmother had been of unsound mind, and that the family's current medical adviser believed she was affected with homicidal madness. She had expressed to her fellow students at school her jealousy of the favoritism shown to the children of the second marriage. There was every reason to believe that the murderer was in nightclothes, and one of Constance's nightdresses was missing. She had the required physical strength to commit the murder, being a "very powerful young girl." Unchallenged by a prosecuting counsel, Edlin made the argument that "nothing had been adduced which was not compatible with the purest innocence." Constance was discharged by the magistrates, though her father was obliged to post a bond of £200 to guarantee her presence should she ever be needed. Sometime later the nursemaid was also examined by the magistrates and discharged.[25]

In 1862 the Road Hill House murder remained unsolved but not forgotten. Popular interest in middle class murderesses was reignited by the charge of willful murder against Ann Cornish Vyse. *The Times* had considered it "too appalling for belief" that a "highly and virtuously bred young lady such as" Madeleine Smith could be a killer. Similarly, it was difficult for elements of the press to believe that a young woman of

Constance's position, who had "the training of a lady," could drop in a moment to "so low a level as to commit a crime at which the vilest of her sex would shudder." Mrs. Vyse's counsel asked much the same question. Was it believable "that a lady in the position of the prisoner—a position which might be said to be one of affluence—should suddenly destroy that affluence while leaving the jury entirely in the dark as to motive"?[26]

Ann Vyse had earned an extremely rare reputation, that of a "good woman of business." The business had been established by Charles Vyse, who billed himself on advertisements as a "manufacturer of British and Foreign Straws [hats] to the Royal Family." Vyse's wares were extremely popular in Victorian England, and he listed a variety of straw bonnets and imported French millinery. He died in the summer of 1850, and the following year the youngest of his three sons, Valentine, married Ann Cornish Saunders, a chemist's daughter. She ran the shop as its forewoman and took full charge when Valentine Vyse became the sole owner of the business. There were a score of girls producing the bonnets for sale, and Mrs. Vyse attended personally to the shop's customers. Above the shop was a residence with a kitchen, two dining rooms on separate floors, and several bedrooms. The evidence of the family's affluence was their rural retreat in Surrey south of the capital. There Mrs. Vyse arrived every Saturday evening for a brief weekend after a long and tiring week of workdays, each 11 hours long. There also her husband was often found. He was responsible for the outside work, that of negotiating with other manufacturers. This division of labor had two years earlier resulted in tragedy. One of the couple's infants had fallen ill, and the Surrey servants, not thinking the condition serious, did not inform the mother in London. When she reached them on Saturday evening the child was doomed, dying of diphtheria. She became haunted by the thought that had she been on hand earlier she might have saved the child, and the agony of the death was extended by the flooding of the burial vault, which delayed considerably the interment. Aware in May 1862 that she was pregnant once again, and perhaps still unable to escape a sense of personal guilt over the earlier death, she had three of the children brought up to her in London. The infant remained in Surrey with Valentine. The two daughters, Annie and Alice, were little more than a year apart in age, being six and five, indicating the rapidity of Ann's pregnancies, and their brother Charles was 10.

Shortly before noon on Thursday, May 22, 1860, Ann Vyse called at a nearby chemist's store, located perhaps appropriately in St. Paul's churchyard. She told a horrifying tale of infestations of rats and mice. They had destroyed the shop's ceiling, which cost five pounds to repair. More frightening, however—for she feared for the children's safety—was the rodents' invasion of the bedrooms. The vermin were scaling bed curtains, and when she shook them, the rodents dropped to the floor. On the advice of the chemist's assistant, she purchased for a shilling three packets of Battle's vermin killer. She was warned that it was a dangerous poison, for approximately 10 percent of the powder was strychnine. The cautious assistant assumed the children were in Surrey, only to learn they were with her at the shop.[27]

Around two o' clock the maid took the dinner up to the children, who ate it in the upper dining room. Mrs. Vyse helped to prepare the meal by carving slices of cold beef while the cook made a rice pudding. The boy, Charles, then left, perhaps for school. The maid was instructed by Mrs. Vyse to go to the chemist's for an additional packet of vermin killer and there had to wait several minutes, it being out of stock. On her return she was unable to persuade her mistress to admit her to her bedroom and turned for help to Sarah Saunders, Ann's sister, who was visiting. On forcing the door open, they saw her standing over a washstand with a razor in her hand. "Pray, what are you doing?" Sarah asked. Ann pulled a letter from a pocket, which perhaps answered the question, and gave it to her sister, to whom it was addressed. She then declared that she was mad and wished to die, before adding that her daughters were in heaven. The maid went into the neighboring bedroom and found the girls in bed dressed with the bedclothes over them. She thought they were asleep and set off in search of medical assistance. She went back to the chemist's shop and found a gentleman there who turned out to be Dr. Edwin Payne, and together they returned to the house. He found Mrs. Vyse standing over a bloodied washstand and, seeing the injury to her throat, removed the clot of blood that was interfering with her breathing. He fetched William Scobell Savory, an assistant surgeon at St. Bartholomew's Hospital. Together they dressed the wound, which was on the right side of the neck and extended towards the middle and might have been self-inflicted with the razor. It was neither deep enough nor in the right place to prove fatal. He asked what the children had taken and their mother, speaking with great difficulty, replied, "Battle's Vermin Killer." Savory made a brief examination of the bodies of the two girls and on the following day, Friday, conducted a postmortem. On removing the skullcap he found vessels congested with blood. Then he removed both stomachs and sent them for analysis and noted symptoms indicative of death by strychnine. For the next three days he and Payne jointly attended to Mrs. Vyse and decided that she should remain in her house. A female searcher, Mrs. Harrison, was placed there by the police, but her presence so agitated Vyse that she was replaced by a nurse.[28]

Five. A Question of Class

The City of London coroner conducted the inquest. To it Dr. Payne recounted his arrival on the scene, the very excited state of Mrs. Vyse, and the considerable force required to control her. While he and Savory were dressing her wound, he was told that the children were dead in the next bedroom and, suspecting poisoning, asked what they had taken. She answered Battle's Vermin Killer. John Attfield, demonstrator of practical chemistry at St. Bartholomew's Hospital, reported finding strychnine in both stomachs. Dr. Payne indicated his willingness to give evidence on the state of the mother's mind, only for the coroner to decline to hear him. The jury could not go into that question, he stated, for it was likely to arise in another court. The question the inquest's jurors needed to answer was whether there could be any moral or reasonable doubt that the children died by their mother's hand. After 10 minutes, they agreed that the poison had been administered by Ann Vyse, which amounted to a verdict of willful murder. Throughout she had remained at home, which was unusual, the medical men declaring her in such a precarious state that conversation was prohibited and she was forbidden to raise herself from her recumbent position for fear this would reopen the neck wound. This anxiety seemed odd given Payne's original opinion of the injury.[29]

The prisoner stood charged on the coroner's inquest with the capital crime of willful murder, consequently the magisterial committal hearing promised to be a formality. The chair, Alderman Wilson, realized a defense of insanity would be set up at the criminal trial and announced, as had the coroner, that it would "form no part of the investigation here." He suspected that this accused murderer was being mollycoddled, so he dispatched the surgeon at Newgate Prison to the house to assess her condition, and in his opinion there would be no serious injury if she were brought up to answer the charge. That the medical man in attendance on her, Payne, declined to accept any responsibility for her removal did not deter the resolute Alderman from instructing the police to bring her before him at the Guildhall Police Court. She eventually arrived late in the care of two hospital nurses, a female attendant from the police station, and Payne. He informed Wilson that she would be "totally unable to bear up under a protracted investigation." In the interests of humanity, the chairman adjourned the proceedings. She was not, however, to be returned to the comfort of her house. Instead, arrangements were made with the governor of Newgate Prison for her reception there. She was conveyed from police court to prison by cab under the care of a police inspector; her sister, Sarah; two female attendants; and the ever-present Payne. Excluded from this group and any connection with her was Caroline Boyce, the hospital nurse who had been with her from the day of the deaths. The nurse's inability to give the police court "any information whatever" excited the Alderman's suspicion that she was withholding evidence out of sympathy.

William Smith fell under the same suspicion. He had served the Vyses as a manager and a porter for 28 years, and Mrs. Vyse had sent for him the day after the deaths. He had urged her to keep quiet and had told her that he would lay down his life not to recall what she had done the day before. "It is done and cannot be undone," she responded. Wilson fancied that this long-serving, loyal employee was withholding the truth of that meeting or had been so drunk at the time that he did not know what had taken place. The cook assured the prosecuting city solicitor that there had been no poisonous substance in the kitchen nor in the rice pudding. She confirmed Mrs. Vyse's complaint of a rodent infestation and their invasion of the bedrooms, which explained the need for Battle's Vermin Killer. In his turn Payne remembered the prisoner asking as her wound was being dressed "why they were all looking so sedate ... they looked as if they were at a funeral or a laying out." But there was no report of an investigation of the letter handed by Ann Vyse to her sister Sarah on May 22. The alderman then committed her for criminal trial.[30]

The trial opened at the Old Bailey on July 6, 1862. Indicted for the murder of both girls, Ann Vyse stood charged with the willful murder of the younger, Alice. Speaking almost inaudibly, and grief stricken, she answered not guilty to the charge. The prosecution's evidence was essentially that delivered at the committal hearing. At its conclusion the prisoner's defense counsel, the formidable Mr. Sergeant Ballantine, described this case as one of the most extraordinary ever brought before a court of justice. He should be able to relieve the prisoner of any contemplation of the crime, there being no motive for it, he assured the jury. He would show that disease was as much the cause of the deaths as the hand of the prisoner and that at the time she was not responsible for her acts, being insane. She had weaned her latest infant, now in the care of her husband in Surrey, for 18 months until April only to discover in May that she was again pregnant. That was "a circumstance and a time calculated to produce great depression of the brain," the medical evidence would show. What is more, he would show that members of her family suffered from insanity, and it was a "well known fact that the taint of disease continued in the blood through different generations." This taint was in the blood of the prisoner. She had sunk into a mental depression on the death of the infant in 1860, expressed in fits of passion during which she smashed crockery and destroyed furniture.[31]

Ballantine was as good as his word if not better. Sarah Saunders among others spoke of her sister's great affection for her children and great pride in them. A police female searcher's clear recollection of what the prisoner said to William Smith the day after the deaths was disputed by the attending doctors, Payne and Savory, who could not understand what their patient said until she had repeated the whisper time after time. That she had laid out the children on the bed probably after the death was further evidence that she was not in her right mind. Witnesses identified those of her relations who had been "affected in the mind." A boot maker swore that three days before the deaths Mrs. Vyse had descended into a wild tantrum in his shop, stamping around it with her eyes in a "mad state," over her complaint, which he could not verify, that the boots she had ordered were not perfectly identical. He thought she was out of her mind. That was the opinion of a regular customer who, on the fatal Thursday, sought to purchase a bonnet. Her criticism of a flower saw Vyse tear it out in a "smouldering fire" that had been ready to burst out. Her staring look had indicated that she was not in a proper state of mind.[32]

Confirmation that she was then insane was provided by medical specialists. William Hood ended in 1862 his decade-long position as resident physician and superintendent of Bethlem Asylum. He was appointed the lord chancellor's visitor of chancery lunatics, one of three full-time visitors, two doctors and the third an attorney, whose patients—like Mrs. Vyse—were affluent. Hood appears to have seen her in Newgate Prison, where she exhibited "subjective evidence" of her disease. There was "perspiring of the brain" when she was "worried by her business transactions." This was a symptom "often complained of by patients who suffer from mental disease," he added. Moreover, the absence of a "sane motive" made the accused "by definition insane." Hood demonstrated "a correlation between her business anxiety, the strain of suckling a child," and the irritations in her head. He raised in court the mental illness of one of her relations to which alienists had given the name "paroxysmal." Sufferers were at times quite beyond reason, at other times quite docile and sane. This condition led to suicide or homicide. An "exciting cause" on a patient of this description would be likely to bring about a paroxysm. And the profession, he declared, recognized insanity that continues from generation to generation.[33]

Augustus George Merritt, the regular medical attendant of the prisoner's children, remembered her being subject to "sudden irrational impulses" and exhibiting "almost undue anxiety" following the death of the child in 1860. At the beginning of the present year, he had urged her to wean the new infant and "partially relieve herself from the duties of her business." He could not attribute the tragic event that had occurred to anything other than the "state of mania" she was then in. Forbes Winslow, the author of books on insanity, stated that with the fresh pregnancy the suppression of menstruation affected the brain. Such women became victims of puerperal insanity. Asked if fits of despondency and impulsive madness following the loss of a child were evidence of an unsoundness of mind, Forbes replied that if there was evidence of hereditary madness in the family this would excite his suspicion. Madness called paroxysmal frequently took a suicidal form and very frequently was homicidal. Ann Vyse had attempted to cut her own throat after poisoning the girls. Such a patient would undoubtedly be incapable of distinguishing right from wrong. The jury agreed, finding her "not guilty being insane." She was an inmate of Fisherton House, the private asylum on the outskirts of Salisbury. Early in 1863 she gave birth to the child she had begun to carry during the trial, a boy named Sydney. In 1867 she was released as recovered by order of the home secretary, and by 1871 she was living in Wimbledon with her husband and ever-growing family. She died in 1889 and was buried in the grave of the two daughters she had murdered.[34]

In 1865, as Ann Vyse sat in the Fisherton House asylum, there was an apparent solution to the Road Hill House crime. Constance Kent made a public confession to her young stepbrother's murder. She had, she swore, acted entirely alone. A strong mental effort was required to understand how one "so young and gentle could imbrue her hands in her brother's blood." The *Western Daily Press* summarized for its readers the response of the national dailies to the confession, for the general tendency was to question its credibility. *The Times* was something of an exception, for it presumed that the unburdening of her mind was free and spontaneous given that she was residing among a "society of religious ladies." The *Daily News* found the explanation for what had happened in "hereditary disease impelling her to violence or delusion." Of much the same mind was the *Daily Telegraph*, whereas the *Standard* thought the public would want "proof, in a practical form, of [the confession's] authenticity." The question for newspapers and the public, the *Paisley Herald* argued, was whether she insanely murdered her half brother or was insanely owning up to the crime of which she was innocent. For others another problem was the language of the confession. The *London Evening Standard* thought it more fitted for an attorney's office, since it had the language of an affidavit and bore the impress of a "too zealous persuasion." The confession needed to be "searchingly investigated," for there was a possibility that certain persons "were interested in dragging forth" from Constance Kent "some incoherent avowal of guilt."[35]

Five. A Question of Class

The cathedral city of Salisbury was crowded by the time the trial opened on July 21, 1865, so the excitement probably penetrated Fisherton House. Constance's defense counsel made but two statements on her behalf: that the guilt was hers alone and that her father and others who had long suffered unjust and cruel suspicions were "wholly and absolutely innocent." The attempt to clear her father's name was not entirely successful, however, and in 1866 he was driven to bring a legal action against the proprietor, printer, and publisher of the Edinburgh *Daily Review* for damages of £5,000 "for certain words and passages" false and calumnious contained in an editorial commentary on Constance's confession. Presumably it dwelt upon the father's possible guilt. The action appears to have been settled out of court. She had not been driven to this act by unkind treatment at home, her counsel asserted, where she had met "nothing but tender and forbearing love." The judge then donned the ceremonial black cap and, having sentenced her to death, immediately dissolved into tears.[36]

The home secretary came under heavy and sustained pressure to advise the Queen to commute the death sentence. The argument of her hereditary insanity was revived, as was her youth at the time of the crime. But her confession naturally limited the clemency she received. To be excessively generous to this young woman of social status would heighten lower class resentment of the inequality of justice. She was sentenced to life imprisonment, which was now extended by five years to a total of 20. Shortly after passing the midpoint of her sentence, she requested an early release. This was refused. She served the full term and was released on July 18, 1885, and emigrated to the other side of the world, Australia, where she joined her brother William and several other members of the family. Under the name Emilie Kaye, she earned a high reputation as a "pioneer nurse." In February 1944 she received the customary message from the monarch on the occasion of her 100 years of life, only to die shortly afterwards.[37]

Chapter Six

Class Beyond Question

Talk of Constance Kent's hereditary insanity, promoted as it was by her stepmother and her father, he being under suspicion in his young son's death, was based upon her biological mother's alleged and unproven lunacy. Seven years later, in 1872, it was to be the basis of the defense of Christiana Edmunds. She was the first child of a middle class couple, her father a successful architect whose designs of a variety of public buildings earned him a handsome income. Three siblings followed her, but her father's later infection of her mother with syphilis proved fatal for two infants and perhaps contributed to the epilepsy and violent eruptions of the seventh child, a boy, who was eventually institutionalized. The family was dogged by tragedy. William Edmunds's career and mental health foundered, and the doctor admitting him to an expensive private asylum judged him a dangerous lunatic. Unable to afford his continued residence there, his wife briefly accepted him back home before securing his admission to a far less pleasant and less expensive asylum where he was one of 250 patients until his death in 1847. Throughout this period of intense family stress, Christiana grew up, having in 1842 returned home from her private schooling. She witnessed her father's instability and his removal from the home in a straitjacket. The house had to be sold and the family reduced to humbler accommodation in Canterbury, which brought it unpleasantly close to the line separating it from the lower orders. Christiana's behavior became worrisome, and her mother sent her off to London to consult a doctor who specialized in hysteria. Upper middle class women were thought to be most vulnerable to it since their sexual feelings were considered more developed due to a "want of necessary employment to occupy the mind." Another diagnosis was "erotomania," the components of which were to be listed in the following century as arrogance, a personal belief in a high special status, hypersensitivity to slights, and an inclination towards paranoia.[1]

Christiana perhaps experienced the "notorious" treatment for hysteria, which was a genital massage to orgasm by a physician in the belief it would relieve her sexual energy. This may help explain the very close relationships that developed between some Victorian women and their doctors. For spinsters, these were the only men with whom they could discuss intimate problems and these the only male hands permitted to touch the most private parts of their bodies. Having spent some time in Canterbury, mother and daughter moved on to a Brighton resort recommended for the therapeutic value of sea air. They rented rooms in a large house in the center of the town across the street from the house and practice of Dr. Charles Beard. A graduate of Trinity College, Cambridge, he had a medical degree from St. Bartholomew's Hospital, was a member of the Royal College of Physicians, had a practice at the Sussex County Hospital, and established his personal practice in 1861. To him Christiana took her problem of neuralgia, which many medical men linked to hysteria. For Beard she quickly developed intense romantic feelings, which unfortunately he did nothing to discourage. She often wrote to him several times a week. Her passion for him at the age of 42 alarmed her mother, for this was also the age at which Christiana's father had begun to exhibit mental instability. So she moved to rooms a little farther away from Beard. Nevertheless, Christiana became a close friend of the doctor's wife, Emily, from whom she may have learned of the stresses and strains from which the Beard marriage suffered. Beard was unattached to his wife, who in turn suspected him of infidelity. During one of Beard's extended absences in London, Christiana called with chocolate creams purchased from a prominent local confectioner, Maynard, a gift for the Beard children. One of the creams she contrived to have Emily take, though she quickly spat it out, offended by the taste. Christiana immediately departed, and that night Emily suffered from excessive saliva and diarrhea. On his return home, Beard, sensing what might have happened given Christiana's romantic feelings for him, which he had kept from his wife, instructed Emily to stay away from the Edmundses. He lost no time calling on her and her mother himself and asked why there had been an attempt to poison his spouse. The daughter denied any such intent and claimed that she had herself been ill after eating a number of Maynard's chocolates.[2]

Anxious to expunge from the mind of the doctor she loved every thought that she was seeking to remove the obstacle to their union, his wife, Christiana saw in food poisoning a means to her end. Butter and bread were colored with copper, lice and bedbugs were found in ice cream, and additives were particularly common in confectionaries. Arsenic in peppermint lozenges sold in Bradford in 1858 had poisoned 220 sweet-toothed persons. Such alarming episodes saw the passage of the Adulteration of Food and Drink Act in 1860, but it was not compulsory, which inevitably led to its evasion. Two years later the Privy Council estimated that one-fifth of the meat sold by butchers was from diseased animals. The need for a diversion became more pressing in January 1871, when Beard repeated his accusation that Christiana had attempted to poison his wife. This she denied and with her mother called at the Beard house and threatened legal action if he did not retract it. Alive to the acute embarrassment to which this would give rise if her letters were exposed during a court case, he destroyed 20 of them. Christiana then embarked on a complex strategy to ensure that a poisoning was not laid at her door. She first tested it callously by giving a bag of Maynard's chocolate creams, which she had infected with poison, to a young lad of 13. He gave one of them to a friend, who spat it out, but his throat soon burned, he vomited, and his limbs stiffened. Two days later his frightened mother took him to hospital, and there he remained for a week before recovering.[3]

Christiana had some knowledge of poisons and initially rejected the most popular, arsenic, because of the well-known scientific tests for its detection. Strychnine was far more powerful, but its bitter taste made difficult its use in food and drink. Yet it might be obtained without great difficulty. A recent Pharmacy Act regulated its sale to a buyer whom the vendor knew or was accompanied by a witness with whom he was acquainted. The poison was to be labeled as such, and the name and address of the purchaser was to be entered in the pharmacist's poison book, which was to be signed by buyer and witness. Christiana's supplier was chemist Isaac Garrett, who dispensed her neuralgia medication, although he knew her as Mrs. Woods. He sold 10 grains to her for the alleged purpose of putting down noisy perhaps feral cats, and it was to Garrett she returned for fresh supply. "Her social background afforded her all the protection she needed to continue poisoning." As a middle class, respectable lady, she was above suspicion. What she lacked was knowledge of the amount to administer, and the bitter taste of strychnine naturally inclined her not to use too much in order to lessen the chance of its detection by the victim. This would help explain why so many adults survived, among them Emily Beard, yet one of her four children died.[4]

Christiana intended to make Maynard's store responsible for any poisonings, including that of Mrs. Beard. This seemed simple enough. She supplied money with which young boys bought some creams. They handed them to her, and she laced them with strychnine before telling the boys to return them as they were not the chocolates she wanted. The shop assistants added them to the shelves of the sweets on sale, and some were bought by a visitor to Brighton, Charles Miller. He gave one to his young nephew Sidney Baker, who died in agony after a few hours. Miller survived, having been made comfortable by a doctor who suspected poison. Richard Rugg had also attended the unfortunate child. He had qualified as a member of the Royal College of Surgeons, was the first house surgeon to the Brighton Dispensary, and served for years as the surgeon to the workhouse. In short, he was a doctor of local distinction. He had a reputation for medical skill, kindness of manner, and charitable activities among the poor. The day after the child's death, June 13, 1871, he collected the body for a postmortem. He found nothing to explain the death but gave the stomach and its contents to Inspector Gibbs, who was present, and the policeman delivered them to London for analysis by Henry Letheby. Although compromised by the controversy over his evidence in the Anne Merritt case, he remained a well-known analytical chemist at the London Hospital and a public health official for the City of London. His test for arsenic proved negative, but he found one quarter of a gram of strychnine. This would be fatal for an infant, and he was sure more would have been taken. Some, he observed, would have been absorbed by the body.[5]

The certainty of an inquest saw Christiana visit Maynard and claim to have been another victim of the chocolates. She complained that they had caused her and a friend to fall ill. In response, Maynard suggested that she have them analyzed, which she did, but the analyst did not detect poison. Hearing of this exchange, Gibbs made sure Christiana attended the inquest as a witness and told her story. The coroner could find no evidence with which to hold either Maynard or the manufacturer of the creams responsible, for, as the latter carefully pointed out, while his creams had been distributed widely, only in Brighton had there been a problem. What was clear, the coroner remarked, was that the child had been a victim of strychnine poisoning. The mystery was how he had come by it. Nevertheless, Christiana made sure that both Beards knew she had been a victim and as such had been required to give evidence before the coroner. Anonymously, she wrote to the dead child's father urging him to sue Maynard. She spoke also of a young lady who as an inquest witness would willingly come forward being entirely dissatisfied with Maynard's failure to analyze and destroy the chocolate creams. The father took no legal action given the verdict of the inquest.[6]

The Beards invited Christiana for tea on July 12, during which Charles revealed that he had shown her letters to his wife. In fact, Emily may have had prior knowledge of them, for, suspecting him of infidelity, she had opened his mail when he was away in London. Their disclosure to the wife came as a shock to Christiana, for they were of an intimate nature. So did his statement that he had not "respected her so much" since the attempt on his wife's life the previous September. He had much earlier in the year closed the door on their connection and now seemed about to padlock it. She redoubled her efforts to remove the obstacle to their eventual union, Emily, and convince Charles that the town was plagued by poisonings of which she was herself an innocent victim. She contrived to obtain brief possession of the chemist's relevant poison book and removed those pages that recorded her purchases of strychnine under the name Woods. She switched from strychnine to arsenic and artfully circumvented the Arsenic Act by turning to a chemist, Bradbury, who was planning to close his Brighton pharmacy. She sent a boy messenger with a note, ostensibly from the large chemists, Glaisyer and Kemp, requesting three ounces of the poison. This being a transfer not a purchase, the provisions of the act did not apply and the boy returned with a three-ounce packet that would have been enough to kill a great many of the town's residents.[7]

Her fresh campaign of poisonings was no longer to be random, and she was confident it was practically foolproof. On August 8 she took the train to Margate, where she rented a room for two days but remained only one. There she made up parcels of fruit and sweetmeats, which she carried to London and deposited with the Brighton railway line for delivery in the town. On August 10 a railway van delivered a parcel of cakes, preserved fruits, and gingerbread nuts to Emily Beard. They were for the children, an explanatory note said, but those that had been made up together were for their mother. These were dusted with arsenic. Later that same day a railway van delivered a similar parcel to the Boys family who lived nearby. Christiana had mistakenly identified them with those of the same name who had made difficulties for her father during his career in Margate. Surgeon Nathaniel Blaker was called when two servants who sampled the contents fell seriously ill, and he moved on to the Beard residence, where he found another two domestics unwell. All four exhibited symptoms of an irritant poison, so he collected vomit and the handkerchief of one servant who had used it to clean her mouth. He took them to the Sussex County Hospital, and the chemist found arsenic. Blaker gave the evidence to Inspector Gibbs, who was informed by surgeon Frederick Humphrey that his patient Christiana Edmunds was a victim of "deliberate poisoning" having received a parcel of fruits. Gibbs called at the Edmundses' rooms, where the mother gave him the parcel and he found the daughter lying on a couch and—in her own words—"nearly poisoned" yet again. Overconfident, she patronized him, remarking that this mystery was beyond his ability to solve. Additional parcels were received by chemist Garrett; by the editor of the *Brighton Gazette*, whose reporting of the mystery she did not approve; and by the surgeon George Tatham, who was also a borough magistrate. Gibbs had little difficulty retracing the poisoner's steps and identifying her. He took the labels from the parcels and the notes in them and consulted a handwriting authority on the similarity between them and Christiana's script as found in one of her letters to Charles Beard. On August 17, he arrested her, and she was remanded until a committal hearing,[8]

When she went before the magistrates, Christiana had legal counsel, but the evidence heard was too strong to be dismissed. Emily Beard revealed the extent of the accused's feelings for her husband, and the letter she sent to him after Sidney Barker's death was read aloud, furnishing Christiana's motive for wanting Emily dead. There was the evidence of the lads used to obtain the chocolate creams and of the shopkeepers who had found bags of Maynard candies at their stores immediately after Edmunds left their premises. There were the reports of the medical men and experts, their finding strychnine in the stomach of the dead child and dangerous quantities of arsenic in the cake intended for Emily Beard and in the fruit of other parcels. The servants who ate portions of the cake and fruit had quickly exhibited symptoms of the poison. Moreover, at the time of Sidney Barker's death, Christiana had access to strychnine. So, on September 7, she was charged with his murder and became one of the 254 women accused of murder or attempted murder by poisoning between 1750 and 1914.[9]

She was sent for trial at the Sussex Assizes, Lewes, on the charge of murder of the boy, and of the attempted murders of Emily Beard, Elizabeth Boys, and Isaac Garrett. The intensity of the local hostility towards her prompted an application for a change of trial venue. This was granted, and the trial opened in the Central Criminal Court, the Old Bailey, at 10:00 a.m. on Monday, January 15, 1872, with Mr. Justice Martin presiding. Long before that hour, all available public accommodation was occupied, with the "fair sex predominant." Since Christmas the accused had been held in the neighboring and notorious Newgate Prison, where she constantly complained of conditions utterly inappropriate for a "lady" of her social position. On entering the dock, she affected not the slightest interest in the proceedings. "She displayed a vacant stare, and not a muscle of her face moved." To the charge of the willful murder of Sidney Barker, she pleaded not guilty. The jury was sworn and not one of them was challenged. Sitting in the well of the court were two formidable legal talents.[10]

William Ballantine and John Humffreys Parry were powerful barristers. Both were serjeants-at-law, an elite body dismissed by Lord

Chief Justice Campbell as a "very degenerate race." Their more general reputation was that of "well educated gentlemen, with an average ability, equal to any of the same number of members of the bar, and amongst them, there were those entitled upon many grounds to claim professional distinction." Ballantine and Parry were two of that number. Ballantine was proud of his performances as a defense counsel yet excelled as a prosecutor. He advocated deterrent punishments, convinced that criminals were waging a deliberate war of reckless violence against society. There was "no example of a criminal under a capital sentence," he wrote, "who would not with joy exchange the [death] penalty for any other form of punishment known to our laws." He was skeptical of the truthfulness of witnesses. Even those with no intention to deceive often succumbed to the temptation to exaggerate facts favorable to the case they were supporting. Thankfully, it was believed that skillful cross-examination would expose falsehoods and correct exaggerated statements.[11]

Ballantine opened the prosecution with a brief address that lasted barely 45 minutes. The press applauded his "able exposition of the facts" so quietly rendered and his avoidance of any opinion "as to the enormity" of the crimes or introduction of "extraneous matter" to ensure a conviction. He repeated the case made before the magistrates, that the prisoner had conceived a violent passion for Dr. Beard and whether from jealousy or some other motive attempted to remove Mrs. Beard. In response, the doctor, convinced she had attempted to poison his wife, broke off his acquaintance with her. To divert suspicion from herself the prisoner added poisonous matter to the "sweetmeats" sold by Maynard, causing the death of a child and several mortal illnesses. He called 27 witnesses, their depositions carefully prepared by the clerk to the magistrates. The final pair were the Beards. Since their evidence would "involve topics of a peculiar character" that made the presence of ladies undesirable, most women left the courtroom. When Emily Beard entered the witness box, the judge observed that it would be better to hear from her husband first. But as soon as Charles Beard— a "tall, fine looking, broad chested man" whom onlookers could easily believe able to excite the passion of Christiana—replaced his wife in the box, Parry immediately objected that evidence regarding the alleged attempt to murder Mrs. Beard could not be adduced to support the charge that his client had murdered Sidney Barker. The judge agreed, and after a brief consultation with the lead counsels he excused the Beards from testifying. At that point, Ballantine suddenly closed the case for the prosecution. Taken by surprise, Parry requested and received leave to open the defense the following morning.[12]

Six. Class Beyond Question

John Humffreys Parry was the son of a barrister who was also an eminent scholar of the Welsh language and a promoter of movements whose motto, when translated, was "May the Welsh language endure as long as the world endures." Following his father's unexpected death, Parry first tried a life in commerce but soon wearied of it and welcomed an appointment to the Printed Book Department of the British Museum. While there he concentrated on law books and eventually, in 1843, was called to the bar. Politically an advanced Liberal, he twice failed to win election to Parliament but excelled in the courtroom. He possessed in abundance the qualities of a successful advocate. His commanding presence, "singularly dignified bearing," almost unique charm of voice and delivery, "warm and generous disposition," and a highly developed sense of honor excited wide admiration of him as the truly "finished advocate." His retention by Mrs. Edmunds as her daughter's defense counsel was an inspired decision.[13]

Parry knew before the trial opened that he would have an uphill battle against the "exigencies of the case." He intended to argue that there was no legal proof that the accused had caused the death of Sidney Barker. Where was the direct evidence that she had laced with poison the chocolate cream that killed him? Not that he expected this defense to succeed given the wealth of circumstantial evidence. His best chance of rescuing her from the hangman was to prove she was insane. In preparation he had several specialists interview her in Newgate Prison. William Wood had in 1845 become the principal resident medical officer to the asylum now known as the Bethlem Royal Hospital, where he implemented more humane treatment of the mental patients. Henry Maudsley, who had been appointed professor of medical jurisprudence at University College, London, was the author of two important books, and was a leading British "alienist." Charles Lockhart Robertson was the recently retired first medical superintendent of the Sussex County Asylum. Parry had wished to add a fourth to this team, J. Beresford Ryley, the surgeon of the Woolwich division of the Metropolitan Police. Unfortunately, the prison surgeon typically present as an observer on such occasions was absent. Consequently, Ryley was denied access to the prisoner. He was present, however, throughout the trial.[14]

Acknowledging his client's "unmistakable guilt," Parry insisted it was "part proof of her insanity." Were she not insane she would not have taken the life of a child for whom she had no malice. His experts in mental diseases then gave their opinions. Wood had been struck and amazed by her apparent indifference to her peril and his inability to impress upon her its seriousness. He concluded that she could not judge between right and wrong. Robertson had difficulty reaching a conclusion and situated her case on the borderline between crime and insanity. Although her intellect was clear and free from delusion, her "moral sense" was deficient as it was in descendants of insane parents. He would not on the basis of his interviews with her sign a certificate of lunacy, however. Maudsley agreed that she lacked a "sense of morality," then added—unhelpfully to the defense—that every person who committed a crime "exhibited some want of moral feeling." The experts were subjected to penetrating cross-examinations by Ballantine. An indignant Lockhart Robertson took to the public his bitter criticism of the prosecutor's conduct. His ethics and professional evidence had been called into question, he protested. Ballantine had treated the experts' scientific evidence in a manner that would "pervert the course of justice." The press was inclined to agree that the "pretensions made by medical experts to decide questions of sanity or insanity on general grounds" had been disposed of off-handedly by Ballantine.[15]

Parry's principal witness in support of the prisoner's hereditary insanity was her mother, who suffered "mortal agony" in giving testimony on her family's tragic history. Her husband had become insane in the prime of life and was condemned to an asylum. Her young son had been an "epileptic idiot" and died in an asylum. Her father had died an epileptic cripple, while one of her daughters had attempted suicide and lost her life to hysteria. As for the prisoner, she had suffered from paralysis and hysteria, and her mother had watched the ominous symptoms of the "hereditary malady" stealing up on her. In the midst of this, Christiana cried from the dock, "This is more than I can bear." But the corroborating evidence of insanity was judged "singularly weak" by the press. Witnesses who might have given testimony to it—and to the prisoner's "strange maladies"—were "almost all dead or had disappeared." Until now the mother had kept to herself her fears of her daughter's insanity and could not supply positive testimony from independent sources of the "prisoner's eccentricity." Nor in his summing up was the judge convinced of the accused's hereditary insanity. He emphasized how rarely accused poor persons were afflicted with insanity whereas the plea was "a common enough defense when people of means were charged with the commission of crime." In his opinion every person of either gender should be held responsible "until it was shown to the contrary." The jury should acquit the prisoner only if they were convinced that at the time of the crime she did not know right from wrong. In no more than 45 minutes, the jury found her guilty without a recommendation for mercy, and the judge sentenced her to death for the murder of Sidney Barker. Asked if she had anything to say to alter the sentence, she declared that she was pregnant, "a statement, astonishing as it was for a woman of her position" who had spent the previous five months in prison. The "absurd and obsolete custom" was now followed. A jury of matrons was formed, for whom J. Beresford Ryley provided the essential medical assistance. He and they quickly concluded that she was not quick with child. The decision reduced the prisoner to a "terrible state of woe," recognizing as finally she did the peril of her situation, and in this she was joined by the 12 matrons. Distraught, she was hurried off to a Newgate cell and the following day sent by rail to Lewes. The impaneling of unskilled matrons in such cases was assailed by the Metropolitan branch of the British Medical Association, for it had "positively humiliated" the country.[16]

No sooner had Christiana reached Lewes to prepare for her execution than Judge Martin altered his opinion on the case, perhaps reconsidering Serjeant Parry's argument with its evidence of her hereditary insanity. He informed Home Secretary Bruce that he believed her insane "to a considerable extent." Although she may know right from wrong, she was affected by "an hereditary taint of insanity." He and the majority of experts agreed that it would be a public scandal to put to a violent death a person "commonly deemed insane." So, he suggested an investigation of her mind by competent and disinterested medical men. She had a motive, the *Lancet* observed, and her conduct to that end was implemented with infernal cunning, yet it was not inconsistent with the worst forms of madness. Then there was her "needless aspect" throughout the trial, her false statement of pregnancy, her family history—all of which amounted to prima facie evidence of insanity. *Reynolds's Newspaper* and the *Pall Mall Gazette* were among those who opposed the home secretary's intervention in this case. He named Sir William Gull and Dr. William Orange, the medical superintendent of Broadmoor Hospital, to examine mentally the condemned woman. Gull, a physician to the royal family and society, which brought him vast wealth, had just been knighted for his cure of the heir to the throne's typhoid fever. They examined the condemned woman for a few hours, which, as the *British Medical Journal* reported, led them to the "most absolute and unequivocal conclusions" that she should not go to the gallows. The social status and privileged background of the condemned had brought about the reprieve, the *Spectator* commented. Had she been a poor woman she would have been hanged. A more general concern of the press was that this decision, as the judge implied, would give people of means the impression that they could get away with murder. Of course, the Broadmoor asylum to which she was now sent did not amount to an escape of punishment.[17]

Christiana arrived there in July 1872, but the surgeon at Lewes

Prison, who had supervised her for some 10 months, was not at all convinced of her insanity. He also considered her responsible for her actions. She was prone to hysteria. At the asylum she was added to the more trusted patients, and her life ended in 1907 when she was 78. There was an element of irony in the fact that the object of her obsessive passion, Charles Beard, was another who ended his days a lunatic. He was admitted to a Northamptonshire asylum in 1886, after 15 years of mental illness. Its origins might have been found at that moment in time when Christiana launched her poisoning campaign in an unsuccessful effort to convince him that she had not attempted to poison his wife. He died in the middle class Holloway Sanitarium, London, in 1916, at the advanced age of 88.[18]

Among the women patients who fell in love with their doctors, Florence Ricardo stands as an exception. Christiana Edmunds's obsessive passion for Dr. Charles Beard may not have been requited, whereas the highly distinguished, elderly, and married Dr. James Manby Gully entered into a lengthy and profoundly intimate love affair with young Florence. Born in Australia in 1845, she and her family moved to England in the middle of the century and her father set about establishing himself as a member of the landed gentry. He acquired Bruscot Park, an estate of 3,500 acres in Berkshire, and a fashionable London residence. Florence was raised in the "world of wealth, leavened with piety and a sense of duty," which prepared her for society life and a suitable marriage. While traveling in Canada with her parents she met Captain Alexander Ricardo, a physically attractive military officer serving in a socially prestigious regiment, the Grenadier Guards. His family was one of "great culture and intellectual power, and no less important great wealth and social prestige." His mother was a sister of the Earl of Fife. On his return to England the marriage was arranged, and in the settlement she received from him a first life interest on £40,000, while her father settled on her £20,000 in which she also had a life interest. Florence soon realized that her husband was an alcoholic. Rarely sober, he fell victim to *delirium tremens* during which he became so violent that a male attendant became necessary to limit the danger to those near him. Mrs. Campbell, his mother-in-law, recommended a period of therapy at the hydropathic clinic of Malvern under the care of Dr. Gully and his partner. Florence rented a house in which Ricardo was not often to be found, and when he was there, she was afraid to remain under the threat of his drunken violence. One of her sisters came to be with her, and together they sought greater refuge in the home of Gully and his two sisters. Florence fell under the spell of the famous man, whose patients had included the poet Tennyson, the author Dickens, and the nurse Nightingale. Although short, bald, rotund, and 37 years older, he fascinated her not least with his "warmth, sympathy and understanding of her situation." He embraced her and told her he loved her, only for such scandalous impropriety to be seen by a maid. Mrs. Campbell was informed by Gully that it was a danger to her daughter's sanity "to leave this man [Ricardo] with any power of compelling her to live with him." Far better, he added, that Florence secure the protection of a legal separation from the violent drunkard. For that purpose he recommended an independent solicitor, Henry Brooks, who negotiated the terms of the separation with Ricardo's representative. Gully signed it as one of the witnesses. Although Ricardo had agreed to support her at £1,200 a year, this arrangement was unacceptable to her parents.[19]

Florence's father, a believer in the "sanctity and permanence of marriage," opposed a legal parting from her husband. In his opinion she should forgive Ricardo and return to him. Then there was her employment of Henry Brooks instead of the family's solicitor, and her decision to lodge with the Brooks family. Her furious father threatened to withhold the interest on her marriage settlement only for Brooks to advise her that this would be illegal. Subsequently, she entered a charge against her father, who quickly retreated. Adding to the parental discontent was her close relationship with Gully. Her mother feared her daughter was infatuated with the famous elderly man, who was married but legally separated from his far older wife currently a resident of a mental asylum. Florence's parents saw the doctor as the driving force behind both the legal separation and her suit against her father over the settlement. They fretted that the frequency of the hydropath's visits to her at the Brooks' home would spark gossip. Her father instructed her to cease all contact with Gully or be cut off from the family. In Gully's own words, "she discarded her family for me in the spring of 1871." This decision was made easier for her with the news that Ricardo had finally drunk himself to death in Germany. Under his will she inherited £40,000. Now a widow of immense wealth, the impropriety of her relationship with the physician would be a little less stark. She acquired a furnished house not far from that of the solicitor, and Gully took one facing it. Mrs. Brooks, who had strongly disapproved of Gully's ceaseless calls on her guest and their "private engagement" was further scandalized by this new arrangement, which would facilitate an "intrigue." Her remarks he countered with the threat of an action for slander. He and Florence may have discussed marriage, but in the meantime they traveled together, accompanied by a pair of servants, first to Paris and then to Italy. Ostensibly they had separate hotel rooms, which proved no obstacle to passionate intercourse. Later they went to Bad Kissingen, and while Gully had thoughtfully kept note of her periods, Florence became pregnant. This Gully terminated, remarking to those who inquired that he was doing no more than removing a small tumor. The pain of the abortion and the experience brought to a halt their highly active sex life. As Florence put it, this terminated her "improper intimacy" with Dr. Gully.[20]

Florence was later to state that she owed her life to the care of Mrs. Jane Cannon Cox at a time when she suffered "acute physical" pain. She had met the widow in the Brooks family home, where she was the daily governess of the children. They liked each other, and, segregated from local society, Florence saw in this woman a trustworthy companion. For Cannon Cox the wealthy widow's household offered far more comfort and security with an annual salary initially of £80, which was far higher than that of other paid companions. Her care of her mistress during the abortion led to a high degree of intimacy, that of using first names and treatment as if a member of the family. Cox was a woman of limited means following the death of her husband, a civil engineer in Jamaica. She received modest financial assistance from the flourishing Jamaican businessman Joseph Bravo; the pair had had an indirect connection in the colony. He advanced loans that saw her three sons gain entry to St. Anne Asylum School for the Sons of Impoverished Gentlefolk. In her dealings with Florence, Cox promptly proved herself an excellent nurse—thoughtful, quick-witted, tireless, calm, and totally loyal. With her Gully discussed Florence's excessive consumption of wine, but it is not clear that she reduced it.[21]

Wearying of waiting for the death of the elderly Mrs. Gully, the obstacle to any union with the doctor, anxious to reconcile with her parents, and keen to reenter a society where tongues had wagged over the nature of her relationship with the famed master of the water cure, Florence may have seen in Charles Bravo her solution. She was introduced to him when she called at Palace Green, the Bravos' London residence, to collect her companion, who happened to be visiting there. Here was a match that would surely satisfy her father and reestablish her socially. Bravo was the only son of an insignificant gentleman and the only child of three who was not disabled. One sister was confined in a mental institution and the other was deaf-mute. On his father's death his mother married, probably in Jamaica, the wealthy Joseph Bravo, who treated his stepson with a measure of generosity. He sent him to Oxford for a higher education and opened a modest bank account for him. Charles took the Bravo name in gratitude and was called to the bar, where he earned a very modest annual income of £200.[22]

He entered adulthood having been doted on as a child. His public image was that of an attractive and appealing young man—high-spirited, good-natured, urbane, and witty. He had ample ability and ample common sense. There was, however, a far less attractive and darker side to his character. At times overbearing and arrogant, frustration excited childish temper tantrums. He was both cynical and devious, and those who knew him well considered him ruthless and rarely if ever given to sentiment. Worst of all was his obsession with money, which Mrs. Campbell considered a "mania." Here lay the attraction of marriage with Florence Ricardo. He had very large ambitions and planned a parliamentary career. His total income from a variety of sources amounted to £1,200—not enough to finance a political life—whereas her wealth would relieve him of dependence on his stepfather, whose financial aid was usually modest. The news that she intended to take advantage of the recent legislation that finally permitted women to keep whatever assets they brought into a marital union infuriated him. He threatened to walk out of the planned marriage and sought the assistance of her father. This Mr. Campbell provided, and a compromise was arranged. Privately, Gully had urged it. Florence retained control of her fortune but made a will in Bravo's favor and surrendered to him the lease on her new home, the Priory, together with its furnishings, and control of her carriages, horses, jewelry, and art.[23]

Charles Bravo treasured his elevated social position, but his entrance into marriage with a woman of equal social rank yet with a compromised personal reputation was further evidence of his prime concern. They agreed to a mutual revelation of personal secrets. His was nothing truly unusual among men of his station. He had kept a mistress for five years and she had borne a child. Florence's, on the other hand, was deadly for a woman. Her intimacy with Gully, which they had always sought to mask as innocent, was too notorious to deny. She admitted they had been lovers only once during a visit to Germany in 1873. Charles accepted this on the condition that she break completely with Gully. The abortion escaped mention. James Ruddick in *Death at the Priory* asserts that Florence told Bravo everything, but this is unlikely. She did leave the decision on their future to Bravo, although it was on the basis of her limited confession. "We all make mistakes," he admitted generously and stated that he still wanted her for his wife. He had broken with his mistress. Was this the response of a fortune hunter? Perhaps it was to escape this demeaning label that his stepfather later declared Charles totally ignorant before their marriage of Florence's intimate relationship with Gully. And it was a carefully edited version of Mrs. Ricardo's past that the Bravos, mother and stepfather, received from Charles. Hence, he assured Florence on November 1, 1875, that his mother had agreed to the announcement of their engagement, although there was never any doubt of her low opinion of Florence. His stepfather settled on him a life interest in £20,000. The wedding was expedited and took place in Kensington on December 7, 1875. His mother was conspicuously absent.[24]

The absence of genuine romantic passion in this suddenly expedited matrimonial venture may help explain its demise just five months later. Charles's love letters, Florence told her mother, were "cold and undemonstrative as possible." The marriage began unhappily with a miscarriage in late January, yet he remained "curiously unsympathetic" to her distress and disappointment. She had informed her parents on January 9 that she was pregnant, which led to the suspicion that they had slept together during at least one of his brief overnight stays at the Priory prior to the nuptials. Conflict followed. The knowledge that the discarded Gully had acquired a house no more than a few minutes' walk away angered the groom. This a "vile" anonymous letter intensified, accusing Bravo of marrying his bride for her money and referring to her as the doctor's mistress. Bravo believed Gully to be the author, which he privately denied to Cox. Another Bravo complaint was his wife's growing alcohol consumption; his commitment was to economy. The product of a Joseph Bravo household, "he looked somewhat too narrowly at both sides of a penny." He protested the size of the staff and insisted it be cut, and the servants were pruned. Even shortly before the wedding, he dismissed George Griffith, Florence's coachman for the past four years after his lengthy service to Gully. Florence resented being told how to run her home, she being its paymistress. His critical eye even fell upon her friend and companion whose cost, along with that of the horses and carriages, was in his opinion excessive. He could rely upon his stepfather to urge Mrs. Cox to return to Jamaica from whence came pleas of her aunt that she be on hand to ensure her eldest son's inheritance of her property. The ceaseless penny-pinching infuriated Florence. He rejected as an unnecessary expense her plan to rent a house in Worthing, where she believed the sea air would be therapeutic. His meddlesome mother, who had told Florence she had ruined her son's life, supported his resistance to expenditures. What is more, she added the sale of the ponies Florence loved as another essential economy. When Florence threatened to write to her mother-in-law to advise her to mind her own business, Charles struck her so firmly that she fell to the ground. Although he immediately wept and apologized, Florence left for her parents' home and he took off to London. She returned to the Priory with her father's strong encouragement on the receipt of a conciliatory letter from her husband. A second legal separation would be a scandal, her angry father warned. In the second week of March her husband told her he was returning to their bed and, coincidentally, he was violently ill, vomiting into the gutter while on his way to the rail station. He continued to town, went to his parents' house, and rested there before going on to his chambers. From time to time he made childishly insincere threats to depart the Priory but was easily dissuaded by Cox from deserting his wealthy wife.[25]

Then on April 6 Florence suffered a second miscarriage, which left her ill and physically frail for more than a week. She told him to sleep across the hall, and Cox became her bed companion. Exhibiting a measure of compassion, Charles sent for his cousin and friend Royes Bell, a prominent surgeon. He recommended that her regular family doctor, Harrison, who lived in nearby Streatham, be called in and that she have a therapeutic dose of Worthing's sea air. Six days later Charles was nursing his painful face and asked Florence for something for his neuralgia, and she recommended laudanum. To this point Harrison had not been summoned. When later Charles complained that he had obtained no relief, she and Cox suggested he rub his gums with chloroform. On Good Friday, April 14, Florence decided to go down to lunch for the first time in eight days. After the meal they withdrew to the morning room only for the restless Charles to go out and in so often that an exasperated Florence ordered him to leave. This peremptory exclusion of him, the master of the house, who was currently excluded from the bedroom, so annoyed him that he denounced her to Cox as a "selfish pig" and despised himself for having married her. On Easter Sunday he again complained to Florence of his neuralgia, for which she now recommended "a hot toddy of brandy and lemon." By Tuesday, April 18, both were well enough to go to the city, she to shop and he to have a Turkish bath and then lunch. She returned to the Priory in the early afternoon, while Charles came home two hours later. He decided to go for a ride, only for the horse to bolt, which brought him back to the house in evident pain from multiple aches and limb stiffness, not to mention his hurt pride. Florence again recommended a hot bath, which he took, and she dressed for dinner. The meal was delayed slightly while they awaited Cox, who had gone off to Worthing to rent a furnished house for Florence's sea air cure. What was served was tasty enough, but the conversation was little short of a disaster. Charles erupted on being handed a letter from his stepfather about one of his investments that had lost a little money. The "Governor," he fumed, had no business meddling in his affairs. The trio withdrew to the morning room, and a little after nine o'clock Charles reminded his wife that she had passed her bedtime. With Cox she withdrew and at the bottom of the stairs asked her companion to fetch a little marsala diluted with water. This took several minutes. Not long afterwards she instructed the maid to bring her yet another tumbler of marsala and water. That the decanters of marsala and sherry on the dining table had been emptied may have led Charles to reprimand his wife yet again on her heavy drinking. This Florence later denied.[26]

A few moments after entering his bedroom Charles flung open the door shouting, "Florence, hot water, hot water." Clearly, he realized he had taken something he needed to be rid of, being, as his stepfather said, "better acquainted than any barrister I know with medicine and medical jurisprudence." Neither Florence nor Cox heard this cry, perhaps because the main bedroom was virtually soundproof. The frightened maid quickly banged on the door and, on entering, found the mistress apparently asleep and her companion sitting in a chair knitting. Cox went to Bravo's room, where he was vomiting out of the window onto the leaded roof below and screaming again for hot water, and then collapsed. Cox resorted to first aid, massaging his chest, hands, and feet, and sent the maid for mustard and hot water. This was initially used as a foot bath, but a subsequent quantity she and the maid struggled to get into his mouth and down his throat. He immediately vomited. The maid was next dispatched downstairs to instruct the coachman to go to Streatham, perhaps a 30-minute drive away, to summon the family doctor, George Harrison, who had little knowledge of the husband. Florence, when finally roused from her bed, sent for the nearby Balham doctor, Moore. Following his quick arrival, he immediately suspected poisoning and was profoundly pessimistic about a recovery. This was a diagnosis with which Harrison agreed when he reached the house and was told by Cox that she believed Bravo had swallowed chloroform, having smelt it on his vomit. When Harrison asked if there was poison in the house, he was told there was rat poison in the stables. Florence then sent for Royes Bell, who on his arrival was accompanied by George Johnson the senior physician at King's College Hospital and vice-president of the Royal College of Physicians. He took control. Charles showed signs of consciousness and finally opened his eyes. Asked what he had taken, he said a little laudanum for toothache, only for Johnson to announce that it would not have produced the symptoms he was experiencing. Suspecting a case of poisoning, the doctors inexplicably did not seize the bottles that were close by. The blood in Bravo's vomit and bowel movements suggested an irritant poison, and he was advised of his moral obligation to confess if he was seeking to take his own life. This he did not do. Cox then intervened, telling Bell that when she first went to Charles's aid, he announced that he had taken poison but instructed her not to tell Florence. Of this she had so advised

Harrison on his arrival, she claimed. This he denied. Instead, he countered that she told him Bravo was an ill man and had swallowed some chloroform. No doubt Cox's revelation was intended to help Florence, but since Charles fell unconscious to the floor even as she entered his room, how could he have made the confession?[27]

Cox's sudden recollection had a forensic impact. Samples of vomit were collected for analysis. Bell telegraphed the coroner and the Detective Department of the Metropolitan Police. He took samples of food and wine; searched the stables and greenhouse; and collected specimens of the rat poison, weedkiller, and worming tablets. Antimony was used for worming horses. A group of Bravos led by Joseph had responded to Florence's telegram informing the family of the seriousness of Charles's condition. The stepfather denounced as rubbish the talk of self-poisoning and observed that the wife "did not seem much grieved in any way." Two additional doctors were soon on the scene. Henry Smith, FRCS, Mrs. Joseph Bravo's brother-in-law, was one, and Sir William Gull the other. The latter had responded to a last-minute appeal from Florence, he being a friend of her father. He ordered the gathering of the vomit on the leaded window of Charles's room; it was sent off for analysis. He questioned the patient on how he had come to be poisoned, but Bravo could tell him nothing more than that he had inadvertently swallowed some laudanum while rubbing it on his gums. Asked by Florence where he had gotten it, he said it was out of her bottle. "If there was anything else in it, I don't know what it was," he added. Questioned yet again by Gull, he wearily replied, "I've taken laudanum. Before God I've taken only laudanum. If it wasn't laudanum, so help me, God, I don't know what it was." This from a patient who knew more of medicine than most barristers. Later the residue in the bottle was tested and no poison was detected. Nevertheless, Gull remained convinced Bravo had poisoned himself. The royal physician left on Thursday evening, and Charles Bravo died in the predawn hours of Friday morning.[28]

The day after the death the postmortem was conducted by Joseph Frank Payne, FRCP, watched by Moore, Harrison, Royes Bell, and Johnson. Part of the intestines and portions of the heart were sent for analysis to Professor Theophilus Redwood, a professor of chemistry with the Pharmaceutical Society of Great Britain. The reason for the death was clear. Bravo had consumed more than enough poison to be fatal. It was suggested that it could have been administered in water, being soluble and tasteless. This drew attention to the water jug that the maid filled each day, for it was a ritual of the deceased to drink from it each night. The police made an extensive search of Surrey pharmacies and found that a large sale of tartar emetic or antimony had been made to a man in

Streatham, who was none other than George Griffiths. He had used it in his treatment of Florence Bravo's horses. Indeed, he had acquainted her with it in Malvern while employed by Gully during one of her visits to the stables. It is possible she was aware of its use in minuscule doses to minimize alcohol abuse. She may even have discussed it confidentially with her favorite physician, who prescribed it in such doses as a homeopathic medicine. Had she been tempted to add it to Ricardo's multiple daily alcoholic beverages in the knowledge it would prove an aversion therapy by producing nausea and vomiting? But the police were understandably reluctant to focus, as a person of interest, on a young widow of high social standing at a time when the most famous of the many medical men, Sir William Gull, made public his opinion that the deceased committed suicide.[29]

How likely a suspect would Florence have been? She had motive aplenty, despite the facade from time to time of domestic bliss. The marriage was, in truth, painfully and hurtfully unpleasant, her husband often obnoxious with violent temper tantrums and verbal abuse. On a single occasion the abuse was physical, and she was knocked down to the floor. She may never have loved Bravo, but by now she surely despised him. She had made "grave charges" in January, to her former Brighton doctor, of Charles's "persistent line" of sexual conduct. Since she was then in the early weeks of pregnancy, he may for that reason have insisted on anal intercourse. If she had motive, did she have the means? She knew of tartar emetic and often visited the stables to see her horses in whose welfare she was constantly interested, and where Griffiths kept the four ounces of the poison in a cupboard. An unanswered question was whether the coachman had taken all of it with him when he quit the premises in early January for his new job in Herne Hill, Kent. Florence also had the opportunity to mix tartar emetic with the water in the minutes she was alone upstairs having sent Cox for more diluted marsala, and it would have had time to dissolve before Charles came up later to his bedroom. Its effect was immediate, hence his shouts for hot water and his vomiting out of the window. Perhaps to deflect suspicion, Florence posted a reward of £500 for the discovery of proof of the sale of antimony or tartar emetic "to throw satisfactory light on the mode by which her husband came by his death."[30]

The inquest was a disaster. The coroner for East Surrey, William Carter, had taken the office in 1836 as a comparatively young attorney. He was to hold on to it for more than half a century. He appears to have accepted Gull's conclusion that the death was a suicide and was certainly keen to limit the inconvenience of the families, the Bravos denying suicide and the Campbells stressing Gull's opinion in support of it.

He was especially conscious of the bereaved widow in whose house the inquest was being held. His restricted list of witnesses included Dr. Harrison; the pathologist who conducted the postmortem; and the highly experienced analytic chemist Theophilus Redwood, to whom important organs had been sent. Both confirmed that antimony had been taken into the body in sufficient quantity to cause death. Excluded to the amazement of most observers were Gull and Florence and the leader of the doctors attending the patient, Johnson, who was snubbed when he sought to give evidence. The jury concluded that Bravo had died from the effects of antimony but had lacked sufficient evidence on how it had entered his body. Carter was excoriated for the "secret and unsatisfactory" manner in which the "singularly incomplete" inquiry into the death had been conducted. Before long there was a deafening demand for a second inquest. Many of the deceased's friends and a great many lawyers took their doubts to the lord chief justice. They pressed for a reopening of the hearing, and memorials were delivered to the Home Office requesting a fresh inquiry into the circumstances under which Charles Bravo died.[31]

The widow and her companion were for obvious reasons prime suspects in the death, they having been the only interested parties present when Bravo fell seriously ill. For this reason, Robert Campbell urged his daughter and her companion at least to make voluntary statements to the Treasury solicitor, which they did. They were so similar in most respects that they may have profited from the same legal advice. Florence told the sad story of her two marriages. She described how Charles had pressed her to put down her two hobbies, her garden and her horses, and discharge her friend and companion. She said that he required her to put down her maid and had struck her physically largely as a result of his mother's interference in the household arrangements. He got into an awful passion because she was so weak and bedridden after the second miscarriage and yet she "got quite to like him and forgot his meanness, which had previously disgusted" her. He constantly spoke of Gully and verbally abused him, constantly upbraiding her although her attachment to the elderly hydropath had been "quite innocent" and nothing improper had ever passed between them. This was untrue, as was her claim to have given up sherry to please her husband. The marriage had been unhappy, and in her own statement Cox corroborated this. She did, however, amend her evidence to the coroner. She now added three words to Charles's confession that he had taken poison and his order that she not tell Florence. He had taken poison, she now recollected, "for doctor Gully." This was certain to lead to an unpleasant and socially disastrous investigation of Florence's relationship with Gully in the event of a second inquest. Cox told of Charles's temper tantrum on Good Friday, when he admitted despising himself for marrying Florence, described his wife as a selfish pig, and declared, "Let her go back to Gully!"[32]

A second inquest opened in July 1876 in the billiards room of the Bedford Hotel, near the Priory. The death was now a topic of conversation in almost every inn in the country, for over the past two months gossips had run amok. The better class of society "shamelessly" exerted influence to secure seats at the inquest, and off-duty barristers and members of Parliament found themselves rubbing shoulders with ladies of fashion. So great was the crowd and the crush that the nervous coroner asked a surveyor sitting on the jury to check the floor to ensure there was no danger of its collapse. What followed was perhaps the most spectacular inquest in English legal history. The jurors were given a little antimony to taste, and all but one immediately spat it out as directed. The crowd kept a morbid watch on the individual who had swallowed a little. Forty-three witnesses were called over the course of 23 days, each examination being "prolonged to the limits of human patience." They were then cross-examined by a glittering battery of high-priced barristers led by the attorney general. Carter again sat as the coroner but with a legal advisor. Each significant figure had his or her own illustrious counsel. The final witnesses, Jane Cannon Cox, Florence Bravo, and James Manby Gully, were subjected to intense scrutiny and captured the greatest public attention. Not that this solved the case. Cox had received a gruesome drawing from an anonymous artist that showed her swinging from a gibbet, and, fearful she was coming under deep suspicion, she "rounded savagely" on Florence during four days of testimony. She gave full details of her friend's association with Gully and repeated the amended confession allegedly made to her by the dying man that he had "taken poison for Dr. Gully." This caused an uproar. She behaved calmly throughout even when questioned why, on being told by Bravo that he had taken poison, she had emptied and cleaned the basin into which he had vomited.

When Florence's turn came, she was ruthlessly probed on her affair with Gully, which caused her to flee the courtroom. On her return and in tears she appealed to the coroner and the jurors for protection when she refused to answer more questions on the master of the water cure. Referring to her former companion Cox, for they had now separated, she curtly declared: "I think she might have spared me many of those painful inquiries to which I have been subjected." Gully was another who emerged with his personal reputation in tatters. *The Times* accused him of abandoning himself to a "selfish intrigue." The jury of 16 members by a vote of 12 to four found that Bravo had been murdered by a person or persons unknown. The verdict angered the crowd, for the mystery had not been solved. The suspicion of murder had not been identified with a suspect.[33]

An alternative suspect was Jane Cannon Cox. "Surely there can be no doubt," Taylor and Clarke argue in *Murder in the Priory* "that Jane Cannon Cox was the murderer of Charles Bravo." She, they write, "put the tartar emetic into Charles Bravo's drinking water." They are scornful of a different theory. Cox's motive, in their opinion, was the retention of her position as Florence's companion. Her salary had risen to £100 along with full bed and board. This provided her with comfort and the means to support her three sons. But once married to Charles Bravo, would Florence need her anymore? Does this explain her suggestion to Charles that he inform his possessive mother of his intended bride's immoral past, which as he realized would have scuttled the marriage? Once the wedding had taken place, was she the author of the anonymous letters that mother and son received depicting Florence as unworthy of the union? Soon, Charles recommended with his mother's encouragement that Cox should be let go for reasons of economy. The contention that Florence was "almost certain" to dismiss her companion lacks evidence, as does the assertion that Cox "must have felt a growing hatred for Charles" and that his violent illness while on his way to his office in March was her first attempt to poison him. That she possessed the means to kill him is far from clear. Florence had been introduced to antimony, tartar emetic, at Malvern. Cox, on the other hand, might have purchased it without great difficulty or procured it when Griffiths was Florence's coachman. As for the opportunity to add it to the water bottle, that was when before dinner on the fateful Tuesday she was alone on her return from Worthing, or when after the meal Florence was preparing for bed and Charles remained for a while downstairs.[34]

Florence, by no means cleansed of suspicion, was, according to much of the press, lolling on cushions at a spa on the Ems river in Germany, happily serenaded daily by the bands for which the nation was famous. This the *Manchester Evening News* contradicted in a widely republished report. She was at her parents' home living in great seclusion "neither receiving visitors nor paying visits." In 1878 she rented a villa at the far end of the Southsea beach, using the name Turner, Bravo's family name at birth. She had been attended by Dr. Henry Robert Smith, and under his urging she became for almost two months a total abstainer. Was it guilt or despair that caused her to resume heavy drinking? September found her confined to bed for three weeks. A third such bout proved fatal. Her maternal uncle James Orr was staying at a nearby beach hotel, and she refused to allow him to summon Dr. Smith or telegraph her mother. She died in his presence and that of two servants. Dr. Smith conducted the postmortem, and the cause of death was obvious, excessive consumption of "alcoholic stimulants." An inquest was held because of her name and reputation, and, satisfied there was no evidence of an irritant poison, it reached the same conclusion.[35]

Chapter Seven

Class Has Limits

Chloroform, which played a role in the death of Charles Bravo, was a decisive factor in the murder trial of Adelaide Bartlett. Indeed, the murder she was accused of committing was believed to be the first case of homicide by that particular drug. In fact, there had been a case seven years earlier in Ontario, Canada, probably the work of Dr. Thomas Neill Cream. He went on to become a serial killer of London's East End prostitutes in the immediate aftermath of the Ripper killings. Combined with the peculiar love triangle that appeared to lie at the heart of the Bartlett crime, and the woman's mysterious background, the case aroused "considerable [public] interest." She had arrived in England from France at the age of 19 carrying the name of an aristocratic French family. In truth she was the illegitimate daughter of a wealthy, socially prominent Englishman who was determined to escape recognition as her father. His plan was to marry her off discreetly to a respectable suburban London grocer, thereby placing her comfortably in the lower middle class. The selected groom was Edwin Thomas Bartlett, second and favorite son of Edwin Bartlett. A cabinetmaker, the father had made a good marriage himself, for his wife stood a step above his own on Britain's long social ladder. His son entered the grocery trade and so impressed his employer, Edward Baxter, that he made him his partner. Young Edwin's contribution to the partnership was an ambition to establish a chain of grocery stores in London's proliferating suburbs. The first two were in Dulwich and Brixton, and they taxed the partners' capital to the limit. Hence Edwin was receptive to an offer of fresh financial support in a marriage settlement, this being a business rather than a romantic decision. Relatively young, having celebrated his 29th birthday in 1874, his business reputation was sound, as was his health. His position was secure, and he was trustworthy. There could be no doubt of his drive and work ethic, and his name "would obliterate the degrading fact of [his wife's] illegitimacy."

The unidentified father's representatives wrote the terms of the marriage settlement. The wedding was to be secret and take place in Croydon on April 6, 1875. Only two witnesses were to be present, one apparently an uncle of the bride the other Edwin's elder sister, who happened to live in that suburban town. The bride, Adelaide, had seen her groom only once before the day she wed him. In appearance he was pleasant looking and inclined to be shy and reserved in his relations with women, with whom he had little experience. He was obliged under the settlement to accept sole responsibility for his bride, never to make any references to her origins, and to supervise the completion of her education. This condition ensured they would not live as man and wife until she was 21. She entered a boarding school in Stoke Newington for a year and then spent 18 months in a Belgium Protestant convent. This allowed her to slip quietly from the Roman Catholic fold, for Edwin was a devout Methodist. Her extended educational absence allowed him to square his conscience with his promise to his partner to remain a bachelor for three years, thereby concentrating his full attention and energy on the expansion of their business. In 1877 Adelaide returned to England and life as Bartlett's wife. They had corresponded regularly during her finishing process, and perhaps during school holidays shared apartments. They now lived as man and wife in rooms above the original Herne Hill store. This humble abode was unlikely to draw unwelcome attention to them.[1]

Edwin Jr.'s reward was his wife's handsome dowry, which he immediately invested in Baxter and Bartlett grocery stores. Eventually they numbered six and a London warehouse. But there was one harmful blot on the marriage. His father could never forget that he had not approved of the bride nor even been invited to the parish church wedding. This became an enduring grievance for which he blamed his mysterious daughter-in-law, not his favorite son. The bride's life was no bed of roses. The Married Women's Property Act of 1870, which was extended in 1882, convinced her that she had been the victim of the marriage settlement. Although she had consented to it and had not dissented from the terms, she complained that she had not understood their meaning. Under them she was left entirely dependent on Edwin, who devoted most of his time and energy to the grocery business. He did purchase a piano on which she could indulge and develop her musical talent, and she walked and played with his prize dogs. Alone and bored, Adelaide left the home on learning that her husband, without consulting her, had invited his hostile widowed father to live with them. Ostensibly she visited an aunt whose identity was a mystery given the circumstances of Adelaide's birth. When the family noticed the coincidental disappearance of the youngest Bartlett brother, Frederick, they put two and two together and concluded that they were involved in a sexual relationship. Frederick was packed off to the United States. On Adelaide's return the elder Edwin accused her of having an affair with Frederick, for which she demanded a formal apology. This was made, however reluctantly, by the father at the request of son Edwin. If a somewhat pyrrhic moral victory, Adelaide exhibited no enthusiasm for sexual intimacy with her husband. His long developing dental problems—involving decayed teeth—may have explained the aversion. She nevertheless became pregnant in 1881, but after a stillbirth she asserted that that pregnancy would be her last. She fell under the influence of the American Mary Nichols, whose second husband, Thomas Low Nichols, was the author of *Esoteric Anthropology*, a copy of which Adelaide owned. Mrs. Nichols set up a practice in London as a "medical consultant" and taught women trapped in loveless marriages to insist on sexual abstinence. Whether or not the Bartletts' life became platonic is unknown, though Edwin's possession of contraceptives casts doubt upon it. Another of Adelaide's grievances was Edwin's will. Under it she would only obtain his property following his death if she remained unmarried. The will, much to Adelaide's resentment, ignored the Married Women's Property Act of 1882. This permitted a wife to retain her assets even if she remarried after her husband's death.[2]

The couple's troubled relationship was further complicated by George Dyson. The Bartletts were residing in Merton in 1885, and the nearby Wimbledon railway gave Edwin speedy connection to the center of his business at Herne Hill. They joined the congregation of the young, probationary Wesleyan minister George Dyson and quickly came to enjoy his company. Dyson's graduation from Trinity College, Dublin, with a bachelor of arts convinced Edwin that he was the solution, as a highly respectable young clergyman, to Adelaide's isolation during his frequent business absences. Moreover, Dyson might continue, if not complete, her education. He was to move in September to a larger chapel in Putney, while the Bartletts after a holiday in Dover moved that same month to Pimlico, a suburb of the capital. While at the port, Edwin covered Dyson's frequent travel costs by rail to Dover and made a significant amendment to his will. The remarriage clause was deleted, and Adelaide would inherit his property and possessions. What is more, he named Dyson as one of the two executors. The Bartletts' Pimlico rooms were in the home of Frederick Doggett, a registrar of births and deaths. Adelaide informed the landlady that Edwin's dyspepsia made him restless at night, which required that he sleep in a single bed. They would also be dining once a week with a clergyman, she mentioned. Yet Dyson had earlier admitted to Edwin his ever-deepening attachment to Adelaide, and this might require a prudent cooling if not an end to their association.[3]

The young clergyman's visits soon exceeded one a week, he on occasion arriving early and staying rather longer than was anticipated. He behaved very much as if at home, donning a blue serge coat and slipping his feet into carpet slippers. He continued to be greatly assisted by Edwin, who provided him with a season ticket for his travel from Putney to Waterloo Station, a short walk from Pimlico. He and Adelaide were seen by a maid in a romantic if not a compromising position in a room whose window curtains were carefully pinned together. The door, however, was never locked, and Adelaide later denied adultery. Such a breach of a commandment would have been calamitous for the young clergyman. She told Dyson that Edwin's life would not be long, explaining that he was suffering from a mysterious internal complaint. Dyson was under the impression that he was the selected successor of the terminally ill husband and may well have advised Adelaide of the date on which he as a Methodist probationer would be eligible to marry.[4]

In mid–October there was a slow deterioration of Edwin's health. A month later he began to suffer from nausea and diarrhea; in early December he started vomiting. The threesome decided to attend a dog show, where Edwin collapsed, and on December 10 his wife summoned the doctor who had opened a practice a short walk along the street. Dr. Alfred Leach was young, had little experience, had no knowledge of the Bartletts, and was probably influenced by the wife's observation that her husband was something of a hypochondriac. Initially, he diagnosed sub-acute gastritis. The condition of his mouth and teeth, butchered by an earlier dentist, had resulted in foul breath, which raised the possibility that he had resorted to mercury, also a therapy for syphilis. There being no evidence of this notorious disease, Leach's revised diagnosis remained mercurial poisoning notwithstanding Edwin's denial of ever taking it. A skillful dentist was imported to repair the damage. All the while, Adelaide maintained control of medicines and drugs; rejected the employment of a professional nurse; and effectively isolated Edwin from his father, his business partner, and his friends. Not surprisingly, there was a demand for a second medical opinion, though the choice was left to Leach. He chose Dr. John Gardner Dudley, who found no physical signs of disease and no evidence of sub-acute gastritis, concluding that the patient was suffering from little more than dyspepsia. In his opinion Edwin was of sound health and would benefit from fresh air by taking a daily walk or a carriage drive.[5]

By December 22 Leach considered this patient's physical recovery nearly complete but remained concerned about his mental condition in light of his wife's comment that often he spoke of dying. A planned trip to Torquay was canceled with her report that Edwin had passed a roundworm, an intestinal parasite, which deepened his depression. Informing Dyson that there was every likelihood of Edwin becoming violent, Adelaide impressed upon him the necessity of chloroform to ensure his sedation. Dyson dutifully shopped in and around Putney for small bottles of the drug, explaining to those who queried his purchases that they were needed to clean spots on his clothes. A well-known clergyman he had little difficulty obtaining the poison. The contents of the small bottles he transferred into a large one for delivery to Adelaide. She turned to Edwin's business partner, Baxter, for brandy, having read in her medical book that it was an excellent solvent for the drug. Dyson, questioning the wisdom of his purchases, unsuccessfully recommended she employ a professional nurse. Yet Edwin was eating heartily and apparently in better spirits. He had taken a walk with Leach and a drive with his wife and had called on the dentist to have another painless removal of an aching tooth. Both his father and his partner were pleased and reassured with this evidence of a restoration of his physical and mental health by New Year's Eve. That evening Edwin ordered a formidable breakfast for the celebratory first day of the New Year. A distraught wife awakened the housemaid at 4.00 a.m., however, and sent her for Leach with the news that Edwin was dead.[6]

Flabbergasted by the sudden death, Leach stated that a postmortem should be held. He had the backing of the landlord, Doggett the local registrar, who announced that he would be unable to register the death in the usual manner. Adelaide appeared to ask that the postmortem take place immediately. There was the odor of brandy on the body's chest, and Adelaide may have said that she had sought to resuscitate Edwin by striving to force the liquor down his throat. Dyson arrived the following morning, January 2, and later that day a team of five doctors, one of them present on the insistence of the suspicious elder Edwin, conducted and observed the operation. Once it was completed, the Bartletts' rooms were locked and sealed and nothing was to be removed because the contents of the stomach needed to be examined further. Leach, one of the observers, disclosed that on the opening of the stomach there had been a strong smell of chloroform. Unnerved by the news, Dyson scurried home and threw away the four small bottles in which he had bought the poison. He then learned that the senior pathologist, Dr. Thomas Green of Charing Cross Hospital, had concluded that the drug was the cause of death. An inquest was certain to be held, and Dyson was issued with a subpoena to ensure he was present. The brief opening was long enough for the elder Edwin and widow Adelaide to make it plain that they detested one another. The coroner adjourned until early February, by which time the senior Home Office analyst, Dr. Thomas Stevenson, was expected to be ready with the results of his analysis of the removed organs. But it was January 12 before they actually reached him. Fearing he would be seen as a dupe of the widow and that the association would bring a scandalous end to his short ministerial career, Dyson went in search of a witness who would confirm the innocence of his purchases of chloroform. He arrived at the inquest on February 4 in the company of his father, who was a senior Wesleyan divine, and the counsel for the ministry. Adelaide sat between her solicitor, Edward Wood, who had served her husband, and attorney Edward Beal. Aware of the suspicion of her, and having witnessed her aggressive performance a month earlier, he intended to keep her silent. On the periphery of this team was George Lewis, who had gained a reputation and respect as the Bravos legal hatchet man during the second inquest on that unsolved crime.[7]

The Bartlett inquest ended badly for both suspects. The coroner issued a warning that if the widow declined to give evidence it would have a heavy and unfortunate influence on the jury. Stevenson gave his findings. He had discovered a fraction of a grain of copper and lead. There was no other poison apart from the chloroform, which had been taken in a large and fatal dose, in the stomach. Despite the drug's hot and fiery taste, it would be possible to mitigate it with a bland fluid. Brandy, he added, would act as a solvent. The person known to have obtained the poison and the brandy, and who had total control of medicines and drugs, was the widow. This the jury surely realized. That Adelaide remained mute led the coroner to announce that he would call Leach "to depose to his conversations with her." Her counsel immediately objected to the conversations being received as evidence unless Leach could quote the "exact words" used during them. This he admitted he could not do so was given time to refresh his memory. He recalled that, on January 26, Mrs. Bartlett had said that the deceased "gave [her] to Mr. Dyson," only to subsequently and surprisingly seek to assert those marital rights he had never earlier claimed in a relationship designed to be platonic. Clearly implied was her acquisition of chloroform to "curb Edwin's sexual demands." This explanation of the drug's use allowed her to be considered a sympathetic figure, but not immediately.[8]

Although the coroner had yet to summarize the evidence for the jury, the foreman announced that it was their unanimous opinion that the widow should be taken into custody. This done, she was charged with suspicion of poisoning her husband. To all intents and purposes the jury had convicted her. Then Stevenson, in his reply to the coroner, declared that it would be quite possible to render a person insensible with the drug and then pour it down the throat while the victim was oblivious to the severe pain it caused. However, he was surprised that the very large quantity administered had apparently not caused vomiting. The jury then returned verdicts of willful murder against Adelaide Bartlett and the Rev. George Dyson, he as her accomplice before the fact.[9]

The Westminster Police Court, where magistrate Partridge presided, was the next destination of the two prisoners. She had been detained on February 11 and he eight days later. Adelaide appeared appropriately attired in deep mourning, while George was in clerical dress. The case had become one of national public interest, given the extraordinary revelations brought to light from time to time. Admission to the crowded court was by ticket only, and a large, loud gathering could be heard outside. The prosecution was conducted on behalf of the Treasury by Mr. Molony, a solicitor who qualified as a barrister the following year. Beal continued to act for the widow, while Frank Lockwood, QC, recently elected as a Liberal member of Parliament, represented Dyson. The pair sat apart in the dock, a jailer between them. Molony briefly described the intimate relations of the deceased, his wife, and the minister and the "sort of tacit understanding" that, on Edwin's death, Dyson would become the widow's husband. He alluded to their possible motive, the fact that Edwin was a "man in a considerable way of business" who on his demise was "worth a good deal of money for a man of his position." The possibility was strengthened by the revised will and also by the fact that during the night on which he died the only person in the room with him was his wife. Dyson had purchased the chloroform in his neighborhood with the untruthful explanation of its want for "different purposes." He had handed it to Mrs. Bartlett without the knowledge of her husband. The circumstances "caused very great suspicion against both prisoners," Molony continued, which was so grave that they might be sent for trial before a jury on the capital charge. Thomas Stevenson drew attention to the length of time that elapsed between the postmortem and his analysis of the body organs, estimating that another 35 to 40 hours passed between the death and postmortem. As for the quantity of chloroform he had found, he expressed the "certain opinion" that there was far more of it in the stomach at the time of death. There must have been a very large dose, he commented, much greater than any medical dose. Unsaid but nonetheless clear was the doctor's belief that the administration could not have been accidental.[10]

The pair were committed for trial, which opened at the Central Criminal Court of the Old Bailey on April 12 before Judge Wills. A week earlier he had told the Grand Jury that a strong case of suspicion had been made out against both prisoners, and he had emphasized their duty to return a true bill of indictment against the pair. Conspicuously present in the uncomfortably crowded courtroom, and exciting severe and caustic remarks, were women. Those who had obtained tickets took their seats an hour before the judge took his, behaving as if securing places at a "free and fashionable theatrical performance." The circumstantial evidence pointed heavily to a conviction, and not the least because the case was to be conducted by Attorney General Sir Charles Russell, the Crown's senior law officer. The child of a devout Irish middle class Catholic family—three of his sisters entered a convent and a brother became a Catholic priest—Russell moved to London and was called to the bar in 1859. His intense ambition, inexhaustible industry, immense ability, "resonant voice," "flashing eyes," and "forcible impressiveness" were the sources of his courtroom triumphs. In addition, he was considered the "cutest cross-examiner." A colleague commenting more truthfully observed that Russell "produced the same effect on a witness that a cobra produces on a rabbit." The *Pall Mall Gazette* offered a mocking assessment of the bar's most prominent performers, naming Russell both the ablest of the QCs and the most expensive, estimating his annual fees in excess of £10,000. He was knighted on accepting the attorney-generalship in the third Liberal government headed by William Gladstone. Not that he was popular among his fellow barristers; he was often "overbearing in his manner; and to his clients contemptuous even offensive." Nor was he always a great success as a criminal advocate. When difficulties arose unexpectedly, "he became impatient and irritable, and would often compel a reluctant client to an unsatisfactory compromise." What is more, he had powerful and time-consuming distractions. Ten days after his appointment as attorney general, he was in court defending Sir Charles Dilke, a leading Liberal who saw himself as Gladstone's possible successor. The attraction of the Dilke case was the "phenomenal" fee of 300 guineas. Dilke was cited as the co-respondent in the Crawford divorce case. By keeping his client off the stand, Russell protected him from cross-examination on his amatory history. The judge's decision struck the public as farcical. He granted the divorce on the grounds of the wife's adultery with another co-respondent but cleared Dilke. To remove this blot on his moral reputation, Dilke secured a rehearing of the case by the Queen's Proctor, but this removed Russell as his barrister and ended disastrously. The Bartlett trial was held against the background of this sorry event and "violent political unrest." The Gladstone government introduced a bill to establish Home Rule for Ireland just four days before the Bartlett trial opened. The debate went on for five nights in Russell's presence. The measure dissuaded some prominent figures from accepting office and alienated elements of the rank and file. The government's days were numbered. During the Bartlett trial, Russell left the presentation of the bulk of the evidence to his supporting counsel, Harry Poland, and restricted himself largely to the examinations of the leading scientific expert, Stevenson.[11]

Less encumbered with distractions was the lead defense counsel, Edward Clarke, who had been retained as the inquest closed, his fee probably paid by Adelaide's mysterious father. Rarely present in the Commons during the debate of the controversial Home Rule Bill, Clarke postponed other cases and returned a number of briefs. As a result, he freed a week or more during which he concentrated on the approaching trial of Adelaide Bartlett. Certain questions of medical science "would be of supreme importance," so he spent his time in the British Museum or in his own library studying "all that was known about the qualities and effects of chloroform and the methods of its administration." He was well equipped to cross-examine the principal scientific authority, Stevenson, and believed it would be the "turning point of the case." Almost as important was the surprising agreement among the counsels to try the two prisoners separately, which the judge approved. Then the attorney general made the unexpected and "remarkable" decision not to prosecute Dyson but to have him found innocent and call him as a prosecution witness. Clarke approached his cross-examination delicately. He was seeking to imply that on Dyson's evidence the jury was being asked to convict the prisoner, yet yesterday the clergyman had stood beside her in the dock. He emphasized the impropriety of his moral conduct with Mrs. Bartlett given his position as a Christian minister. From Dyson he drew the deceased's strange ideas on married life, but ultimately the cross-examination of Stevenson proved more decisive. The great expert equivocated when questioned about whether the administration of liquid chloroform to a sleeping man was too difficult and delicate a task to be effected without the great pain it would cause awakening him. And if some chloroform went down the windpipe of a man too insensible to suffer pain, Clarke asked, would there not be traces of its passage? None had been detected on the dead man's windpipe. Clarke's decisive point was Stevenson's agreement that, had the postmortem been held immediately after death, as the prisoner had urged, "there would have been still better opportunity of determining the cause of death."

In his closing address to the jury, which must have seemed interminable to the 12 men, Clarke observed that his client was a model wife who had lived for years in friendship and affection with her spouse. She had nursed him day and night during his illness and had summoned doctors, yet suddenly she was transformed into a murderess. Admittedly, her marriage was in no sense a model. She was young and convent educated, whereas her husband was a man of "strange ideas," one of which was that a man may have two wives, one for service and the other for companionship, and there was little doubt she was the latter. He was familiar with the controversial book *Esoteric Anthropology; or the Mysteries of Man*, which asserted that sexual passion was permissible only for the continuation of the species and that abstinence was the means of preventing childbirth. The exception to this rule was the prisoner's pregnancy, which resulted in the delivery of a stillborn infant. Then Dyson entered the relationship. The deceased effectively bequeathed his widow to the minister and did not object to their ever-deepening intimacy. But when he sought to assert his marital rights so long abandoned, she protected herself with the chloroform supplied by Dyson. With it she expected to induce his sleep whenever that was necessary. Both she and Dyson were ignorant of its effect, however, and of the way it could be used successfully.

Clarke's anticipatory study of chloroform before the trial opened—and his penetrating cross-examination of Stevenson during it—formed the core of the defense. This was the first case the world had ever heard of, he assured the jury, ignorant of the colonial trial in Ontario, Canada, in which it had been suggested that a person had been murdered by the administration of liquid chloroform. The difficulties of its use taxed the skill of the greatest experts, and he left the jurors to ask themselves a simple question: Could they believe that this entirely unskilled defendant would be able to transition the victim from sleep into insensibility without awakening him to the deep pain the drug was certain to cause? The best medical men thought it to the "highest degree improbable." Furthermore, there were no indications of inhalation of chloroform, which, if present, would probably have been discovered during the postmortem had it been conducted immediately as the prisoner had urged. Nor had there been any evidence of the vomiting that the administration of the drug generally produces. In effect, could the jury believe that this woman, that night, all alone with her husband, performed on him a "marvellous operation," which expert Stevenson acknowledged would even for him have been difficult and delicate? The judge's summing up, "which throughout was favourable to [the] prisoner," had in the opinion of the press made impossible any verdict other than an acquittal.[12]

Not that the decision was clear-cut. When asked by the clerk of the court if the jury found Adelaide Bartlett guilty or not guilty, the foreman replied, "We have well considered the evidence, and, although we think grave suspicion is attached to the prisoner, we do not think there is sufficient evidence to show how or by whom the chloroform was administered." The clerk then commented that the jury had concluded that she was not guilty, and this the foreman repeated. Although it was not recognized under English criminal law, the jury was implying a verdict of "not proven." This was wildly popular within the courtroom and without, and the audience cheered Clarke loudly when he went to the theater that evening. His political reward came a little later. The Liberal government fell with the defeat of the Home Rule Bill, and when the Conservatives returned to office, Clarke was appointed solicitor general. That the jury effectively delivered the Scottish "neutral" verdict may explain why it attracted such attention in the Scottish press. After all, this case was reminiscent of that of Madeleine Smith two decades earlier. Here was another young, middle class poisoner who, notwithstanding the strong circumstantial evidence, escaped the fate she deserved.[13]

One upper middle class alleged poisoner whose rank failed to protect her was Florence Maybrick. She had been born in Mobile, Alabama, in 1862, during the American Civil War. Her father, William Chandler, a senior partner in the city's largest bank, had died two months earlier. She was christened Florence Elizabeth Chandler, and there ensued a long, itinerant chapter of her early life. Not one of the three subsequent husbands her mother selected was capable of developing her daughter's emotional well-being and providing affection, protection, and security. Nor did her mother fill the void. Scant attention was paid to Florence's preparation for adulthood. Her mother and grandmother judged her too delicate for college, which young women of her class were increasingly beginning to attend. Instead, they believed that women were better suited to instruction in "social trivia," and this was the task of her governesses and tutors. What she possessed was youth; physical attractiveness; knowledge of the United States, Germany, France, and Russia; and a command of French and German as well as English. She would have little difficulty shining socially in the role of hostess.

In March 1880, Florence was not yet 18 when she and her mother took first-class passage on the SS *Baltic* for the transatlantic crossing to Britain. She caught the eye of a middle-aged Englishman, James Maybrick, who was much the same age as her mother. He learned she was the daughter of a German baroness, that the mother had inherited a very large estate, and that the pretty, petite girl was one of its two heirs. A cotton broker, his business was in need of investment, and this the girl appeared capable of providing. To her, he appeared to be the quintessential English gentleman—well dressed, well-spoken, well-mannered, well-educated, and seemingly well-off. He was also good-natured, amiable, and generous and had a reputation in business as honest, upright, and always honorable in his dealings. In appearance quite homely, he did not cut a romantic figure. Instead his appeal was more subtle, for he was diverting, solicitous, and undemanding. Here was a middle-aged man with whom she was certain to enjoy the affluence and stability lacking in life with her mother. Marriage to this fatherly figure may have aroused in her a "sanguine expectation of happiness." Since both of them stood to gain from a partnership, they reached a sensible understanding. They would continue to see each other and steadily progress towards a life together. In preparation for it, and she being the daughter of a baroness, the groom gave his own social image a quick polish. He secured from the College of Heralds in London a coat of arms. They were married in London in July 1881; he was 43 and she 18.

Very close friends within the wedding party were skeptical of the marriage's chances of success. The cynics were led by the best man, Michael Maybrick, a bachelor and a star singer. Talented and arrogant, he had, in the opinion of one American family friend, acquired a superiority complex, confident "that he had forgotten more than anybody else did know." He did not consider the young American bride a suitable partner for his brother. Perhaps the motto on the new Maybrick coat of arms, "time reveals all," brought to his mind the "slough underneath" their union. The groom had an illegitimate family composed of a long-time mistress and several children. Should this be revealed, it would be an embarrassment and create a profound domestic crisis. How would this young, immature American girl react to so blatant a contradiction of the wedding vows? The disappointing discovery of her inability to invest in the Maybrick cotton brokerage compounded the criticism of an alliance for "economic and class considerations." Even the baroness, whose requests for loans from her son-in-law were unwelcome and an annoyance "did not believe any good would come of the [marriage]." Maybrick could ill afford the luxurious lifestyle his wife had anticipated when she accepted his proposal. Her spendthrift personal habits quickly exhausted her small private annuity derived from her grandmother's properties. She was soon seeking spending money from private lenders who charged high rates of interest.

Initially, Maybrick rented a house from his personal friend, Mrs. Matilda Briggs, and there the couple's first child, a son, was born eight months after the wedding. They soon set off for Norfolk, Virginia, where Maybrick strove, without great success, to revive his failing cotton business. In the spring of 1884 they returned permanently to Liverpool, leasing another house from Briggs where their second child, a daughter, was born. Meanwhile, Maybrick was quietly supporting his growing illicit family at a cost of £100 a year. In 1888, however, he leased Battlecrease House, which sat in a leafy Liverpool suburb and was, in the opinion of a visiting American, a classic example of residences "beloved of the merchant, the flash stock-broker, the professional man and the wealthy shop-keeper." A middling mansion of 20 rooms, it symbolized worldly success, while a staff of four live-in servants and a gardener proved the family stood in the "ranks of the socially superior." To care for the children there was a nursemaid, Alice Yapp, who was assertive among her fellow servants and inquisitive about her mistress with whom she was not on the best of personal terms. The other domestics considered the master's young, inexperienced foreign wife "ignorant in matters of domestic management."[14]

The Maybricks' pleasant and prosperous life was in reality based upon diminishing income and mounting expenditures. Florence's lavish purchases of fashionable clothes and adornments gained her a reputation for careless extravagance. Nor did James count his pennies carefully, joining the Palatine, a Liverpool version of London's gentlemen's clubs. There he rubbed shoulders with politicians national and municipal, local peers and gentry, visiting ministers of the Crown, and judges on the Northern Circuit. In short, he entered the society of the city's elite. As such, he lived the life of businessman and racegoer, and the maintenance of status was costly. The cotton business, now managed in the United States by James's youngest brother, Edwin, continued to flounder. Economies were necessary, but his lessening of Florence's household allowance, which she had always considered miserly and from which the servants were paid, was deeply resented. Not that it induced a reduction in her lavish expenditures. What she suggested was the surrender of Battlecrease House in favor of a far more modest residence. This was the one economy James rejected out of hand, revealing as it would the precarious state of his cotton business.[15]

Florence's discovery of James's other woman and family extinguished any lingering hope she may have had of the idealized Victorian home as a "well spring of true happiness" in which a monogamous, patriarchal husband was the core of a civilized community. He had betrayed her since their marriage by adding to his illegitimate family. What is more, she surely suspected that this was known to some of his friends and members of his family, if not to the servants. Her vanity had suffered a severe blow. She excluded him from their bed, and he had one made up in the dressing room. What would the servants make of this?

James hosted a dinner party for an American friend and sitting at the table was Alfred Brierley, a senior partner in a cotton house. A bachelor, tall, comparatively slim, fair complexioned, with a full head of hair and a well-trimmed reddish beard, he was a popular figure among the ladies. On the other hand, an American who met Brierley in Savannah had difficulty believing he made a favorable impression on the fairer sex, being a "raw-boned, uncouth young gentleman and anything but an Adonis." Florence almost goaded him, as she later confidentially admitted, into a sexual adventure. No longer having "connexion" with the unfaithful James, she could not have been ignorant of the danger of what she had in mind. Adultery violated a commandment and the professed code of upper middle class Victorian rectitude. Discovered, it would almost certainly result in marital and social disaster. Using the names of her brother-in-law Thomas and his wife, she personally booked rooms in a fashionable London hotel popular with cotton men. That in itself was reckless. The other purpose of her visit to the capital was to take advice of a legal separation. This Matilda Briggs had acquired a separation her husband along with financial maintenance and custody of the children. A meeting with an attorney was arranged by a friend of some years who understood she could no longer live with James "on account of keeping this woman in Liverpool." The lawyer drafted a letter in which she sought a legal separation and an adequate annual allowance, but there is no evidence it was ever handed to James. The following day, Brierley arrived at the hotel under the name of Maybrick and the couple spent three days together. With his departure she shopped in preparation for the Grand National, Liverpool's famous and highly dangerous steeplechase.

James had organized a race party, and Brierley was one of its members. Florence angered her husband, perhaps deliberately, by wandering off with Brierley, contrary to James's instructions, and an argument erupted when they returned. It continued loudly and physically once they both returned home, which they did separately. The following morning, Florence sported battle scars: a black eye and bruises. Accompanied by Matilda Briggs, she called on the family doctor, Hopper, who volunteered his services as a mediator. James was persuaded to apologize for the violence and to pay off Florence's personal debts. He traveled up to London in mid–April and settled them. While there he mentioned to his brother Michael his recurrent bouts of ill health and consulted Michael's personal physician, Charles Fuller. He could detect nothing more serious than indigestion. Nevertheless, convinced he was seriously ill, James on April 25 replaced the will made only four months earlier. The benefit that on his demise might accrue to Florence was at best very limited. He envisaged her living on her small annuity and the interest on his two life insurance policies. How much she knew of this will is unclear, but one friend believed it so infuriated her that it became a motive for murder.

Just two days later, James vomited severely, having double dosed himself with the medicine Fuller had sent down from the capital. Foolishly he insisted on riding in foul weather to a race meeting, where on his arrival his etiolated appearance shocked an acquaintance. James told him he had overdosed on strychnine, and this Florence had long suspected as she had informed both Hopper and Michael Maybrick. He returned home in poor condition, so Florence summoned the local general practitioner, Richard Humphreys. He had attended the children and, on one occasion, James. The upper middle classes kept to their homes when ill instead of entering hospitals, for the domestic sickroom was depicted, at least in fiction, as a "haven of comfort, order, and natural affection," a place of "marital reconciliation." The wife's duty was to nurse her husband calmly and compassionately back to health, but this couple's recent violent quarrel ensured that many an eye in Battlecrease House watched the mistress very closely for any evidence of insincerity in her commitment to the ailing master's full recovery. How long would it be before Mrs. Maybrick sought more experienced medical assistance? Richard Humphreys, young and inexperienced, brought to the sickroom the belief common to the profession that men who worked hard for visible evidence of success depleted their reserves of nervous energy. The stress of keeping competitors at bay, meeting financial obligations, and the daily management of their affairs jeopardized social status and produced nervous exhaustion and prostration. James Maybrick must have seemed to young Humphreys a classic example, and he initially concluded that the patient was simply out of sorts. Summoned back to the house that evening, April 28, he found the patient in severe discomfort with painfully stiff limbs. He immediately suspected "hysterical" paralysis. This was a psychological condition often attributed to women. If difficult to diagnose it was often linked to psychological stress and thus consistent with Humphreys's estimate of the strains on Maybrick's nervous energy.[16]

Writing to Michael the following day, James moaned that he felt more like dying than living and guessed that what ailed him would not be determined until he was dead. Hence in that event a postmortem should be held. This letter rooted in Michael's artistic mind a profound suspicion of nurse Florence. As it happened Humphreys, Fuller, and a third doctor, Drysdale, who had seen James four months earlier, were in agreement that the patient's intestinal problems resulted from nothing more than acute indigestion. As for his stiff legs, which he likened to "bars of tin stretched out to the fullest extent," this could be attributed to his ride to the races two days earlier. Humphreys also fixed on the "nux vomica" prescribed by Fuller, it being derived from the nuts of the "strychnine tree." But attention was also drawn to the flypapers Florence had recently purchased in quantity. They were seen by the maid and the nursemaid soaking in her bedroom. This was the means of extracting arsenic from them, and for this there was an innocent explanation. Florence was to attend a masked ball with James's younger brother Edwin, who had just returned from the United States, and an arsenic solution would clear her skin of unsightly blemishes.[17]

A steady diet of invalid food had by Wednesday, May 1, allowed James to return to his city office, where home-prepared meals were delivered to him. Two days later he was again plainly unwell. Humphreys prescribed morphine and recommended a Turkish bath for the relief of painfully stiff limbs, but on reaching home James went straight to bed. When the nursemaid suggested the mistress secure a second opinion of the illness, Florence dismissed it as unnecessary. She changed her mind a few days later, however. She left to Edwin the choice of the physician, and he named Dr. William Carter. He was a "highly respected specialist in cases involving medicinal overdoses of arsenic." On his arrival at the house, he consulted with Humphreys and spoke with the patient. What he diagnosed was indigestion and prescribed a mild medication. That Florence had been open to a second opinion should have raised reasonable doubt of her lack of interest in her husband's full recovery.[18]

A far from gallant lover, Brierley suddenly decided to take a Mediterranean cruise in order to ensure he had no embarrassing confrontation with Maybrick should the assignation in London be discovered. Upset by this news, Florence assured him that flight was unnecessary, that James believed her innocent account of her visit to the capital. In the letter she admitted adultery and unwisely gave it to Yapp to post. Instead, claiming that the infant Gladys, who was carrying the letter, dropped it in mud, the nursemaid opened the soiled envelope in order, she said, to place it in a clean one. On reading what it contained, she carried the letter back to the house and handed it to Edwin. She also disclosed its compromising contents to the two sisters, Mrs. Briggs and Mrs. Hughes, who were in the house asking after James's health. Michael arrived hotfoot from London that evening in response to alarming telegrams from Edwin and Briggs, the latter insinuating that strange happenings were afoot. Edwin handed the letter to him.

Michael's dark suspicion of Florence, first aroused by James's letter of April 29, was now confirmed. Into it he read Florence's wish to be free of James in order to wed her lover, and thus her motive for murder. Michael quickly knocked on Humphreys's door and raised the possibility of poisoning. Next he ensured that Florence was no longer entrusted with the administration of all foods and medicines. A professional nurse was to handle that task. His discovery that she had purchased and soaked flypapers probably called to his mind the trial and execution of two Liverpool sisters who, five years earlier, had by this means done away with their victims. The servants clearly understood that the brothers did not believe Florence was committed to James's recovery, and this sinister suspicion shaped the attitude of much of the domestic staff. Professional nurses were engaged; one of them, Ellen Ann Gore, had in fact been employed with Florence's consent hours before Michael arrived on the scene.[19]

There was no improvement in the condition of James following the isolation of his wife. Nurse Gore thought suspicious Florence's handling of a bottle of meat juice, so Michael asked Carter to analyze it, despite having been assured by Humphreys that no arsenic had been detected in his brother's feces, urine, or invalid food, Carter did find it in the meat juice. Not that there was evidence of its administration to the ill man; nevertheless Humphreys and Carter agreed that under the circumstances they could not certify James's death on Saturday as natural, and the police were so informed. Meanwhile, the brothers and close family friends scoured the house for possible evidence. In Florence's room they reportedly found a number of love letters, the majority from Edwin Maybrick. Michael ensured that these would never be seen in court. The police called first on Sunday evening and again on Monday when the senior officer, Superintendent Bryning, treated the house as a crime scene. He searched it sensibly and methodically. The postmortem that the deceased himself had suggested weeks earlier was now conducted by Humphreys, Carter, and Professor Alexander Baring of University College, Liverpool. They agreed that an irritant poison had ended Maybrick's life, though the circumspect academic did not join his colleagues in specifying arsenic. The inquest opened in a nearby public house with Samuel Brighouse, the coroner of South West Lancashire, in the chair. He was expected to determine the cause of death, to determine the nature of the act that led to the death, and to see a charge brought against the person or persons responsible for the death. At the formal opening, little was done apart from the formal identification of the body by Michael Maybrick. The inquest then adjourned. Startlingly, Superintendent Bryning immediately strode up the street to Battlecrease House and detained Florence on suspicion of causing her husband's death. The intercepted letter, the brothers' profound suspicion of their sister-in-law, Carter's finding arsenic in the meat juice, and the evidence collected by the house searchers within hours of the death satisfied Bryning that this was a case of murder and that he had sufficient grounds on which to detain the widow as the culprit. Was he doing the coroner's work before the inquest commenced its investigation? Arsenic was the cause of death, which was a murder, and Florence Maybrick was the responsible person.[20]

Michael Maybrick had retained as legal counsel solicitor Douglas Steel, who then briefed his barrister brother, Alan Gibson Steel. The solicitor raised with the Maybrick brothers the advisability of their sister-in-law having independent representation. They did nothing. Overhearing the conversation, Humphreys called on the Cleaver brothers, Richard and Arnold, the former the president of the Liverpool Law Society. He in turn briefed barrister William Pickford, a member of the Northern Circuit. Perhaps decisive in his selection was his role as defense counsel of the earlier flypaper murderers Flanagan and Higgins. According to local talk and malicious gossip, Florence had committed the same crime and by the same means. But the coroner's decision to delegate to Bryning the organization and questioning of witnesses ensured that this inquest would be more prosecutorial than investigational. Carefully selecting his moment, the superintendent raised the suspect's assignation in London. In what way, Pickford asked, was that "unfortunate episode" germane to a determination of the cause of James Maybrick's death and by what means he met his end? The coroner had Florence's correspondence with the management of the London hotel on hand, however, and this was read aloud so that the jury understood how much she needed to conceal from her husband. In his summing up, Brighouse urged the jury not to be guided by suspicion alone no matter how strong. The three requirements generally considered essential for a successful criminal conviction were motive, means, and opportunity, and they shaped the coroner's conclusions. They were not entirely consistent with an inquest's purpose but gave the summation a strong prosecutorial tone. The coroner's 13 jurors were unanimous. James Maybrick was poisoned, but one of them did not agree that the poison was administered by Florence Maybrick. He refused to convict her on "circumstantial evidence alone." Brighouse was satisfied, however, as coroners were instructed to be, with a unanimous decision of 12 jurors. To many present in the courtroom, the verdict sounded "as tragical as a death sentence," and Brighouse sent Florence to trial on the capital charge.

On June 12 Florence was escorted from Lark Lane Police Station to the County Sessions Court for a committal hearing before two magistrates. If the *Norwich Post* could be believed, she traveled in style not in a police van, a Black Maria, but in a private brougham, with the blinds drawn for privacy and driven by a man in livery. This was certain to alienate any lower class sympathy for her. She had already received during the inquest "grave consideration" that would never have been shown to a woman from the lower orders. Excused from sitting effectively amongst the public in the courtroom, she was provided with a comfortable chair in a neighboring room. Who could be surprised that this generated class resentment, the *Daily News* asked. The parade of witnesses was led by the malevolent Alice Yapp, a "good looking girl of about twenty-four years of age," who adorned her recollection of the quarrel between husband and wife on the day of the Grand National with suddenly remembered quotes harmful to her mistress. The nursemaid was followed by Michael Maybrick, a handsome celebrity. "Tall, broad-shouldered, muscular, and bronze featured," he was a natural target of the women equipped with opera glasses. Pickford exposed under cross-examination how often this witness's suspicions of his sister-in-law were unfounded and the lengths he went to avoid uttering a single word that might in some way prove helpful to her.[21]

The ubiquitous Bryning summed up the case for the committal of the widow on a charge of willful murder. Pickford then "practically asked the magistrates whether there was any case for him to answer." If in their opinion this case ought to go before a jury at the assizes, he would not waste their time with a defense address. His "unique attitude" gave them pause, and they withdrew with their legal counsel, William Swift. Whether they were satisfied with the evidence in support of the capital charge was not apposite. Swift had long believed that the evidence against Florence Maybrick was very strong. Moreover, as Pickford surmised, the magistrates considered themselves duty bound by the verdict of the coroner's jury. Understanding this, he followed the customary practice and reserved the defense.[22]

The trial opened in Liverpool on Wednesday, the last day of July, and Florence's social status was not forgotten. She was not held in a cramped cell while awaiting her summons to the dock but in the relative comfort of the warders' kitchen. There was on this occasion no comfortable chair in the dock but a plain, hard one. Even less comfortable were the jurors in their box, being so "crabbed, cabined and confined" that this might prejudice them against the "least guilty" accused. Moreover, what reasonable man or woman, the press asked, would wish to be tried for his or her life by a plumber, a painter, a baker, a grocer, or an ironmonger? Most of them, however, would be familiar with this widely reported crime, including the deceased's published last will, which exhibited no great concern for his wife's welfare. Asked her response to the indictment, Florence replied firmly and clearly, "Not Guilty." The lead legal combatants were an ill-matched pair. Sir Charles Russell had accepted the brief to defend the accused, and he came with a refurbished reputation following his triumphant defense of the leader of Irish nationalists in Parliament, Charles Stewart Parnell. The general opinion following this success was that few barristers could "conduct the defense of an unfortunate client for his life with greater ability than [Russell], and no one knows better how to handle a jury without recourse to excess of sentiment." His opponent was John Wentworth Addison, who had been called to the bar more than a quarter of a century earlier and had recently become a Conservative member of Parliament. He had an undistinguished record in capital crime cases but was especially adept in breach of promise suits and had won substantial cash awards for his female clients. In a pedestrian address to the jury, he declared that between April 27 and May 11 the deceased became seriously ill. He credited Edwin Maybrick with the summoning of a second opinion, whereas the accused had taken the initiative, and Carter seemed to have concluded on May 9 that the symptoms "were those, and those only, of an irritant poison." Addison informed the jury that it was not the arsenic detected that killed but that which had "passed away."[23]

The first witness was, naturally, Michael Maybrick. Under cross-examination by Russell reasonable doubt was raised about this important Crown witness. Under pressure he was obliged to accept that his suspicion of the accused had affected the household's view of her, that his denial of knowledge that she had sent for a professional nurse was compromised by the presence of one when he arrived at the house, and that a second opinion on the illness had been sought a full day earlier. Michael was reduced to sheltering under the leaky umbrella of a poor memory. Nor could he avoid admitting that only in the bottle of meat juice had arsenic been found, not a dose of which was administered to his brother. Of the accused's letter in March referring to James's use of a mysterious powder, which Michael insisted was so unimportant he destroyed it immediately, Russell made the obvious point that the powder was perhaps dangerous. Michael knew of the couple's marital problems and of their joint complaints of infidelity but knew nothing of Brierley's involvement. He was certain James died ignorant of his wife's London assignation but did know of Florence's investigation of a legal separation. That Victorian prudery halted discussion of the other woman and illegitimate family tipped the scales of justice against the prisoner. Her adultery alone would influence the jury. Dr. Hopper stated that he had not considered James hale and hearty, always excessively attentive to the "smallest change" of feeling in his body. He consumed medications recklessly, not least those recommended by friends that were contrary to a doctor's prescriptions. But Hopper never suspected James of an arsenic habit while the poison taken as a tonic was usually in solution.

Edwin Maybrick's anxiety about his brother's health on May 8 equaled that of the accused and the ubiquitous Briggs. The intercepted letter had been handed to him by the nursemaid, and he had shown it to Michael when he reached Liverpool that evening. Yet Russell saw him as a prosecution witness potentially helpful to the defense. Frequently at the house, often sleeping there, he was a far more reliable assessor than Michael of Florence's nursing care. She had swiftly summoned a doctor; had sat up many a night caring for James, which had prompted Edwin's suggestion of a professional nurse; and had also initiated his selection of a second medical opinion. The letter handed to Edwin by the nursemaid, however, saw him ally with the dominant and intensely suspicious Michael in measures hostile to the accused. The second day found Dr. Fuller on the witness stand, and, based upon his two consultations with James, he diagnosed him as a sufferer from acute indigestion. He had never heard of the consumption of arsenic for pleasure in England; nor of its addition to food, drink, or medicine; nor of its use as an aphrodisiac. But Russell obliged the nursemaid to amend her testimony on the master's general good health. He then strove to divert the jury's attention from the contents of the letter Yapp intercepted to her venomous behavior. Reexamined by Addison, she stated that her reading of the letter caused her to rethink the possible alternative uses of the flypapers recently acquired by the prisoner and seen soaking in water in the mistress's bedroom. With the aid of the kitchen staff Russell established that the flypapers had never been hidden and the slops of those used were kept on the orders of the prisoner to make possible Humphreys's examination of it. The cook did acknowledge that the papers were not needed to control flies. The young doctor denied ever instructing Florence alone to administer all food and medicines, or of telling her that her husband was sick unto death. Yet the day after Michael Maybrick's appearance he had advised him to ensure that his brother's affairs were in order, implying he had not long to live. On Saturday Carter informed him that he had found arsenic in the meat juice. With the assistance of Carter and Barron he had conducted the postmortem and attributed the death "to some irritant poison, most probably arsenic, but I would not like to swear that it was." Russell saw his opportunity to raise other possible irritants but was largely frustrated by the judge's resolve to adjourn overnight. Had he not meant to say, the judge inquired of Carter, that the symptoms were consistent with arsenical poisoning? They were "consistent, taking the symptoms collectively," he replied.[24]

On returning to the stand the following morning, Humphreys appeared to have convinced himself overnight of Florence Maybrick's guilt. He declined to praise her nursing care of her husband. His inability to detect arsenic in the feces and urine did not prove the absence of the poison, he stated. The negative results were attributable to his inexperience as an analyst. Omitting his conversation with Michael Maybrick on Wednesday evening, May 8, he stated that the possibility of poisoning occurred to him as early as Wednesday or Thursday. Carter in turn admitted that he had detected arsenic only in the meat juice and justified his failure to act immediately to try to save the ill man's life. He asserted that it was already too late to protect the patient with an antidote. Russell quickly challenged his experience as a poison expert. This postmortem was his first on a suspected victim, and never before had he attended a patient supposedly suffering from arsenical poisoning. This was a case of acute not chronic poisoning, he continued, thereby explaining the absence of symptoms during the eight days Maybrick lived following the alleged fatal dose on May 3. Russell informed the jury that symptoms such as diarrhea would normally be obvious within two hours of administration. Consequently, he was confident he had strengthened reasonable doubt of the credibility of Carter's evidence. Indeed, Professor Barron believed that arsenic symptoms, diarrhea and intense vomiting, would have been apparent within 24 hours or sooner. Clear from the evidence of Edward Davies, the public analyst, was how little poison had been found in those organs examined by him. Nevertheless, he had frequently expressed his personal confidence that there had probably been a great deal more. The defense feasted on the "minute" and "distinct" traces of arsenic found in the body. If the evidence was unmistakable, the trace was distinct, Davies answered. When Russell requested the test tubes containing the evidence of the traces, there followed a scene reminiscent of a Christmas pantomime. Neither Russell nor the judge could identify in them, though the latter was equipped with two magnifying glasses, the traces of the poison from the liver and the kidneys. Russell then challenged Davies's calculations and competence, announcing that the amount of arsenic in this case was half that detected by the analyst in the trial of the flypapers murderesses five years earlier.

Thomas Stevenson was the Crown's final witness. There had "probably" been a fatal dose of arsenic in the body of the deceased, he stated, but the amount was a little more or a little less than that found in other fatal cases of arsenical poisoning. Nonetheless, the man "died from the effects of arsenic." The symptoms were either collective or individual, and in this case they were the latter and very anomalous, which might explain their delayed appearance or nonappearance. He went on to draw a clear distinction between arsenical poisoning and food poisoning and dismissed as a factor in Maybrick's illness the arsenic he had received while in the United States. Finally, he disputed the poison's employment as a beauty aid for it was a skin irritant. Russell's relentless and at times sardonic cross-examination of the Home Office's senior scientific analyst may have been inspired by the expert's contribution to his loss as attorney general of the Adelaide Bartlett case. After a number of probing questions, he concluded, "You cannot give me a case where death followed from the administration of arsenic, where you assisted in the post-mortem, and followed this up with analysis." The prosecution, he continued, lacked the "undeniably distinct evidence" of guilt necessary for a safe conviction on a capital offense. Although a "dark cloud" that had passed over the accused's life and "must for all time rest upon her character as a woman and a wife," unfaithfulness was not in this case a motive for murder. A handful of witnesses documented the dead man's arsenic habit, among them a retired druggist who now repeated under oath what he had told a reporter of the *Liverpool Daily Post*. The deceased had come to his store daily for increasingly strong arsenic pick-me-ups. Russell introduced Home Office medical scientist Dr. Charles Meymott Tidy, hailed by the press as the "chief ornament of chemistry." He documented his experience of poisonings, which greatly exceeded that of Stevenson. While agreeing with his colleague that symptoms were on occasion anomalous, Tidy listed four to which he attached particular importance. The absence of one might alter a diagnosis, but the want of all four certainly would. This was an exceptionally rare case, a "toxicological curiosity," an ironic Tidy observed to the amusement of those present in the courtroom. Not one of the postmortem examiners had noted the "most distinctive characteristics of post-mortem appearances of arsenical poisoning": red spots, petechiae, over the surface of the stomach. Turning to the weighable quantities of the poison Davies and Stevenson had obtained from the liver and intestines, Tidy insisted that they had made a calculation error by failing to mash the liver and intestines and then analyzing samples of each. The cause of this death, he concluded, was "undoubtedly not arsenical poisoning." To drive home the defense assertion that Maybrick died of gastroenteritis caused by an irritant other than arsenic, Russell called a distinguished Irish physician who had gained great experience with the poison as the senior surgeon of Dublin's Lock Hospital, founded for the treatment of sexually transmitted diseases. This fatal case of gastroenteritis was in no way related to arsenic, he declared.

Mr. Justice Stephen was one of the judges who permitted an accused, who was still denied the right to give evidence, to make a statement from the dock before the jury deliberated on its verdict. There was to be no assistance of counsel, no prepared document, but she might speak from her own notes. Being an unsworn statement, this intervention was a gamble, for it might be criticized severely, without contradiction, by both prosecutor and judge. Reflecting on how well the trial had gone, Russell doubted the wisdom of Florence speaking, but she was determined to have her say and may have been confident of her ability as an attractive young widow to arouse the sympathy of the 12 men in the jury box. She addressed two defense difficulties, the purpose of the flypapers she acquired and the reason there was arsenic in the bottle of meat juice. She spoke of her German friends who soaked flypapers in water to obtain a solution they applied to their faces with a handkerchief to remove blemishes. There had been a blemish on her face before the ball to which Edwin had escorted her. To the meat juice she had added an insignificant amount of her husband's powder 48 hours before his death. Initially, she had refused his repeated pleas for it, but overwrought, terribly anxious, miserably unhappy, and totally unnerved by his frantic requests, she accepted his assurance that it would do him no harm. She did what he asked. She had not consulted the attending nurse, who had made no mention in her evidence of the husband's agitation. On returning with the bottle, she discovered that James had lost interest in the powder, and to her knowledge he had not taken any of the meat juice. This explanation left two difficulties unsolved. First, she was on record as fearing that the powder was dangerous, possibly strychnine, so why administer it? Second, she had not raised the powder with those caring for her husband. Only after his death did she hear of the discovery of arsenic in the meat juice and suddenly realized the possible significance of her action. Surprisingly omitted from her statement was her informing her solicitors of what she had done during the early investigation of the death. She claimed in her statement that she had admitted her "marital impropriety"—a discreet reference to her adultery—to her dying husband and that he had forgiven her. Neither judge nor jurors appear to have believed this account of the couple's final conversation. When Florence sat down on the hard chair, Russell immediately rose to remind judge and jury of her consultation with Richard Cleaver on May 23, and of the willingness of several witnesses to give evidence on it. This the judge did not permit.

Florence's admission in her statement of adding a tiny amount of the mysterious powder to the meat juice Russell countered with the reminder that not one drop of it was administered. The fatal dose of poison, which in Carter's opinion had been taken on May 3, presumably in the lunch prepared at home and sent down to him in his office, was effectively dismissed by Russell. That particular meal had been forgotten and remained in the house, he informed the jury. Why did it take so long for the classic symptoms of arsenical poisoning to appear, he asked, if, as Carter contended, it was administered on April 17 and May 3? There was no diarrhea until May 9, and the loose bowels Carter had noted two days earlier was a "very different thing" from diarrhea. Finally, he addressed the moral elephant in the courtroom. There was a great difference between adultery and murder, he repeated to the jury. Nor did he forget the gender inequality in the punishment of it. The unfaithful husband was "often regarded with toleration," whereas the adulterous wife was treated as a pariah. In this case, following his hints of another woman, the deceased's long-term mistress and family, was there not something to palliate the accused's offense? As for the capital crime of willful murder, there was too much reasonable doubt of her guilt for a conviction to be safe, not least because of the deceased's arsenic habit. Valid as this was, Florence's ultimate misfortune was her judge.

Mr. Justice Stephen opened his summation with a list of the trial's "leading dates," the first March 21 and the last May 13, which made clear the importance he attached to the accused's adultery for a true understanding of her husband's demise. Stephen delivered his summation over two days, on the second of which, no doubt to the silent dismay of the perplexed and weary jury, he announced that overnight he had reexamined the medical evidence and was confident of his ability to enhance their understanding of it. He sharpened the differences between the two sets of experts and indicated which he found persuasive, but he must have puzzled the jury when he announced that the case would be decided not by "medical refinements" but by a "great number of different things." A matter of "very first importance" was Florence's powerful and immoral motive. Stephen had been a scholar of the criminal law before his elevation to the bench, and it was in his opinion the "most powerful instrument which society [had] at its disposal." The protection of society from "disintegrating immoral forces" was for him a matter of profound concern. Adultery, especially by wives, was "vile, hateful and treacherous," nothing short of sexual depravity. His opinion may have been hardened by the minor stroke he suffered in 1885. Solicitor Edward Clarke, who appeared before him in a libel case on the eve of the Maybrick trial, noticed his failing powers, while the anxiety to which this gave rise was increased "by some peculiarities in his behavior."[25]

He found the prisoner's powerful and immoral motive in her adultery and hinted injudiciously at other possible instances of unfaithfulness. He insisted incorrectly that the London assignation occurred after, not before the reconciliation of husband and wife after the Grand National. He disputed the accused's commitment to reconciliation with the startling error that she wrote the intercepted letter two weeks after its negotiation. He rejected her explanation of the addition of the deceased's mysterious powder to the meat juice. He did not believe that she had confessed her adultery to her dying husband and received his "entire forgiveness." He accepted Stevenson's evidence that the symptoms of arsenical poisoning were anomalous, thereby accounting for the delay in their appearance. The proof of this woman's evil intent was her "terrible letter" to Brierley. As her husband lay in her care, his life trembling in the balance, she wrote to the man with whom "she had behaved so disgracefully." This the jury should bear in mind when deliberating on a verdict and consider how far the moral circumstances corroborated the other evidence given. The judge's preoccupation with the accused's immorality simplified the jury's task. They no longer had to make a choice between the great medical experts on the cause of death. They could focus instead on the defendant's common enough adultery, something even jurors who worked all day with their hands could understand, as her motive for murdering her husband.[26]

The public response to Florence's conviction and sentence to death was sympathetic, while the newspaper reporting of the investigation of the death and of the trial seemingly placed tens of thousands of readers "in possession of every point of evidence adduced, and in a position to form a fair opinion upon the issues at stake." *Y Genedl Gymreig* observed that although a preponderance of newspapers and journals were satisfied that justice had been done, the vast majority of their readers were not. The source of the massive public criticism of the verdict was a combination of long-standing opposition to the capital punishment of women, especially those who belonged to the middle class, and serious doubt about her guilt. Would the Home Secretary intervene, the *Welsh Nation* asked, and commute the death sentence? The wisdom of this action in light of an aroused public was the essence of Russell's private letter to the home secretary immediately after the trial. He carefully addressed the conduct of Mr. Justice Stephen, observing that his ordinarily fair judgment had in this instance been overwhelmed by the accused's adultery.[27]

The death sentence was commuted to penal servitude for life, which was approximately 15 years behind bars. The decision was influenced by political considerations. The unending stream of memorials and petitions suggested a "state of burning agitation" over the punishment of this individual, and it was "fast becoming unbearable" in the House of Commons. Penal servitude for life would be a fitting penalty for a woman who, by her actions and words, had confessed at least her intent to kill. Surely this would delete the topic from the parliamentary agenda. What it did not halt was the public agitation for her release. Not until 1904, three years after the death of the Queen, was she set free, and then for good behavior. She returned to the United States. Victoria had regretted that this wicked woman had escaped the hangman by a legal quibble and repeatedly discouraged her cabinet ministers from recommending additional leniency. Not that they were so inclined, for home secretary after home secretary emerged from periodic examinations of the case convinced of Florence Maybrick's guilt.[28]

Chapter Eight

Late-Century Female Poisoners

The lower orders had long been instructed to emulate the middle class in their commitment to morality and law and order. Indeed, the law was often seen as a means of fostering a "middle-class character in the general population." Perhaps the "fastest growing section of the population" in the final third of the century was the lower middle class. Their ranks were open to the most ambitious of those beneath them socially. The Elementary Education Act of 1870 required the schooling of all children between the ages of five and 12, which was of particular benefit for those born in the lower orders. As the economy expanded and became more complex, a wide variety of "white collar" workers increased exponentially and rose socially, among them even some shop assistants. All middle class women were idealized, the assumption of men being that their ambition was to wed well and care for the family. They had long been portrayed as beacons of respectability, the home's moral and spiritual guardians who nurtured and educated the children to whom they gave birth. The legal position of the wife was distinctly inferior to that of the husband, but improvements in her status were progressing during the century's final third. The gentle and moral nature of middle class women was sullied by the likes of Christiana Edmunds, Adelaide Bartlett, and Florence Maybrick. Edmunds, a spinster, was willing to scatter death indiscriminately throughout Dover and exhibited a "cold-blooded indifference" to the safety of the children whom she employed in her plot. Bartlett and Maybrick were wives guilty of adultery, and both were alleged poison murderers, though only the latter was convicted. Maybrick's death sentence, the *Liverpool Courier* declared, was a stern "warning to women who have severed themselves from women's attributes."[1]

The trials of these middle class women were reported in great detail to the ever-growing readership of both metropolitan and provincial newspapers. The prosecutions were oddities, rare events that exposed the apparent frailty of Victorian society as presently constructed. The popular press, such as the *News of the World* and *Reynolds's Newspaper*, devoted special attention to crime, especially murder. The supposedly commonplace homicides of the lower orders were often assumed by the national media to have scant attraction for the public nationally and usually received sparse coverage. Where they were reported more fully was in the burgeoning local and regional press. What is more, the organization of the new police across the land in 1856 brought more reliable figures on homicides during the second half of the century. Between "1857 and 1890 there were rarely more than 400 homicides reported to the police each year, and during the 1890s the average was below 350."[2]

Ever present, it seemed, were a number of lower class women with the motive, means, and opportunity to engage in poisoning. An apparent increase in crime led "to the emergence of criminology." This amounted to "the self conscious application of scientific principles to the study of crime and criminals, embracing such issues as causation, correction and prevention." Nevertheless, there continued to be severe complaints about the way scientific evidence was handled in criminal trials. Barristers were accused of distorting truth, blending fact and fiction, and reducing justice to a mere hypothesis. All the while there were attempts to curtail easy access to dangerous poisons. This was one intent of the Pharmaceutical Society, which in 1862 held examinations and issued certificates that restricted to its members the right to dispense dangerous drugs. Many of those who had been selling them continued to do so as druggists and chemists, however. The revised Pharmacy Act six years later again sought to restrict the persons who could sell poisons and required the recording of sales in poison books. The Arsenic Act had been the initial step, and now there was a lengthening list of fatal drugs to which restrictions applied, including strychnine, cyanides, prussic acid, and tartar emetic or antimony. Unfortunately, enforcement was weak, and the restrictions on rat poisons, or vermin killers, many of which were combinations of strychnine and arsenic, continued to allow sales in penny packets.[3]

Alice Holt was a case in point. She, her mother, and her common law husband lived in two rooms of the slums of Stockport. Her mother, who was chronically ill, complained that her daughter did not treat her well. Alice created a motive to be rid of her grumbling mother by insuring her life with the Wesleyan Insurance Company for £26. The company required a medical certificate of health before issuing a policy, and, given her mother's illness, Alice persuaded a friend to stand in for her at the examination. Alice then acquired a quarter of an ounce of arsenic with the aid of the wife of the lodger who occupied the cottage's other two rooms. She served as her witness of the sale, which the law required. They repeated the purchase the following day, Alice informing the druggist that the poison was required to protect her mother from vermin. She probably administered it to her mother—who died the following evening—in a cup of brandy. One of the two doctors who had attended the deceased, without knowing another was being consulted, issued a death certificate giving gastroenteritis as the cause, and the funeral went ahead. But the gossip that the medical certificate of health had been fraudulent reached the Wesleyan Company and it withheld payment until there had been an investigation. So, three months after the death, the body was exhumed and found to be saturated with arsenic. Tried, convicted, and sentenced to death, Alice implicated her "husband" as the driving force of the crime. He was not charged as either organizer or accomplice. Her execution by hangman William Calcraft was cruelly botched, becoming a horrifying spectacle as slowly she was strangled to death while screaming piteously "make haste."[4]

Mary Ann Ashford lived in greater comfort than had Alice Holt. She had been married for 20 years to husband William, a cordwainer with a staff of journeymen and apprentices. She heard talk of her husband's savings account, estimates of which rarely dropped beneath £100 and which by some guesses exceeded £300. Her motive was greed and a sexual passion for one of the young apprentices. Angered by Mary Ann's behavior with the apprentice, William dismissed him and wrote her out of his will. Patiently, Mary Ann spent the next two years persuading him to reverse both decisions. She became William's sole beneficiary, he reemployed the apprentice, and the pair resumed their illicit relationship. The circumstantial evidence of the prosecution was in the opinion of the press "most complete." Her motive was the removal of the husband as the obstacle to her designs on the apprentice and her inheritance of his savings. She realized that a slow death was more likely to escape investigation, and this might well have been the case had she not lived next door to the village constable, Butt, and his highly inquisitive wife.[5]

Mary Ann in all likelihood added small doses of arsenic and strychnine to her husband's meals, and he was soon suffering from vomiting and diarrhea. A daily presence was Mrs. Butt, who noticed a gritty blue powder in the tea she was asked to administer and in the medicine William's brother Thomas administered. She took some of the powder and gave it to her husband. The following day William died, and Mary Ann was arrested by Constable Butt on a charge of murdering her husband. For their part, the two doctors who had been consulted over the illness declared a postmortem necessary. The stomach and liver were sent for analysis, and the analytical chemist was none other than William

Herapath. He found quantities of poison, and after a short trial during which Mary Ann was represented by a Queen's Counsel the jury convicted her in a mere 15 minutes. Sentenced to death, she admitted her guilt and the justice of her sentence but attempted to strangle herself with a handkerchief in a desperate effort to avoid the public gallows. Two wardresses prevented this. As in the Holt case, it was the ordeal of her execution that captured public attention and was witnessed by thousands. The cap was drawn over her face, the noose was placed around her neck, and the chair on which she had been sitting on the trapdoor was withdrawn, as was its bolt. Calcraft's short drop of the rope did not break her neck, so, as Holt had, she struggled violently for a number of minutes and spent several more in obvious terror before her frantic writhing eased. "Such prolonged suffering excited the greatest horror in those who beheld it," but "the state's retributive power continued to override imaginative compassion."[6]

The popular press could not have been blind to the appalling conditions under which a large section of the working poor were obliged to live or exist. Priscilla Biggadyke was an example. A "good looking" woman "with small regular features and a fresh color," she had been married to her husband, Richard, a well-sinker, for 13 years. They lived in a cottage in the Lincolnshire village of Stickney with their three children and two male lodgers, one a ratcatcher and the other a laborer. There was a single bedroom "occupied in common nightly" and two beds. Richard left earlier for work than either of the lodgers, which inevitably gave rise to gossip. Certainly, Richard became suspicious of his wife's relationship with the ratcatcher, Proctor. There was talk that she often wished Richard were dead, and this he was after taking tea and milk and a piece of cake. Richard had summoned a doctor, who swiftly suspected poisoning and insisted that he conduct a postmortem. At the inquest the doctor attributed the death to an irritant poison, and the stomach and its contents were sent to London for analysis by Alfred Swaine Taylor. This "case was so conclusive," Taylor reported, "that some arsenic found [was] in a perfect state." That all food and medicine had been administered by Priscilla made her the natural suspect, and she was arrested. Her chance of an acquittal was prejudiced by the press commentary on the Biggadykes' living conditions, into which she had been forced by grim necessity. She was accused of rejecting Victorian morality. There was no innocence in the way they chose to live, the *Lincolnshire Chronicle* criticized, instead immorality was invited. Such degraded conditions forbade any expectations of "moral or rational conduct." No punishment, however terrible, would "deter such abject creatures from the commission of crime." *Reynolds's Newspaper* stood apart from much of the press. Priscilla was poor, ignorant, and perhaps immoral, it allowed. Had she been "the wife of a gentleman, a member of a family of the ruling class, then the scientific evidence would have been forthcoming as to her insanity."[7]

While detained in a house of correction awaiting trial, Priscilla made a statement to the governor in which she averred that she had seen Proctor put white powder of some sort into Richard's teacup and then in the prescribed medicine. Since he was a ratcatcher, he was assumed to have ready access to a vermin killer, although he favored a ferret over the poison. Arrested, he together with Priscilla appeared before magistrates at a committal hearing, and from there both were sent to trial. The grand jury at the county assizes removed him from the indictment on the advice of Mr. Justice Byles, who was to preside at the trial. The evidence against Proctor being the accusation of his lover, he could not be convicted on it and an acquittal would prevent his being tried for the murder should additional evidence come to light. Proctor's deathbed confession to the crime 14 years later has seen Priscilla named to the list of innocents unjustly executed. Yet, as the judge asked, why did Priscilla administer her husband's tea and medicine, having seen her lover add white powder to them?[8]

Priscilla's trial opened on December 11. The judge requested an attorney attending the assizes, named Lawrence, to watch the largely circumstantial case on her behalf. Although he did little cross-examination of the prosecution's witnesses, in his address to the jury he strove with some success to raise reasonable doubt of her guilt. Where, he asked, was the evidence of poison in the house at the time it was allegedly administered? Where was the proof of an adequate motive? Why had the arsenic made a dramatic appearance in no more than 30 minutes after the deceased took tea, whereas the eminent Dr. Taylor had stated that it was usually a full hour before the poison took effect? Where was the evidence that it was given at that time? There was no proof Priscilla did the poisoning, Lawrence concluded, only the possibility that she may have done it. Was this sufficient grounds on which to send her to the gallows? In his summation the judge stressed that the secrecy of poisoning made its proof by direct evidence improbable and that the crime was often brought home to a murderer by indirect or circumstantial evidence. In this case he judged that evidence solid. But Lawrence's argument had impressed the jurymen. They returned with a conviction and a recommendation for mercy. The judge's query of the recommendation caused some confusion. The foreman consulted his 11 colleagues before replying "because it is circumstantial evidence." Mr. Justice Byles halted any further discussion.

The jury had found her guilty of willful murder, he observed, and then sentenced her to death.

There was no campaign for a commutation of the sentence. Moreover, there were to be no more public executions, most members of Parliament having voted for their abolition. This was less a matter of sanitizing them than a conviction that, often witnessed by massive celebratory crowds of spectators, they were a disgrace to civilization. The "legal strangling" would now be done out of view of the multitude, the *Manchester Examiner* was pleased to report. No longer would the gallows be cited as "an important piece of our educational machinery." Not that Priscilla Biggadyke's private hanging was humane. Terror-stricken, she had to walk 200 yards from her cell to the scaffold erected on the grounds of Lincoln Castle. Once the rope was around her neck, the hangman placed the knot under her chin instead of at the back of her neck. He thought that the head with her drop would be thrown backwards "on to the spine of the back," thereby destroying all sensation. All the while she would continue to breathe and suffer a "slow and agonizing strangulation." In the words of the castle's laconic governor, the hanging might have been done better.[9]

Barely six months after the private execution of Priscilla Biggadyke, this giving her a measure of distinction, a milliner, aged 28, Fanny Oliver, was charged with the willful murder of her "good and kind" husband, a boilermaker. His Whit Sunday death was certified by the doctor as one of "hepatic congestion." The funeral swiftly followed, only for talk of Fanny's intimate conduct before the death with a young man, Burgess, who had courted her before her marriage to excite suspicion. The body of the husband was exhumed and examined by an expert, Dr. Alfred Hill, who found "infinitesimal quantities" of arsenic in the liver. This did not dissuade him from declaring himself "unhesitatingly" convinced that the deceased had died of arsenical poisoning. The wife's two purchases of the poison under the false name of Fanny Burgess, her use of a false address, and a letter to Burgess in which she affirmed her love of him and hatred of her husband strengthened the circumstantial evidence. The prosecution provided her with a motive. Her husband had invested £92 in a building society, and, unknown to him, Fanny had drawn all the money out. The withdrawal would not have come to the husband's attention until mid–May, so the prosecutor argued that Fanny was motivated to kill him in mid–April before the emptiness of the account was revealed. Her mother-in-law, unable to lay her own hands on the £92, accused Fanny of his murder.[10]

The jury convicted her with an unexplained strong recommendation for mercy. Before she was sentenced, Fanny was permitted by the judge to deliver a statement from the dock. She made a defense argument, an impassioned assertion of her innocence, and appealed to the Almighty, which stunned a great many of those in the courtroom and impressed public opinion. "Lord do not leave me in this terrible hour," she cried with hands clasped as in prayer while looking upwards to heaven. It was a clever performance. "The very peculiar circumstances of the case, the purely circumstantial nature of the evidence," and her "daring appeal to God" removed the case "out of the catalogue of ordinary murders." In this age of science there was considerable uneasiness that convictions were still based largely on circumstantial evidence. Not that there was a widespread belief in her innocence. *The Echo* of London debated at length the possibility of her insanity, which was becoming for the working classes as it had for the middle classes, a plea for clemency. The newspaper concluded that Fanny was "partially deranged" yet guilty. A Birmingham petition signed by medical men, scientists, and other members of the liberal professions declared incomplete the chemical reasons for the death. They were insufficient to justify the irrevocable sentence of the law to be carried into effect. Was it safe to rely on the evidence of a single scientist, Hill, who may have made a mistake? Here was a reason for further inquiry, it being well known that the Marsh test for the detection of arsenic was one of great delicacy and that the reagents used could themselves introduce the poison. Furthermore, the continued wide diffusion of arsenic, its presence in so many medicines, colors, and domestic appliances meant that few living persons, if tested minutely, would be free of the poison. Fanny's sentence was commuted to penal servitude for life. The *Daily News*, which like the *Echo* was in no doubt of her guilt, argued it would be wiser "to abolish capital punishment outright than resort individual cases to commutation which distinctly repeal the law."[11]

Notwithstanding the concerns to which the conviction of Fanny Oliver gave rise, she being considered almost certainly guilty beyond a reasonable doubt, what was surprising was how quickly she became a forgotten figure. That could not be said of the far more notorious Mary Ann Cotton. She was born in 1832 into a family life of grinding poverty. The death of her father in a pit accident when she was 10 saw her pragmatic mother urgently wed another miner to escape eviction from a tied cottage. Mary Ann had the limited education available in a mining village; she attended—and eventually taught—Sunday school, her parents being devout Wesleyans. At the age of 16 she entered domestic service, appointed nursemaid to the children of a colliery manager who lived comfortably in a large house. Mary Ann's first exposure to middle class life was one she naturally envied and perhaps hoped to achieve. When the manager's children went off to boarding schools, she was released and returned home. Already pregnant, she sought the security of marriage, wedding a laborer, William Mowbray, who was probably the father of the expected child. The pair moved in his pursuit of work to South West England but eventually retraced their steps to the coalfields of the North East. There now commenced a string of deaths in Mary Ann's households. Fatalities were "natural" given the depressed conditions of life and the poor quality of medical assistance. Infants and children fell victim to gastric fever while Mowbray died of typhus at the age of 39. All of the dead had been insured with the British and Prudential Insurance Company. Mary Ann collected small sums on the children and £35 on her husband. The remaining child, Isabella, she handed to her mother for daily care.[12]

Mary Ann became a fever nurse at the old Sunderland Infirmary, which would probably have given her access to the poison cabinet, and there she cared for a patient, George Ward. On his release, they married, only for him soon to fall fatally ill. The attending doctors diagnosed typhus fever. Mary Ann, now a widow again, became in 1866 the housekeeper of widowed shipwright John Robinson and his five children. On her second day in the household his ill son died, the death certified as natural. Within a year she had made her way into Robinson's bed, only to be called away immediately by the news that her mother was seriously ill with hepatitis. She died nine days after her daughter's arrival, not that this excited surprise given the diagnosis. Mary Ann returned to Robinson with Isabella, who, along with two of Robinson's surviving children, was soon dead. She collected an insurance payment on her own child. Four months later, and five months pregnant, she married Robinson. She might now enjoy relative comfort, if not a middle class lifestyle, yet she revealed an antisocial personality disorder that prevented this social advance. She stole from Robinson's Building Society account and his Post Office savings and even pawned clothes, linen, and furniture taken from the house. What she did with the money remained unclear. Furious, Robinson severed their relationship, and she left with their son George, who was later returned to his father.[13]

Still married, Mary Ann Robinson worked briefly in a Sunderland hostel for distressed women and was taken on as a domestic servant by a Dr. Hefferman and so gained access to his clinic, in which there were poisons. When her thefts led to dismissal, she turned once again to marriage, although bigamous, being again pregnant. Frederick Cotton was another miner, and he accepted responsibility for the child delivered in February 1871. In all likelihood Mary Ann began a relationship with a nearby neighbor, Joseph Nattrass. Her fit and healthy husband—now an impediment—died, apparently from typhoid fever and hepatitis, and Nattrass became her lodger. Frederick Cotton, Jr., died too, allegedly from gastric fever, and Robert Robson Cotton of teething convulsions. Nattrass, who had planned to marry Mary Ann, died on April Fool's Day. She collected small insurance payments on the children and a larger sum on Nattrass. The death of her surviving stepson, Charles Edward Cotton, would be convenient, for he impeded her marriage to a customs official by whom she was pregnant and who would elevate her socially. To collect the insurance on Charles Edward she required a death certificate, so an inquest and postmortem followed, and the latter provided evidence of poisoning.[14]

It was remarkable that, of the dozen children Mary Ann had birthed, only George Robinson survived. Childhood deaths from disease and malnutrition were always high, but the survival rate in Mary Ann's households was extraordinarily low. An ironic *Dublin Daily Express* later remarked that this was "The Working Class Insurance System in England." At her trial, Mary Ann was equipped by the judge with a defense counsel, Thomas Campbell Foster, QC. Although spirited and clever, Campbell Foster had little time in which to prepare a thorough defense. When Charles Russell, the prosecutor, asked the forensic expert, Dr. Thomas Scattergood, about his examination of the three others named in the indictment, the judge permitted him to answer over the stern objection of Campbell Foster. After weighing the evidence for an hour, the jury convicted Mary Ann, and she was sentenced to death.[15]

The press held the condemned responsible for the deaths of her mother, three husbands, a lover, eight of her own children, and seven stepchildren. All had at the time been attributed by doctors to a variety of diseases that were symptomatic of arsenical poisoning. The *Newcastle Chronicle* commented 13 years later that her cold-blooded murders were "singular for the absence of an adequate motive." She killed "husbands and children with the unconcern of a farm-girl killing poultry." The small sums collected from insurance companies were not in the *Chronicle*'s opinion an adequate motive for the deaths of five Mowbrays, four Robinsons, four Cottons, her mother, George Ward, and Joseph Nattrass. Given the number, there was little likelihood of a commutation and no talk of an abolition of capital punishment. She exhibited psychopathic traits, callousness, detachment, and an ability to be charming if not seductive. She was manipulative and totally without empathy. Surprisingly, press interest in her was predominantly regional. A concern of the Cotton case was the poor performance of the doctors called to the bedsides of her alleged victims. Physicians had been publicly "enjoined to be on the lookout for any signs of foul play," but, unfamiliar with the patient, they were frequently misled by Cotton on the nature of the illness. An accurate diagnosis was inhibited by her understanding that the administration of the poison in a series of small doses would deceive a doctor with little if any knowledge of the patient or the case. After all, not many of them kept abreast of "the discoveries of medical jurisprudence."[16]

In the decade following the serial killings of Mary Cotton, a number of more singular poisonings failed to excite the interest of even the regional media. Then, in the autumn of 1883, there was in the slums of Liverpool a truly sensational case that seemed certain to capture far greater attention. The assumption that the lower orders killed for profit, for the sums small and more substantial paid out by burial clubs and insurance companies, had been reinforced by Mary Ann Cotton. The press now reported "alleged whole sale" poisonings by one Catherine Flanagan. For the past two years, 15 persons whom she had insured had died, and she had collected the payments. Neighbors had long been suspicious of her, but no steps were taken until Patrick Higgins, a shoemaker, acted to prevent the rapid burial of his brother Thomas, a bricklayer's laborer. He had married Flanagan's sister Margaret. Patrick let it be known that he had discovered that Flanagan had insured his brother's life for £40 with the Prudential Society, £25 with the Wesleyan Club, £30 with the Victoria Legal Friendly Society, and £20 with the Royal Liver Insurance Company. The grand total, £115, was a princely sum to members of the lower orders. Patrick convinced his deceased brother's doctor, Whitford, of his strong suspicion of poisoning. This was reported to the coroner, and Whitford undertook a postmortem, which strengthened his personal suspicion of poisoning. A chemical analysis of the dead man's intestines provided yet stronger evidence. Mary Higgins, the daughter of Thomas, did not long survive her father. The widow Margaret Higgins quickly collected the £22.5 for which she had insured the life of her stepdaughter. Yet another death was that of Margaret Jennings, age 18, who with her father Patrick had lodged with Flanagan for 10 years. She had died heavily insured on January 23, 1883, and the cause, as certified by a doctor, was pneumonia. Her father and Flanagan collected £50 from the Royal Liver Company, the larger portion going to Flanagan for the father had known nothing of the insurance. Margaret Jennings was laid to rest on January 28, 1883.[17]

As the police prepared to charge Flanagan, confident they had gathered the required evidence on six of her alleged victims, she suddenly disappeared. For several days they were unable to track her down in the port city's impenetrable slums. They finally spied her drinking in a public house, and on Wednesday, October 17, she was placed in the dock of the Liverpool Police Court alongside her sister Margaret. Flanagan alone had counsel. Initially the pair were accused of poisoning Thomas Higgins, although by the end of the month this restricted charge had been amended to one of "wholesale poisoning." They were remanded pending the verdict of the inquest, and the coroner investigated not only the death of Thomas Higgins, but those of Mary Higgins, Margaret Jennings, and John Flanagan. The son of Catherine, he had died at the age of 22 having been insured by his mother in five societies for a total of £95.[18]

Catherine Flanagan and her sister Margaret were jointly committed for trial for the deaths of three of those named, and Margaret alone for that of her stepdaughter Mary Higgins. The sisters had able legal representation. Henry Gordon Shee and William Pickford had been appointed by Judge Butt. The *Liverpool Echo* commented on a curious lack of public interest when the trial opened, but as the day progressed the seats in the courtroom were filled to capacity, more than half of them by women. The *Echo* suggested that men were at work during the day and had no time to waste in court, but the *Liverpool Daily Post* noted not only that there were vast crowds outside the court before the proceedings began but that they remained there all day. John Aspinall, QC, led the prosecution and in opening the case was "hardly at his best." A leg injury made standing painful and accounted for the brevity of his speech. But of the four indictments only one was being tried, that of Thomas Higgins. No sooner had Aspinall commenced than Shee intervened, knowing that the prosecution intended to present evidence of the three other deaths in order to strengthen the case against the pair in the dock. Shee admitted that the legal authorities were conflicted on this point. Mr. Justice Butt summarily overruled the defense objection, as had the judge in the Cotton case. He would be guided by common sense, he announced, which forbade him from excluding this evidence. Aspinall then spoke of the relevance of three other deaths. There was a stir in the court when Ellen Flanagan, Catherine's young daughter, was called by the prosecution. No more than 14, she proved to be remarkably cool and self-possessed. She weighed every question before replying and was plainly determined not to say anything harmful to her mother. As a result, Aspinall was reduced to the embarrassment of cross-examining his own witness. The principal scientific witness was the public analyst, Dr. Campbell Brown, who found considerable quantities of arsenic in the exhumed bodies, administered, in his opinion, in small doses spread over several days. Moreover, he answered the question of how the accused had obtained arsenic, there being no evidence of their

Eight. Late-Century Female Poisoners 181

purchase of it. He dissolved nine flypapers in cold water and reported that the solution obtained was identical to the arsenic solution found in Flanagan's house. Every flypaper contained a large fraction of a grain of arsenic. Both accused were convicted. Catherine in a confession admitted obtaining the poison from a solution of flypapers soaked in water, thereby confirming the "theory of the prosecution."[19]

Summing up, Mr. Justice Butt castigated the insurance companies for permitting such a "pernicious system under any circumstances." When the sums involved were small, the policies were often effected without the officers of the company "taking care to ascertain that the persons whose lives were about to be insured were consenting parties." That agents were paid a commission on premiums was in Butt's opinion the source of the insurance malpractice. The judge's disdainful comment on the money involved revealed his own upper middle class background, whereas for the lower orders the sums were huge. The jury took no more than 45 minutes to convict the pair, and they were sentenced to death and executed on May 3 at Kirkdale Prison, near Liverpool. While awaiting execution, neither of them exhibited sibling loyalty. Hoping for clemency, Catherine offered to give evidence against her sister, and on it being refused Margaret admitted assisting her in poisoning but insisted that she had always acted under her sister's influence. That they were not the only women of the lower orders engaged in poisoning for profit was a point Catherine made by naming a handful. There was a necessity for tighter regulation of arsenical flypapers, she argued. If this was evidence of her public spirit, it is difficult to accept that the sisters murdered for what were to them large amounts of cash in order to ease the grinding poverty of their slum lives. That the victims were members of their own families strongly suggests that they had a number of psychopathic tendencies.[20]

Barely three weeks later, Mary Lefley was hanged at Lincoln Gaol, the last woman executed there. The hangman, Berry of Bradford, sped her swiftly to her end by allowing the body to drop nine feet through the trap door. Yet he was unable ever to forget this ghastly experience. He, the prison's matron, and its governor had together forcibly extracted her from her cell bedstead, to which she was desperately clinging, and dressed her for her date with death. She screamed in terror as she was pinioned and continued her piercing cry on the gallows. She had been convicted of killing her far older husband by poisoning the rice pudding she had left for him to cook and eat while she was away in the local town. She admitted to a witness who gave evidence at her trial that she had not lived on very good terms with her husband, describing him as an old brute. There was evidence that he had told her that there was no need for her to make him a rice pudding as there was plenty of cooked food in their "nice little cottage." But she had insisted. On becoming seriously ill, vomiting heavily, he carried the pudding in a basin to the doctor's surgery, having accused her on another occasion of seeking to poison him. The following day, the doctor tested it and found evidence of metallic poisoning. The ever-present expert Thomas Stevenson did the analysis and found it contained sufficient poison to kill 40 people.

Her protestations of innocence, the Crown's inability to define her motive to kill, and the absence of her possession of arsenic nourished doubts of her guilt. Her implied motive was her desire to get her hands on her husband's money. In addition, he may have suspected her of sexual delinquency, which with the deepening intensity of his religious belief made him a zealous advocate of her moral reformation. The police found no evidence of a lover. She had plainly wearied of his prayers, his exhortations, and his solicitude for her soul. For the judge it was her nonappearance in the sickroom during her husband's last hours of life that convicted her. Did they suppose, he put it to the jury, that her staying away from the bedside that night was consistent with her innocence? Eight years later doubts of her innocence could, in the opinion of the press, "no longer be entertained." Frank Reeson, aged 60, a smallholder, confessed to the woman attending him as he lay dying his complicity in the crime. He claimed he had been one of Mary Lefley's alleged lovers, quarreled with her husband, procured the poison knowing how it was to be used, and taken advantage of the couples' absence from the cottage to sneak in and add the arsenic to the rice pudding. Reeson swore to secrecy the woman caring for him, and she said not a word until she was on her own deathbed. The delayed and complicated nature of the confession impugns its validity.[21]

The case received limited media coverage, the press judging it another run-of-the-mill lower class murder in which there would be little public interest outside of the area in which it was committed. Far more noteworthy was Mary Ann Britland. She, her barman husband, and their two daughters lived in Ashton-under-Lyne. She and daughter Elizabeth worked in a local mill while the other daughter was a domestic servant. Their next-door neighbors were Thomas and Mary Dixon, who also worked in the mill, and "there was an unusual degree of intimacy" between Thomas Dixon and Mary Ann. He was in the Britland house a good deal, and the pair had traveled together to the market in Oldham. Suddenly, on the night of March 8, 1886, Elizabeth suffered a violent illness with bilious vomiting and diarrhea. That same day her mother Mary Ann had purchased a packet of Harrison's Vermin Powder. Elizabeth died on March 9, and her parents collected £10 from the insurance society. On April 30 Mary Ann made certain the insurance premiums on her husband and surviving daughter were fully paid and purchased an additional supply of vermin killer. The symptoms of her husband's immediate illness were similar to those of the deceased Elizabeth, and he died on May 3. Thomas Dixon accompanied Mary Ann to the office of the insurance company, where she collected almost £20. The widow now moved in with the Dixons, and shortly after supper on May 13, Mary Dixon fell ill, her symptoms suggestive of poisoning. She died the following day, and Dixon lost no time obtaining £19 of life insurance. Mary Ann's imprudent questioning of a man, ironically named Law, about whether it could be detected that a deceased had taken "mouse powder" intensified suspicion of all three deaths. A postmortem was held, and the internal organs were analyzed. They showed the presence of arsenic in the bodies of the two Britlands, daughter and father, and strychnine in that of Mary Dixon.[22]

The press laid before the public a case of "Wholesale Poisonings" linked to insurance policies. Even more shocking was the likelihood that greed was not the only motive for these killings. Their origin appeared to lie in a sordid sexual conspiracy. Here was an appalling example of "Depravity and Crime." The coroner's jury concluded that all three deceased died of poison maliciously administered by Mary Ann Britland, adding that the current sale of vermin powders laced with arsenic and strychnine was highly objectionable and dangerous to human life. More stringent regulations were required, and the jury was of the opinion that their urgent recommendation ought to be forwarded by the coroner to the home secretary. Meanwhile, at the committal hearing, the magistrates found insufficient the present evidence to incriminate Dixon, but, as in an earlier case, vowed that, should such evidence come to light, "he will be put upon his trial." This news angered Mary Ann, who on one journey from prison to court asked her police guard if Dixon would "get off." When he replied that some people certainly thought he would, she responded that he did not deserve to escape indictment and would not if she was able to give evidence. "It was him that led me into it," she fumed.[23]

Mary Ann's trial for the murder of Mary Dixon opened on July 22 and lasted two days. The judge provided her with a counsel who denied that a motive had been shown; asserted that her house was infested with mice, which explained the purchases of vermin killers; stressed that she had acquired them openly, thus innocently; and insisted there was no evidence of undue intimacy between her and Dixon. Witnesses proved that she had obtained the poison immediately before the deaths and had received insurance payments soon after them. Others recalled her questioning whether poison could be detected in the stomach of a deceased if taken in tea. Informed that it could, she asserted through her counsel, though it was unclear on what authority, that the bodies of persons poisoned swelled after death, but that was not true of the three deceased. The judge put two questions to the jury. First, did Mary Dixon die in consequence of mouse powder administered to her? Second, in the event that she did so die, had the prisoner administered the deadly powder? After an hour of deliberation, the foreman reported that the jury was unanimous on the first question. Their difficulty on the second was that three persons could have administered the poison. The judge advised them to reconsider the verdict, and two and a half hours later the jury returned without being united. When the judge suggested they see him again the following morning—that is, proposed an overnight confined stay—the foreman requested no more than a brief adjournment. A few minutes later he reported a unanimous verdict of willful murder. Clearly holdouts had been bullied into this decision, raising doubt about its justice.[24]

Mary Ann Britland was the first woman to be executed at Strangeways Prison, Manchester. In his recollections of a career as public hangman, James Berry likened her death to that of Lefley. She began shrieking the moment he entered her cell and continued in this terror-stricken condition all the way on the walk to the scaffold. There she had to be held down forcibly by two female warders while the rope was fitted around her neck. They were then replaced on the trap by two males, who quickly stepped aside following a signal from Berry before she plunged perhaps seven feet to her instant end. He wrote to the town's chief constable requesting a copy of the photograph of Britland that had been on sale outside the prison on the day of her death and received one. Five months later "Lee's Grand Museum, Picture Gallery and Waxwork" had a wax model of Britland on prominent display.[25]

The close relationship of murder and life insurance resurfaced almost immediately in the case of Elizabeth Berry. A widow of 31, she appears to have had hopes of remarriage. Being a nurse at the Oldham Workhouse Infirmary she held the key to the dispensary and thus had access to poisons. When her daughter Edith, age 11, began to vomit violently, she was attended by Dr. Patterson, who was a daily presence at the workhouse. He prescribed a mixture of bicarbonate and creosote, and when the girl failed to improve a second opinion was sought. Both doctors were of the same opinion, that she had swallowed a corrosive poison, a diagnosis supported by the blistering of her lips. Patterson deduced that the mother had on successive days administered massive doses of creosote to her child. So, he declined to issue a death

Eight. Late-Century Female Poisoners 185

certificate and there was an autopsy. Asked if her daughter was insured, Elizabeth emphatically answered no, only to be contradicted by a burial society payment of £10. The chief secretary of the National Sick and Burial Association revealed that the child had been insured at the rate of a penny a week since 1875. An agent of the Prudential Insurance then revealed that Elizabeth had applied for insurance of £100 in April 1886 for herself and her child. Should one die, the survivor would receive the payment. She had been thinking of marrying again, she explained, and thought the insurance would help her daughter. Both were medically examined, but since then no further communication on the application had taken place.[26]

Berry's trial opened at Liverpool on February 21, 1887. The evidence was purely circumstantial, the prosecutor admitted, but went on to contend that the prisoner had administered to her daughter a corrosive liquid, probably sulfuric acid, in order to obtain the £10 insurance on her life. He mentioned by way of a motive that Edith was costing her mother £12 a year for clothing and maintenance and noted that Elizabeth had ample opportunity to administer poison. Circumstantial as this evidence plainly was, the prosecutor casually asserted that it was "not competent for the prosecution to find an adequate motive for such a crime." To this the appointed defense counsel made an effective response. The child's demise was consistent with a natural death; she had had a tendency to tubercular disease and, consequently, was prone to "sudden derangement of stomach and bowels." Where, the defense asked, was the evidence the girl died of sulfuric acid, for no trace of it had been found in the viscera after death, nor was there any evidence of its administration by the prisoner? She had been a kind and affectionate mother, and the theory that she would kill her daughter for an insignificant insurance payment was a "monstrous proposition." William Thompson, an analytical chemist from Manchester, testified that if a person lived for a few days after taking the poison, as Edith had, and had vomited frequently, he would have expected to find traces in the body after death. Nevertheless, many of the symptoms were consistent with sulfuric acid poisoning. The public analyst had examined the child's gullet but had not tested for any other matter than the acid.[27]

Two physicians and a professional analyst were of the opinion that the child had been poisoned even though "no trace of the poison could be found in the body." There is little doubt that the belief, as distinct from evidence, that Elizabeth Berry had administered poison to her young daughter had a powerful impact on the trial and public opinion. "Peculiarly horrible" as capital punishment of women was in Victorian society, the press considered it almost impossible to extend sympathy to this woman. "She subjected her daughter to cruel torture of corrosive poisoning and watched her die before her eyes." This murder, the judge remarked in his summing up, was "cold blooded, merciless, and cruel." He dwelt upon the prisoner's numerous "cruel" statements about the child's health and referred to the insurance on her. To help the jury to make up its mind, which it did in 10 minutes, a photograph of the dead child was handed to them. Plainly, this death was not the result of any natural disease. Sentenced to death, Berry was another woman first to be hanged at a new site for the capital punishments of females. The home secretary had discontinued executions at Kirkdale Prison in favor of Walton Prison.[28]

Before the end of the century there was a case that captured the attention of the entire nation. Its attraction was the means by which the poison was delivered to the victim. Then, following the accused's conviction, the belief that she was insane dominated discussion and led members of her jury to make a singular posttrial intervention. The woman was Mary Ann Ansell, born in November 1877, who had worked for several years as a domestic servant in a Bloomsbury lodging house. Engaged and anxious to marry, she and her young man were short of the funds they needed to "make up a home." They postponed the wedding only for Mary Ann to think of a way to obtain the required money. On September 6, 1898, she approached John Cooper, an agent of the Royal London Friendly Society, for a policy that would pay £22.5 to ensure that her sister Caroline, aged 26, had a proper private funeral when the time came. Caroline, she told Cooper, worked as a general servant at Leavesden Asylum, near Watford. In truth, she was an inmate of the heavily overcrowded and grossly understaffed institution. Had this been disclosed, the policy would never have been granted. For it, Mary Ann was required to pay at a rate of threepence a week. Instead, she made a regular-as-clockwork cumulative payment of a shilling each month. By March 6, 1899, the policy would become profit bearing, with the Society committed to the payment of half its total value. Would this modest sum allow the engaged couple to marry and set up a home together?[29]

The postal service delivered an unexpected food parcel to Caroline, along with a letter informing her that her parents had died. An inquiry by the asylum staff proved that they were still very much alive. Then, three days after the insurance policy's profit bearing date, a cake addressed to Caroline arrived by post. She shared a little of it with fellow inmates, all of whom fell ill. Caroline, who ate far more than the others, became seriously ill and died on March 14. Initially, the cause of her death was thought to be peritonitis. However, an asylum doctor suggested a postmortem to the parents, and the mourning mother while on a brief visit agreed with him. Meanwhile, Mary Ann had convinced her father to refuse permission, but a postmortem was held and phosphorous poisoning was certified as the cause of death. On March 17, Mary Ann advised Cooper of the death, and he instructed her to take the policy and death certificate to the Society's nearest branch office. Several days passed without any action by her. Hearing that the death was regarded as suspicious, Cooper called on her at the lodging house and informed her that in the application she had made misstatements about her sister. She was not in general service at the asylum but an inmate, and the Society would not honor the full claim. If she produced the premium book and the policy, he would at least refund the money she had paid in. She replied that she could find neither document and would await the finding of the inquest.[30]

The inquest opened on April 10 in the asylum's Recreation Hall. Dr. Stevenson reported that his analysis of the deceased's viscera pointed to phosphorus poisoning. A witness told of Mary Ann's purchase of penny bottles of phosphorus paste, and her employer at the lodging house denied that they had been acquired on her instructions to suppress rats. Cooper had handed the agreed insurance policy to Mary Ann on October 6, 1898, commenting on the "admirable regularity" with which she paid the premiums. A handwriting expert stated that the letter informing Caroline of her parents' deaths; the statement made by Mary Ann to the investigating policeman, Superintendent Wood; and the address on the parcel in which the cake had been delivered were all in the hand of Mary Ann. The parcel's cover had been discarded and was found by the police on March 20 in a field adjacent to the asylum. After three hours of investigation, the coroner's jury delivered a unanimous verdict. Caroline Ansell died on March 14 having eaten a piece of the poisoned cake sent to her by her sister. Her motive was greed, the insurance money. She was guilty of willful murder and committed to trial. Here was another domestic murder like those of Bartlett and Maybrick and that of Eleanor Pearcey, who, in 1890, murdered the wife and child of her lover, Frank Hogg, yet enjoyed considerable sympathy in the press and "in the public consciousness." Popular attention in murder cases was turning from the dangerous streets to homes and from the unruly to persons of apparent respectability. Not that Mary Ann as a domestic in a lodging house was considered genuinely respectable. However, like Pearcey, she became an example of class injustice. Mrs. Maybrick's life had been spared, *Reynolds's Newspaper* commented, "because of the social position she had filled."[31]

The investigating superintendent had arrested Mary Ann on April 6 and charged her with willful murder. This was a sensational development, unexpected given the length of time that had passed since the death. The next step was the committal hearing in the Watford Police Court before a full bench of magistrates. The prosecuting solicitor submitted that the chain of circumstances of the accused's guilt was "irresistibly strong," and he requested the bench to commit her for trial on the capital charge. This it did. The Police Court had been crowded, and public interest was further heightened when the grand jury at the Hertford Assizes found a bill against Mary Ann. The proceedings opened in the old Shire Hall before Mr. Justice Mathew, who said that, in his experience, he had never had the misfortune to try a case "in which so cold-blooded and revolting a crime had been committed to obtain so miserable an end." Although she had a competent defense counsel, Mary Ann decided to take full advantage of the previous year's Criminal Evidence Act, which finally permitted defendants to give evidence in their cases. But it exposed her to cross-examination, where she made a poor showing, and the strength of the evidence and the premeditated nature of the poisoning doomed her. The jury took more than two hours to reach a verdict, returning after one hour to the courtroom to ask a question of the judge. He declined to listen to it. He also refused to allow them to have the refreshments that had been prepared for them. The jury then convicted Mary Ann without a recommendation for mercy, and the judge sentenced her to death.[32]

Following the sentence, Mary Ann Ansell became a national sensation with much of the press agitating for a reprieve. There was a belief that she was of too weak a mind herself to be held responsible for her actions. Her treatment stood in stark contrast to that of middle class poisoners such as Christiana Edmunds, whose judge had observed that insanity "seldom affected" a poor defendant but "it was common to raise a defense of that kind when people of means were charged with the commission of a crime." Insanity served as a form of clemency for the middle class. Mary Ann's defense counsel was heavily criticized by the press for his failure to raise the question of her sanity, it being asserted that she had been denied "fair play" because she was a "penniless maid servant without influence or good looks." The visit of Forbes Winslow to examine her was well known. In his opinion she was a "mental degenerate" and therefore ought not to be held responsible in the eyes of the law. "Unable to discriminate between right and wrong she could not appreciate the gravity of her crime." Had a plea of insanity been raised when she went to trial, no jury, Winslow concluded, could have convicted her.[33]

A search for evidence of imbecility in her family tree followed. Two of Mary Ann's aunts had reportedly died in an asylum, while two of her

Eight. Late-Century Female Poisoners

sisters had been certified as imbeciles. Her father, on the other hand, emphatically denied that there was insanity in his family and claimed that Caroline had been as right as rain until her brother was killed. Only then, he said, did she fret so much that her mind gave way. The Police Court "Missioner" had confidentially informed a journalist that he did not doubt Mary Ann's sanity. The trial jury's foreman, Charles Cusworth, stated, however, that, had the evidence of mental instability since published been put before the jury, it would have recommended unanimously a commutation of the death sentence. This led to the question being raised in the House of Commons, where it was suggested that the scheduled execution be postponed to allow an independent inquiry into the prisoner's sanity. The home secretary responded that there had been a full inquiry: two doctors had been named to examine the prisoner, and the judge had been consulted. There was no evidence, he added, that had the question of insanity been raised it could have affected the verdict. Shortly afterwards, and shortly before the execution, a group of jurymen made an extraordinary visit to the lobby of the House of Commons in the hope of having an interview with the home secretary. He refused to receive them. But their petition praying for a reprieve was during the course of the evening signed by as many as 70 members of Parliament representing all shades of political opinion. In a final desperate effort, a petition praying for a commutation was sent directly to the monarch, but she referred the jurors back to the home secretary. Little wonder the safety of her conviction continued to be questioned. Mary Ann Ansell was sentenced to death on June 30, and her execution—the last of a female poisoner that century—occurred on July 19, 1899.[34]

Conclusion

SADLY, THE 19TH CENTURY ENDED as it had begun, with a young woman executed for the crime of murder. Mary York was charged with the willful murder of her bastard infant. She threw the baby into a river. Her distinction was that of being the first woman hanged in the new century. In her defense she made a hesitant claim to deranged behavior at the time of the birth, of not knowing what she did. At the time this was known as "milk fever." Her premeditated disposal of the baby had in the opinion of the judge disqualified her plea of temporary insanity. There was irony in this decision, for over the course of the next half-century medical men and "alienists" who concentrated on a woman's reproductive cycle—on menstruation, childbirth, and postnatal depression—concluded that the tensions to which she was subjected impaired her mental health. During the second half of the century, infanticide ceased, to all intents and purposes, to be judged a capital crime. In 1899 Mary Ann Ansell went to the gallows for the murder of her mentally ill adult sister. The poisoned cake was delivered by the Royal Mail. What York and Ansell had in common was public concern about their mental health. By the time of Ansell's trial, there had been limited advances in the understanding of insanity. The House of Lords had years earlier sought from the Anglican bishops a clearer legal definition of the illness, not that their reply clarified the situation, and juries often had to rely on their own common sense.

Female poisoners were equipped with the deadly drugs readily available in penny packets despite legislation intended to limit access to them. Their victims were invariably members of their own families—infants, children, husbands—to whom they had immediate access. Mothers who gave birth to as many as 13 infants knew they would not be able to nourish them all. Many of them were removed naturally by the diseases that swept through the unsanitary slums in which they were tightly packed. The survivors of these plagues faced tragically grim adult lives, and this certainty induced some mothers to spare them this life of misery by killing them. Those who did not adopt this radical solution might instead send them at a very young age to earn a few pennies working in mills and in mines. To attribute this maternal conduct exclusively to a sense of humanity would be a mistake. Greed often explained the death of either an unwanted child or a husband unwanted for whatever reason. Burial clubs and insurance companies provided opportunities to profit from deaths. Once the policy was fully paid and the death occurred, the sum collected far exceeded the cost of a private burial. The balance remaining helped ease the cost of living. As one coroner remarked, when the death of a burial club member came before him, he always suspected murder.

Sexual passion was another powerful motive for poisoning. The bonds of marriage were often far from strong among the laboring and working classes. For the woman tempted into adultery, the removal of husband and children cleared the path to remarriage. To the extent that the crime went outside the immediate family, it drove the poisoner to remove the wife of the man with whom she had established a sexual relationship. Women convicted of homicide might seek clemency with a plea of insanity. This legal strategy was for many years far easier for middle class women to exploit than the female masses beneath them socially. Class was the structure of British society. Industrialization saw a rapid expansion of the middle classes, including the lower middle class. On those rare occasions in which they found themselves in conflict with the law, they usually had the means to retain counsel. Eventually the women of the lower orders benefited from the deepening Victorian opposition to the execution of women and from the willingness of judges to appoint barristers to defend them when charged with a capital crime. Not that they thus achieved genuine legal equality with the middle classes.

By the middle of the century there was a belief among the middle and upper classes that Britain's criminal law was a "great practical school of truth, morality and compassion...eminently favorable to individuals." The innocent had "every possible security which human institutions can [provide] for freedom from unjust punishment." Trial by jury, the presumption of innocence, the right against self-incrimination, and the requirement that a jury be convinced beyond a reasonable doubt of the guilt of an accused furnished all the protection an accused required in the opinion of the optimists.[1]

How did the alleged female poisoner fare in this society? Undernourished, underclothed, undereducated, she was brought before a hostile court in which her fate would be decided exclusively by men. Without a counsel to cross-examine witnesses, she sped through the trial and was convicted within a few minutes. The evidence was almost entirely circumstantial and thus suspect, although the introduction of a scientific method of detecting the most widely used poison, arsenic, gave more assurance. Evidence of its acquisition was considered proof of its administration. Even much later when the accused were equipped with counsel by judges, this was done at the assizes on the eve of trial. This did not give the barrister sufficient time in which to prepare a proper defense. Not until almost the end of the century was the accused permitted to give sworn testimony on her own behalf.

Under sentence of death, the female poisoner's only hope of escaping a public or a private strangling hung on the growing opposition to the hanging of women—or the belief that she was insane. To these potentially saving graces must be added the press, which influenced the enforcement of the law. It reported trials in such detail that readers considered themselves so well briefed that they were able to comment on the justice of verdicts. Newspapers that claimed to be voices of the working classes complained of their harsh disadvantages when compared to the treatment of middle class offenders. Others, convinced justice had not been done, sought to galvanize public opinion against an execution. Not that this always succeeded, as Mary Ann Ansell discovered in the final months of the century.

What then had changed over the century? The injustice of day trials and lightening verdicts was by the mid-century largely a thing of the past for the lower orders. The equipment of defendants with counsels, and their ability not only to cross-examine prosecution witnesses but also to address the jury, was an important step forward. But the last minute appointment of many counsels by judges at assizes denied them the time to prepare thorough defences. Nor did the lower class accused possess the required education to compose a coherent "statement" to the jury before it reached a verdict. The Criminal Evidence Act of 1898 finally permitted an accused to give sworn evidence in her or his defence. But the Florence Maybrick case a decade earlier had revealed the dangers of statements while the Ansell case proved the possible pitfalls of the Act. Nor could the injustice of ill-conducted trials, such as that of the middle class Maybrick, whose conviction was the work of the judge, be corrected legally and completely until the creation in 1907 of the Court of Appeal in criminal cases.

Chapter Notes

Introduction

1. Frederic Hill, *Crime: Its Amount, Causes and Remedies* (Forgotten Books, 2012), 53, 83; Clive Emsley, *Crime and Society in England 1750–1900*, 5th Edition (London: Routledge, 2018), 21–48.
2. Eleanor Gordon and Gwyneth Nair, *Public Lives: Women, Family and Society in Victorian Britain* (London: Yale University Press, 2003), 13–5.
3. Judith Flanders, *The Invention of Murder* (London: Harper Press, 2011), 226–7; Tal Golan, *Laws of Men and Laws of Nature: The History of Scientific Testimony in England and America* (Cambridge: Harvard University Press, 2004), 90; Helen Barrell, *Fatal Evidence: Professor Alfred Swaine Taylor and the Dawn of Forensic Science* (Barnsley: Pen and Sword Press, 2017), 116–21; Ian A. Burney, "A Poisoning of No Substance: The Trials of Medico-Legal Proof in Mid-Victorian England," *Journal of British Studies* 38 (1999): 66–7, 70.
4. Hill, *Crime*, 53.
5. Emsley, *Crime and Society*, 21, 23, 26, 31.
6. Barrell, *Fatal Evidence*, 122–5; David Bentley, *English Criminal Justice in the Nineteenth Century* (London: Hambledon Press, 1998), 3, 17–8.
7. Stephen Jacobi, *Misjudged Murderesses: Female Injustice in Victorian Britain* (Barnsley: Penn and Sword, 2019), 11; Adrian Gray, *Crime and Criminals of Victorian England* (Stroud: History Press, 2011), 10–1.

Chapter One

1. Naomi Clifford, *Women and the Gallows, 1797–1837: Unfortunate Wretches* (Barnsley: Penn and Sword, 2017), 85–87.
2. Alfred S. Taylor, *A Manual of Medical Jurisprudence*, 2nd ed. (London: John Churchill, 1846), 67.
3. Eric Vallillee, "Deconstructing Infanticide," *Western Journal of Legal Studies* 5, no. 4 (2015); Clifford, *Women and the Gallows*, 76.
4. Davies and Company, *Extraordinary Life and Character of Mary Bateman: The Yorkshire Witch* (Leeds: Stanhope Press, 1811), 28–9, 5.
5. Davies and Company, *Extraordinary*, 9–14, 23; Summer Strevens, *The Yorkshire Witch: The Life and Trial of Mary Bateman* (Barnsley: Pen and Sword, 2017), 19–22.
6. Davies and Company, *Extraordinary Life*, 16–7; Strevens, *The Yorkshire Witch*, 41–3, 47.
7. Davies and Company, *Extraordinary*, 29–31.
8. Davies and Company, *Extraordinary Life*, 33–40; Clifford, *Women and the Gallows*, 93–5; Emsley, *The Elements of Murder*, 70–1.
9. Davies and Company, *Extraordinary Life*, 49–52; Strevens, *Yorkshire Witch*, 101–2; Emsley, *The Elements of Murder*, 71; Clifford, *Women and the Gallows*, 95–7.
10. Clifford, *Women and the Gallows*, 99–101; Davies and Company, *Extraordinary Life*, 52–5; Strevens, *Yorkshire Witch*, 108–15.
11. Stephen Jakobi, *In the Mind of a Female Serial Killer* (Barnsley: Pen and Sword History, 2017), 134–5.

12. Lionel Rose, *Massacre of the Innocents: Infanticide in Great Britain, 1800–1939* (London: Routledge & Kegan Paul, 1986), 7; "The Proceedings of the Old Bailey," www.oldbaileyonline.org, version 8.0, September 1809, trial of Rebecca Merrin; Clifford, *Women and the Gallows*, 191–2, 196.

13. "Eliza Fenning—hanged for attempted murder," www.capitalpunishmentuk.org/eliza.html; Kate Clarke, ed., *Trial of Eliza Fenning* (London: Mango Books, 2020), 2–3; John Marshall, *Five Cases of Recovery from the Effects of Arsenic Relative to the Guilt of Eliza Fenning* (London: C. Chapple, 1815), 4–10.

14. Clarke, *Trial of Eliza Fenning*, 124, 3–4; Flanders, *The Invention of Murder*, 184.

15. *London Medical and Physical Journal* 23 (1810): 448–50; *London Medical and Physical Journal* 39 (1818): 279–82; S.W.F. Holloway, "The Apothecaries' Act, 1815: A Reinterpretation," *Medical History* 10 (1966): 108, 129.

16. Clarke, *Trial of Eliza Fenning*, 103–5, 130; William Ballantine, *Some Experiences of a Barrister's Life* (London: Richard Bentley & Son, 1883), 54–6; "The Proceedings of the Old Bailey," www.oldbaileyonline.org, version 8.0, April 1806.

17. Clarke, *Trial of Eliza Fenning*, 85–100, 109; www.capitalpunishmentuk.org/eliza.html.

18. Clarke, *Trial of Eliza Fenning*, 24, 136–7, 26–32; www.capitalpunishmentuk.org/eliza.html.

19. John Marshall, *Five Cases of Recovery from the Effects of Arsenic Relative to the Guilt of Eliza Fenning* (London: C. Chapple, 1815).

20. *Important Results on an Elaborate Investigation into the Mysterious Case of Elizabeth Fenning* (November 1815), 130–2, 151–2, 157, 185–6; Ben Wilson, *The Laughter of Triumph: William Hone and the Fight for the Free Press* (London: Faber and Faber, 2005), 143.

21. *Circumstantial Evidence: The Extraordinary Case of Eliza Fenning with a Statement of Facts Since Developed Tending to Prove Her Innocence of the Crime* (London: Cowie and Strange); Flanders, *Invention of Murder*, 192; Stratmann, *The Secret Poisoner*, 16–7; Brian Jenkins, *Madeleine Smith on Trial: A Glasgow Murder and the Young Woman Too Respectable to Convict* (Jefferson, NC: McFarland and Company, 2019), 166–7; Clarke, *Trial of Eliza Fenning*, 161–73; *Leicester Chronicle*, July 22, 1857.

22. Clive Emsley, *Crime and Society in England, 1750–1900*, 5th ed. (London: Routledge, 2018), 196, 231–8.

23. James C. Whorton, *The Arsenic Century: How Victorian Britain Was Poisoned at Home, Work and Play* (Oxford: Oxford University Press, 2011), 8; Emsley, *Elements of Murder*, 94, 96.

Chapter Two

1. Ben Griffin, *The Politics of Gender in Victorian Britain: Masculinity, Political Culture and the Struggle for Women's Rights* (Cambridge: Cambridge University Press, 2012), 31, 51, 53; A. James Hammerton, *Cruelty and Companionship: Conflict in Nineteenth Century Married Life* (London: Routledge, 1992), 61, 58.

2. Clifford, *Women at the Gallows*, 197–8.

3. Clifford, *Women at the Gallows*, 208–9; Christina Croft, *Murderesses in Victorian Britain* (Monee, IL: 2021), 143.

4. Clifford, *Women at the Gallows*, 216; "The Proceedings of the Old Bailey," www.oldbaileyonline.org, version 8.0, September 1827.

5. Peter Vronsky, *Female Serial Killers: How and Why Women Become Monsters* (New York: Berkley Books, 2007), 98; Clifford, *Women at the Gallows*, 217, 221–2.

6. Clifford, *Women at the Gallows*, 225; Stratmann, *The Secret Poisoner*, 38; Jenkins, *Madeleine Smith on Trial*, 33, 55–7.

7. Katherine Watson, *Poisoned Lives: English Poisoners and Their Victims* (London: Hambledon and London, 2004), 207; Flanders, *The Invention of Murder*, 325; *Old England*, April 13, 1835; *Preston Chronicle*, April 25, 1835; *Leicester Herald*, April 18, 1835; *Salopian Journal*, April 22, 1835; Susan Thomas, *The Bristol Riots* (Bristol University, The History Association [Bristol Branch], 1974), 10–1, 16.

8. Stratmann, *The Secret Poisoner*, 55–7; *Essex Standard*, April 17, 1835; www.capitalpunishmentuk.org/burdock.html.
9. Stratmann, *The Secret Poisoner*, 55; www.capitalpunishmentuk.org/burdock.html; Watson, *Poisoned Lives*, 13.
10. *Lancet*, August 10, 1838, 264; www.capitalpunishmentuk.org/burdock.html; Stratmann, *The Secret Poisoner*, 58; *Staffordshire Advertiser*, May 2, 1835; *Bath Chronicle and Weekly Gazette*, June 25, 1835.
11. *Leicester Herald*, April 18, 1835; *Preston Chronicle*, April 25, 1835; *Norfolk Chronicle*, May 2, 1835.
12. *Royal Cornwall Gazette*, April 18, 1835; *Essex Standard*, April 17, 1835; *Salopian Journal*, April 22, 1835; Stratmann, *The Secret Poisoner*, 58; Knelman, *Twisting in the Wind*, 214.
13. Stratmann, *The Secret Poisoner*, 59; *Reading Mercury*, April 20, 1835; *Essex Standard*, April 17, 1835; *Berkshire Chronicle*, April 23, 1843.
14. *Salopian Journal*, April 22, 1835; *Staffordshire Advertiser*, May 2, 1835; Flanders, *Invention of Murder*, 325.
15. Stratmann, *The Secret Poisoner*, 59; *Albion and Star* (London), April 16, 1835.
16. *Exeter Flying Post*, April 30, 1835.
17. Watson, *Poisoned Lives*, 14, 207; Flanders, *Invention of Murder*, 325–9; Knelman, *Twisting in the Wind*, 208, 215.
18. *Morning Herald*, April 9, 1836; *London Evening Standard*, April 9, 1836.
19. *The Sun*, London, November 23, 1836; *Morning Post*, London, November 23, 1836; "Proceedings of the Old Bailey," www.oldbaileyonline.org, version 8.0, November 1836; Roger Smith, *Trial by Medicine: Insanity and Responsibility in Victorian Trials* (Edinburgh: Edinburgh University Press, 1981), 21; Croft, *Murderesses in Victorian Britain*, 142, 100.
20. G.W. Keeton, *Guilty But Insane: Four Trials for Murder* (London: MacDonald, 1961), 20; Lisa Appignanesi, *Mad, Bad and Sad: A History of Women and the Mind Doctors from 1800 to the Present* (London: Virago Press, 2009), 23.
21. Keeton, *Guilty But Insane*, 25, 38, 47; John Hostettler, *Thomas Erskine and Trial by Jury* (London: Waterside Press, 2010), 149–50, 150–60; Appignanesi, *Mad, Bad and Sad*, 24, 21; Rachel Dixon, *Infanticide Expert Evidence and Testimony in Child Murder Cases, 1688–1955* (London: Routledge, 2022), 128.
22. Roy Porter, *Bodies Politic: Disease, Death and Doctors in Britain, 1650–1900* (London: Reaktion Books, 2001), 93–4; Keeton, *Guilty But Insane*, 65–6, 70–4.
23. Keeton, *Guilty But Insane*, 65–6, 70–4; Mr. Sergeant Ballantine, *Some Experiences of a Barrister's Life* (London: Richard Bentley & Son, 1883), 163–4.
24. Keeton, *Guilty But Insane*, 65–6, 70–4; Ballantine, *Some Experiences of a Barrister's Life*, 163–4; Rachel Dixon, *Infanticide Expert Evidence and Testimony in Child Murder Cases, 1688–1955* (Abingdon: Routledge, 2022), 9.
25. Appignanesi, *Mad, Bad and Sad*, 54–5, 125, 91; Dixon, *Infanticide*, 48; Knelman, *Twisting in the Wind*, 123.

Chapter Three

1. Clifford, *Women and the Gallows*, 228–9; *Royal Cornwall Gazette*, April 25, 1836; *Kentish Gazette*, April 19, 1836; *Morning Post*, April 9, 1836; https://unknownmisandry.blogspot.com.
2. *Royal Cornwall Gazette*, April 15, 1836; *Worcester Herald*, April 16, 1836; *Morning Herald*, April 19, 1836; *Morning Post*, December 30, 1835; *Bell's Weekly Messenger*, January 3, 1836.
3. *Western Advertiser*, April 20, 1836; *Dorset County Chronicle*, April 14, 1836; *Northampton Mercury*, April 30, 1836; Knelman, *Twisting in the Wind*, 94–5.
4. Jenkins, *Madeleine Smith on Trial*, 57; Emsley, *The Elements of Murder*, 156; Stratmann, *The Secret Poisoner*, 74; Ian Burney, *Poison, Detection, and Victorian Imagination* (Manchester: Manchester University Press, 2006), 88.
5. J.F.C. Harrison, *The Early Victorians 1832–51* (St. Albans: Panther Books Ltd., 1973), 34, 75, 80.
6. Andrew Pettegree, *The Invention of News: How the World Came to Know About Itself* (London: Yale University Press, 2014), 370–1; Alan J. Lee, *The Origins of the Popular Press 1855–1914* (London: Croom Helm, 1976), 42, 53, 59, 69, 99, 106; Knelman, *Twisting in the Wind*, 49.
7. *Northampton Mercury*, September

1, 1849; Sally Hendry, *Mother and Murderer: The Sad True Tale of Rebecca Smith* (Gloucester: Hobnob Press, 2022), 9–25, 37–42.

8. Hendry, *Mother and Murderer*, 69–74.

9. *Weekly Dispatch* (London), August 26, 1849; *Northampton Mercury*, September 1, 1849; *Devizes Gazette* (republished in *Elgin Courant and Morayshire Advertiser*, September 7, 1849; Hendry, *Mother and Murderer*, 65, 86–7, 90.

10. *Banbury Guardian*, January 16, 1845; *Bell's New Weekly Messenger*, August 12, 1849.

11. Christopher Berry-Dee, *Female Serial Killers: Up Close and Personal* (Berkeley, CA: Ulysses Press, 2019), 10; Tori Telfer, *Lady Killers: Deadly Women Throughout History* (New York: Harper Collins, 2017), xi–xii, xvi; Kent A. Kiel and Morrio B. Hoffman, "The Criminal Psychopath History, Neuroscience, Treatment and Economics," *Jurimetrics* 51 (2011): 355–97; Ely Van De Warker, "The Relations of Women to Crime," in *Women Who Killed: Murderous Women From the 18th and 19th Century* (Redditch: Read Books Ltd., 2021), 7–43; Jakobi, *In the Mind of a Female Serial Killer*, 134–5.

12. Vronsky, *Female Serial Killers*, 36–62; *Belfast News-Letter*, August 18, 1843; Croft, *Murderesses in Victorian Britain*, 154–5; Paul Heslop, *Murderous Woman: From Sarah Dazley to Ruth Ellis* (Stroud: The History Press, 2009), 19–20, 25; Patrick Wilson, *Murderess: A Study of Women Executed in Britain Since 1843* (London: Michael Joseph, 1971), 17–20; *Bedford Mercury* republished in *Befordshire Times & Independent*, October 10, 1843; *Hertford Mercury and Reformer*, April 14, 1843.

13. *Morning Advertiser*, January 15, 1844; Wilson, *Murderess*, 21–2, 29–32; *Lloyd's Weekly Newspaper*, December 29, 1844; *Windsor and Eton Express*, January 18, 1845; *Ipswich Journal*, January 18, 1845; *London Evening Standard*, January 13, 1845; *Evening Mail*, December 27, 1844; Wilson, *Murderess*, 32–3.

14. Wilson, *Murderess*, 34–47; Croft, *Murderesses in Victorian Britain*, 157–8; Sanders, *The Invention of Murder*, 237; *Worcestershire Chronicle*, April 30, 1845; *Morning Herald*, April 24, 1845; *Drogheda Conservative Journal*, April 26, 1845; *Morning Herald*, April 24, 1845; *Taunton Courier and Western Advertiser*, April 23, 1845.

15. *Stamford Mercury*, August 6, 1847; *Morning Post*, August 3, 1847; *Staffordshire Advertiser*, August 7, 1847; *Liverpool Mercury*, August 6, 1847; *Ipswich Journal*, April 10, 1847; *Sun* (London), April 20, 1847.

16. Watson, *Poisoned Lives*, 90–1; Flanders, *Invention of Murder*, 228–9; *Morning Herald*, October 24, 1840; *English Chronicle and Whitehall Evening Post*, November 3, 1840; *Morning Post*, October 30, 1840; *City Chronicle*, November 10, 1840.

17. Lee, *Origins of the Popular Press*, 73; *Morning Herald*, August 5, 1841; *Sussex Advertiser*, August 9, 1841; Flanders, *Invention of Murder*, 230; Watson, *Poisoned Lives*, 91, 104; Knelman, *Twisting in the Wind*, 126.

18. *Northern Star and Leeds Advertiser*, April 8, 1843; *Morning Herald*, May 8, 1843; *Cork Examiner*, May 12, 1843; *Manchester Courier*, May 13, 1843; Wilson, *Murderess*, 15–6.

19. *Morning Herald*, August 15, 1848; Wilson, *Murderess*, 58–61; Knelman, *Twisting in the Wind*, 62; Flanders, *The Invention of Murder*, 243; *Morning Advertiser*, August 16, 1848; Jill Louise Ainsley, "The Ordeal of Sarah Chesham," Master of Arts thesis, University of Victoria, 1997, 40–2; Helen Barrell, *Fatal Evidence: Professor Alfred Swaine Taylor and the Dawn of Forensic Science* (Barnsley: Pen and Sword, 2017), 69–72; Hendry, *Mother and Murderer*, 49.

20. Wilson, *Murderess*, 69–72; *Examiner*, May 19, 1849; Barrell, *Fatal Evidence*, 78; Burney, *Poison, Detection, and Victorian Imagination*, 43, 54; Flanders, *The Invention of Murder*, 234n; *Evening Mail*, August 3, 1849; *Bell's New Weekly Newspaper*, August 12, 1849.

21. Flanders, *The Invention of Murder*, 234; *Cork Examiner*, August 31, 1849; *Daily News*, August 13, 1849; *Northampton Mercury*, September 1, 1849; Stephen Jakobi, *Misjudged Murderesses: Female Injustice in Victorian Britain* (Barnsley: Penn and Sword, 2019), 60–1, 69–71, 76; Wilson, *Murderess*, 67–8; Robert

Muscutt, *The Life, Trial and Hanging of Mary Ball* (Milton Keynes: Broadlands Books, 2011), 25, 29, 34, 45, 51.

22. *Morning Post*, August 7, 1849; *Weekly Chronicle*, August 11, 1849; *Warder*, August 11, 1849; *Daily News*, October 19, 1849; *Liverpool Mercury*, October 23, 1849; *Standard of Freedom*, October 27, 1849; *Bradford Observer*, November 1, 1849; *Glasgow Courier*, November 14, 1849; *Morning Post*, May 18, 1850; Ian A. Burney, "A Poisoning of No Substance: The Trials of Medico-Legal Proof in Mid-Victorian England," *Journal of British Studies* 38 (January, 1999): 72.

23. www.oldbaileyonline.org, version 8.0, March 1850, trial of Ann Merritt; William Ballantine, *Some Experiences of a Barrister's Life* (London: Richard Bentley & Son, 1883), 103; London *Evening Standard*, February 11, 1850; *Daily News*, March 22, 1850; *Northern Star and Leeds Advertiser*, March 23, 1850; *Bucks Advertiser & Aylesbury News*, March 23, 1850; *Glasgow Chronicle*, March 27, April 3, 1850; Martin J. Wiener, "Convicted Murderers and the Press Idolatration," www.atmostfear-entertainment.com.

24. Wiener, "Convicted Murderers and the Press Idolatration"; Alison Morton, "The Female Crime: Gender, Class and Female Criminality in Victorian Representations of Poisoning," *Midland Historical Review* 5 (2021); Barrell, *Fatal Evidence*, 85–6; *Cambridge Independent Press*, April 20, 1850; *Daily News*, April 15, 1850; *Newcastle Guardian and Tyne Mercury*, April 20, 1850; *Weekly Register and Catholic Standard*, April 20, 1850; *Northampton Mercury*, March 15, 1851.

25. Karen Farrington, *Murder, Mystery & My Family* (London: BBC Books, 2019), 14–25; Stratmann, *Secret Poisoner*, 127–30, 138–9.

26. Barrell, *Fatal Evidence*, 32, 63–8; Alfred Swaine Taylor, *On Poisons in Relation to Medical Jurisprudence and Medicine*, 2nd and revised ed. (Philadelphia: Blanchard & Lea, 1859); Burney, *Poison, Detection, and Victorian Imagination*, 55, 78, 62; Wilson, *Murderess*, 95–102.

27. Ainsley, "The Ordeal of Sarah Chesham."

28. Farrington, *Murder, Mystery & My Family*, 47–9, 52–5; Barrell, *Fatal Evidence*, 89–90; Ainsley, "The Ordeal of Sarah Chesham," 118, 115; *Northampton Mercury*, March 15, 1851; *Morning Chronicle*, March 26, 1861; *Morning Herald*, March 13, 1851; John Parascandola, *King of Poisons: A History of Arsenic* (Washington, D.C.: Potomac Books, 2012), 150–5.

29. Farrington, *Murder, Mystery & My Family*, 54–5; *Morning Chronicle*, March 26, 1851; Ainsley, "Ordeal of Sarah Chesham," 98; *Huddersfield Chronicle*, March 29, 1851; *Northampton Mercury*, March 15, 1851; *Freeman's Journal*, March 27, 1851.

30. *The Era*, March 30, 1851; *Freeman's Journal*, March 27, 1851; *Preston Chronicle*, March 29, 1851; *Reynolds's Newspaper*, March 30, 1851; Farrington, *Murder, Mystery & My Family*, 56–7; Jakobi, *Misjudged Murderesses*, 55.

31. *Reynolds's Weekly Newspaper*, March 30, 1851; *Staffordshire Advertiser*, March 29, 1851; *John o' Groats Journal*, April 4, 1851; *Dundee Courier*, March 19, 1851.

32. Jan Bondeson, *Victorian Murders* (Stroud: Amberley Publishing, 2017), 7–9.

33. Bondeson, *Victorian Murders*.

Chapter Four

1. Clive Emsley, *Crime and Society in England 1750–1900*, 5th ed. (London: Routledge, 2018), 231–8; John Briggs, Christopher Harrison, Angus McInnes, and David Vincent, *Crime and Punishment in England: An Introductory History* (London: UCL Press, 1996), 73–5, 158–9, 144–5; Haia Shpayer-Makov, *The Ascent of the Detective: Police Sleuths in Victorian and Edwardian England* (Oxford: Oxford University Press, 2011), 41, 38, 53–6.

2. *Cork Examiner*, June 13, 1851; Wilson, *Murderess*, 107–10; Whorton, *The Arsenic Century*, 135; *Nottinghamshire Guardian*, August 21, 1851; *Nottingham and Newark Mercury*, August 22, 1851; *Lloyd's Weekly Newspaper*, August 24, 1851; *Reynolds's Newspaper*, August 24, 1851; *Cambridge Independent Press*, August 23, 1851; *Berkshire Chronicle*, August 16, 1851.

3. Wilson, *Murderess*, 115–8; *Brighton Gazette*, April 15, 1852; *Morning Chronicle*, April 12, 1852; *Preston Chronicle*, April 17, 1852.
4. *Derbyshire Courier*, February 7, 1852; *Bolton Chronicle*, February 7, 1852; *Windsor and Eton Express*, February 7, 1852; *Berkshire Chronicle*, February 7, 1852.
5. *Derbyshire Courier*, April 3, 1852; *Berkshire Chronicle*, February 7, 1852.
6. *Preston Chronicle*, April 17, 1852; *Sussex Advertiser*, April 13, 1852; *Berkshire Chronicle*, April 17, 1852.
7. *Dover Telegraph*, August 16, 1856; *Carlisle Patriot*, August 30, 1856; *Dublin Medical Press*, July 30, 1856.
8. Ian Burney, *Poison, Detection, and the Victorian Imagination* (Manchester: Manchester University Press, 2006), 100; *Bolton Chronicle*, August 16, 23, 1856; Emsley, *The Elements of Murder*, 197; *Fleetwood Chronicle*, August 30, 1856; *Munster News*, August 27, 1856.
9. *Dublin Medical Press*, July 30, 1856; Whorton, *The Arsenic Century*, 134–5.
10. www.oldbaileyonline.org, version 8.0, April 1856; *Cumberland Pacquet*, June 10, 1856.
11. *Elgin Courant*, May 2, 1856; *Cumberland Pacquet*, June 10, 1856; *Sun*, June 6, 1856; *The Queen*, May 3, 1862; *Belfast News-Letter*, June 13, 1856; *Carlisle Journal*, June 13, 1856; Croft, *Murderesses in Victorian Britain*, 86–8; https://criminallunacy.blogspot.com.
12. Burney, *Poison, Detection, and the Victorian Imagination*, 133, 138–9, 141; Burney, *Journal of British Studies* 38: 60–1.
13. Henry Maudsley, *Responsibility in Mental Disease* (New York: Appleton and Company, 1896), republished in the Leopold Classic Library, 101, 77–8, 110–1, 149–50, 164, 187.
14. Ballantine, *Some Experiences of a Barrister's Life*, 113, 165, 176–77, 68.
15. London *Express*, August 10, 1854; *Cheltenham Chronicle*, August 15, 1854.
16. *Cheltenham Chronicle*, August 15, 1854; Ballantine, *Some Experiences of a Barrister's Life*, 165.
17. *Westmorland Gazette*, August 12, 1854; *Cheltenham Chronicle*, August 15, 1854.
18. Smith, *Trial by Medicine*, 13, 31, 33, 103, 59.
19. *Cheltenham Chronicle*, August 15, 1854; *Stonehaven Journal*, August 17, 1854.
20. *Westmorland Gazette*, August 12, 1854; *Cheltenham Chronicle*, August 15, 1854; *Bucks Herald*, August 12, 1854; *Inverness Advertiser*, August 22, 1854.
21. *Morning Chronicle*, March 21, 1861.
22. *Nottinghamshire Guardian*, August 1, 1862; *Lincolnshire Chronical*, July 11, 1862; *Lancaster Guardian*, October 25, 1862; Barrell, *Fatal Evidence*, 177.
23. www.oldbaileyonline.org, version 8.0, June 1862; *British Standard*, October 3, 1862.
24. *Sun* (London), October 24, 1862; *British Standard*, October 3, 1862; Wilson, *Murderess*, 131–2.
25. www.oldbaileyonline.org, version 8.0, September 1862; Barrell, *Fatal Evidence*, 173–7.
26. *British Standard*, October 3, 1862; *Sun*, September 27, 1862.
27. *British Standard*, October 3, 1862; *Saint James's Chronicle*, September 30, 1862.
28. *Nottingham Journal*, October 25, 1862; *Blackburn Times*, October 4, 1862; *South and North Lincolnshire Advertiser*, August 2, 1862; *Nottinghamshire Guardian*, August 1, 1862; *Lancaster Guardian*, October 25, 1862; *British Standard*, October 24, 1862; *Cork Examiner*, October 28, 1862; *Paisley Herald*, November 1, 1862; *Chester Chronicle*, November 1, 1862; *Sun*, October 24, 27, 1862.
29. Barrel, *Fatal Evidence*, 177; Watson, *Poisoned Lives*, 211; Vronsky, *Female Serial Killers*, 107.

Chapter Five

1. Burney, *Journal of British Studies* 38 (1999): 83–4.
2. Appignanesi, *Trials of Passion*, 5; Burney, *Poison, Detection, and Victorian Imagination*, 17, 30, 40, 154; Watson, *Poisoned Lives*, 50, 208.
3. Michael Diamond, *Victorian Sensation Or, the Spectacular, the Shocking, and Scandalous in Nineteenth Century Britain* (London: Anthem Press, 2003), 171; *Leeds Times*, September 2, 1843; *Fifeshire Journal*, September 21, 1843; *The Scotsman*, October 1, 2002; Croft, *Murderesses in Victorian Britain*, 46–8.

4. *Glasgow Herald*, January 15, 1844; Croft, *Murderesses in Victorian Britain*, 48–9.
5. *Fifeshire Journal*, September 21, 1843; *The Scotsman*, October 1, 2002.
6. *Glasgow Herald*, January 15, 1844; Croft, *Murderesses in Victorian Britain*, 49–50.
7. *Glasgow Herald*, January 15, 1844; Croft, *Murderesses in Victorian Britain*, 50.
8. *Glasgow Herald*, June 15, 1857; *Berkshire Chronicle*, July 4, 1857.
9. Eleanor Gordon and Gwyneth Nair, *Murder and Morality in Victorian Britain* (Manchester: University of Manchester Press, 2008), 2–4; Brian Jenkins, *Madeleine Smith on Trial* (Jefferson, NC: McFarland & Co., 2019), 13–4.
10. Gordon and Nair, *Murder and Morality*, 38–9; Douglas McGowan, *The Strange Affair of Madeleine Smith* (Glasgow: Mercat Press, 2007), 3–7; Precognitions of Peter Pollock, Sarah Niven, Charles Alexander Murray, AD14/57/255/5, National Archives of Scotland, Edinburgh; *Dundee Courier*, September 9, 1857; *Glasgow Herald*, December 20, 1857; AS14/57/255/5.
11. McGowan, *Strange Affair of Madeleine Smith*, 20, 22–3, 18; Gordon and Nair, *Murder and Morality*, 39; Madeleine Smith to L'Angelier, February 11, 1856, October 19, November 24, 1855, AD14/57/255/1; Statement of Auguste Vanvert de Mean, April 13, 1857, AD14/55/255/13.
12. Jenkins, *Madeleine Smith on Trial*, 36.
13. Precognitions of Thuau and Thomson, AD14/57/255/13; Register Book of Deaths, AD14/57/255/20; Precognitions of Thomson and Steven, AD14/57/255/13.
14. Precognitions of Stevenson, Thomson, and Steven, AD14/57/255/13; Jenkins, *Madeleine Smith on Trial*, 44, 47–9; Browne, *Reports of Trial for Murder by Poisoning*, 395.
15. John Crabb Watt, *John Inglis Lord Justice-General of Scotland, A Memoir* (Edinburgh: William Green & Sons, 1893), 51, 83, 102; Legal Notebooks of John Inglis, 38.1.17; 38.2.17, National Library of Scotland, Edinburgh; *Cork Examiner*, July 15, 1857.
16. *Kentish Gazette*, July 15, 1857;

Southern Reporter, July 17, 1857; *Newcastle Courant*, July 17, 1857; *Preston Chronicle*, July 18, 1857.
17. *Salisbury and Winchester Journal*, July 22, 1865; Gray, *Crimes and Criminals*, 43; Maunder and Moore, *Victorian Crime, Madness and Sensation*, 73.
18. Yseult Bridges, *Saint—With Red Hands? The Chronicle of a Great Crime* (London: Jarrolds, 1954), 20–2; Joseph Whitaker Stapleton, *The Great Crime of 1860* (London: E. Marlborough & Co., 1861), 15–29, 40–1.
19. *Wiltshire Independent*, May 4, 1854.
20. Bridges, *Saint—With Red Hands*, 47, 54–62.
21. Kate Summerscale, *The Suspicions of Mr. Whicher* (London: Bloomsbury, 2009), 14, 18, 21, 23–4; Bridges, *Saint—With Red Hands*, 66–9, 71.
22. Bridges, *Saint—With Red Hands*, 68–9, 73, 76; Summerscale, *Suspicions of Mr. Whicher*, 33; Shpayer-Makov, *Ascent of the Detective*, 45–6; *Hertfordshire Express*, July 21, 1860.
23. Bridges, *Saint—With Red Hands*, 85–6, 114–5, 123; Summerscale, *Suspicions of Mr. Whicher*, 29–30, 33, 67, 87, 93–4, 104–7, 179; *Hertfordshire Express*, July 21, 1860.
24. *West Somerset Free Press*, July 28, 1860; Bridges, *Saint—With Red Hands*, 116–9, 184–5; Summerscale, *Suspicions of Mr. Whicher*, 115–6, 126.
25. Stapleton, *The Great Crime of 1860*, 125–36; *Bath Chronicle*, August 2, 1860; Bernard Taylor, *Cruelly Murdered: Constance Kent and the Killing at Road Hill House* (London: Grafton Books, 1989), 158, 188–92, 209–34.
26. Flanders, *Invention of Murder*, 283; *Taunton Courier and Western Advertiser*, June 14, 1865; *Hull Advertiser*, July 12, 1862.
27. www.oldbaileyonline.org, version 8.0, July 1862, 3/12, 4/12, 1/12, 2/12; https://londonstreetsviews.wordpress.com.
28. www.oldbaileyonline.org, version 8.0, July 1862, 2/12 to 7/12.
29. *Leeds Times*, June 7, 1862; *Cork Daily Herald*, June 7, 1862; *Suffolk Chronicle*, June 14, 1862; *Northampton Mercury*, June 14, 1862.
30. *Taunton Courier and Western Advertiser*, July 2, 1862; *South London Chron-*

icle, July 5, 1862; *Glasgow Free Press*, July 5, 1862.
31. *Western Times*, July 12, 1862; *Hull Advertiser*, July 12, 1862.
32. www.oldbaileyonline.org, version 8.0, July 1862, 4/12 to 10/12.
33. Smith, *Trial by Medicine*, 69, 122, 112; www.oldbaileyonline.org, version 8.0, July 1862, 8/12 to 9/12.
34. www.oldbaileyonline.org, version 8.0, July 1862, 8/12 to 12/12; www.londonstreetviews.wordpress.com/charles-vyse-straw-hat-manufacturer, 6/10, 9/10.
35. *Western Daily Press*, April 27, 1865; *London Evening Standard*, April 26, 1865; *Preston Chronicle*, April 29, 1865; *Paisley Herald and Renfrewshire Advertiser*, April 29, 1865.
36. *Salisbury and Winchester Journal*, July 22, 1865; *Hull Packet*, July 28, 1865; Summerscale, *The Suspicions of Mr. Whicher*, 249–50; *Sussex Advertiser*, May 30, 1866.
37. Summerscale, *The Suspicions of Mr. Whicher*, 228–30.

Chapter Six

1. Kaye Jones, *The Case of the Chocolate Cream Killer: The Poisonous Passion of Christiana Edmunds* (Barnsley: Pen and Sword Press, 2016), 7–8, 12–4, 17, 20–1, 29; Appignanesi, *Trials of Passion*, 52–4, 63–4.
2. Jones, *The Case of the Chocolate Cream Killer*, 38–39; Appignanesi, *Trials of Passion*, 17, 60–1; Jones, 48–50, 51–2; Sophie Jackson, *Death by Chocolate: The Serial Poisoning of Victorian Britain* (Stroud: Fonthill Media, 2015), Kindle Edition, loc. 1208.
3. Appignanesi, *Trials of Passion*, 14; Jones, *The Case of the Chocolate Cream Killer*, 54–5.
4. Jones, *The Case of the Chocolate Cream Killer*, 58–9, 63.
5. Jackson, *Death by Chocolate*, loc. 113, 120, 128; Royal College of Surgeons England; S. Bland, "Workhouse surgeon Richard Rugg 1851," My Brighton and Hove, https://www.mybrightonandhove.org.uk/topic/workhouse-surgeon-richard-rugg-1851.
6. Jackson, *Death by Chocolate*, loc. 203, 211, 234, 241, 249; Jones, *The Case of the Chocolate Cream Killer*, 73–4, 98, 100.
7. Appignanesi, *Trials of Passion*, 21–2; Jones, *The Case of the Chocolate Cream Killer*, 101, 103–4.
8. Appignanesi, *Trials of Passion*, 31, 33; Jones, *The Case of the Chocolate Cream Killer*, 109–10; 112–3; Jackson, *Death by Chocolate*, loc. 377.
9. Jones, *The Case of the Chocolate Cream Killer*, 119; Appignanesi, *Trials of Passion*, 33–4.
10. *Brighton Gazette*, January 18, 1872.
11. Mr. Sergeant Ballantine, *Some Experiences of a Barrister's Life* (London: Richard Bentley and Son, 1890), 138–40, 142, 146, 69, 84–91; Thomas Edward Crispe, *Reminiscences of a K.C.* (London: Methuen & Co., 1909), 130–1.
12. *Brighton Gazette*, January 18, 1872; *South London Press*, January 20, 1872.
13. *Western Mail*, February 10, 1825; *Morning Herald*, February 22, 1825; *Aberdeen Free Press and Journal*, January 12, 1880; *Aberdeen Free Press*, January 12, 1880.
14. *South London Press*, January 20, 1872; *Tamworth Herald*, January 27, 1872; Appignanesi, *Trials of Passion*, 83.
15. *Greenock Telegraph*, January 16, 1872; Jackson, *Death by Chocolate*, loc. 2798, 2805, 2820, 2844; *South London Press*, January 20, 1872.
16. Appignanesi, *Trials of Passion*, 104–5; *Tamworth Herald*, January 27, 1872; *South London Press*, January 20, 1872; *Manchester Evening News*, February 2, 1872.
17. Appignanesi, *Trials of Passion*, 111–2; *West Surrey Times*, January 27, 1872; *Belfast Daily Telegraph*, January 25, 1872; *Pall Mall Gazette*, January 24, 1872; *Tamworth Herald*, January 27, 1872; *Hull Daily News*, May 18, 1872; Jones, *The Case of the Chocolate Cream Killer*, 146–8, 151.
18. Jones, *The Case of the Chocolate Cream Killer*, 167; Jackson, *Death by Chocolate*, loc. 3441.
19. Bernard Taylor and Kate Clarke, *Murder at the Priory: The Mysterious Poisoning of Charles Bravo* (London: Grafton Books, 1988), 4–9; Yseult Bridges, *How Charles Bravo Died: The Chronicle of a Cause Célèbre* (London: The Reprint

Society, 1957), 23–7, 30; Elizabeth Jenkins, *Dr. Gully: A Novel* (London: Michael Joseph, 1972), 60–1, 68–70, 82–3, 86.
 20. William E. Swinton, "The Hydrotherapy and Infamy of Dr. James Gully," *Canadian Medical Association Journal* 123 (1980): 1263–4; Taylor and Clarke, *Murder at the Priory*, 10–4; Bridges, *How Charles Bravo Died*, 30–4; Jenkins, *Dr. Gully*, 91–4, 99, 112–4, 141–4.
 21. Taylor and Clarke, *Murder at the Priory*, 14–8; Bridges, *How Charles Bravo Died*, 41–2, 36–7; Jenkins, *Dr. Gully*, 127–8, 137, 143.
 22. Bridges, *How Charles Bravo Died*, 54–5.
 23. Taylor and Clarke, *Murder at the Priory*, 23–6; Jenkins, *Dr. Gully*, 137; Antony M. Brown, *Poisoned at the Priory: The Notorious Death of Charles Bravo* (London: Mirror Books, 2020), 16, 18–9; James Ruddick, *Death at the Priory: Love, Sex, and Murder in Victorian England* (New York: Grove Press, 2001), 34, 40.
 24. Taylor and Clarke, *Murder at the Priory*, 30–3; Ruddick, *Death at the Priory*, 38–9; Brown, *Poisoned at the Priory*, 19; Mary S. Hartman, *Victorian Murderesses* (London: Robson Books, 1985), 133–4; William Roughead, *Malice Domestic* (Garden City, NY: Doubleday, Doran & Company, 1929), 8.
 25. Hartman, *Victorian Murderesses*, 138–39; Roughead, *Malice Domestic*, 8; Brown, *Poisoned at the Priory*, 19–23; Bridges, *How Charles Bravo Died*, 80; Ruddick, *Death at the Priory*, 44, 47, 61, 63; Williams, *Suddenly at the Priory*, 50; Taylor and Clarke, *Murder at the Priory*, 36.
 26. Bridges, *How Charles Bravo Died*, 105–22; Ruddick, *Death at the Priory*, 68; Taylor and Clarke, *Murder at the Priory*, 47–50.
 27. Ruddick, *Death at the Priory*, 70–8; Bridges, *How Charles Bravo Died*, 122–33; Taylor and Clarke, *Murder at the Priory*, 151.
 28. Bridges, *How Charles Bravo Died*, 133–48; Ruddick, *Death at the Priory*, 80–4; Taylor and Clarke, *Murder at the Priory*, 61–2.
 29. Taylor and Clarke, *Murder at the Priory*, 68; Ruddick, *Death at the Priory*, 86–8; *Penny Illustrated Newspaper*, August 5, 1876; Bridges, *How Charles Bravo Died*, 136.
 30. Ruddick, *Death at the Priory*, 50, 89, 124–5; *Exeter and Plymouth Gazette*, May 17, 1876.
 31. Yvonne King Fisher, "Coroners of London and Middlesex c. 1820–1888: A Study of Medicalization and Professionalization," PhD thesis, The Open University, 2020, 133, 160–61; Bridges, *How Charles Bravo Died*, 150–61; *Oxfordshire Telegraph*, May 24, 1876.
 32. Taylor and Clarke, *Murder at the Priory*, 88–92, 96.
 33. *Penny Illustrated Newspaper*, August 5, 1876; *Liverpool Echo*, January 11, 1956; *Newcastle Daily Chronicle*, March 22, 1912.
 34. Taylor and Clarke, *Murder at the Priory*, 228–34, 238, 240, 242, 246, 251–2.
 35. *Manchester Evening News*, October 18, 1876; *Gloucester Citizen*, September 19, 1878; *Western Times*, September 21, 1878; *Sussex Advertiser*, September 24, 1878.

Chapter Seven

 1. Yseult Bridges, *Poison and Adelaide Bartlett: The Pimlico Poisoning Case* (London: Macmillan, 1970), 22–30; Kate Clarke, *In the Interests of Science: Adelaide Bartlett and the Pimlico Poisoning* (London: Mango Books, 2019), 1–6.
 2. Bridges, *Poison and Adelaide Bartlett*, 31; Clarke, *In the Interests of Science*, 7, 19; Hartman, *Victorian Murderesses*, 195, 182, 181, 184, 201, 200.
 3. Clarke, *In the Interests of Science*, 20–9.
 4. Bridges, *Poison and Adelaide Bartlett*, 80–3.
 5. Bridges, *Poison and Adelaide Bartlett*, 89–111.
 6. Clarke, *In the Interests of Science*, 47–68; Bridges, *Poison and Adelaide Bartlett*, 131–46.
 7. Clarke, *In the Interests of Science*, 69–83; Hartman, *Victorian Murderesses*, 178–9; Bridges, *Poison and Adelaide Bartlett*, 173–81.
 8. Bridges, *Poison and Adelaide Bartlett*, 196–7, 199, 192; Hartman, *Victorian Murderesses*, 179.
 9. Bridges, *Poison and Adelaide Bartlett*, 202–3.

10. *Liverpool Daily Post*, February 20, 1886; *Western Daily Express*, March 6, 1886; *Abergavenny Chronicle*, March 12, 1886; *Heywood Advertiser*, March 26, 1886.

11. *London Daily News*, April 6, 1886; *London Echo*, April 12, 1886; R. Barry O'Brien, *The Life of Lord Russell of Killowen* (London: Thomas Nelson and Sons, 1980); *Paisley and Renfrewshire Gazette*, August 21, 1886; Thomas Edward Crispe, *Reminiscences of a K. C.* (London: Methuen, 1909), 98–101; Sir Edward Clarke, *The Story of My Life* (London: John Murray, 1918), 328; Roy Jenkins, *Sir Charles Dilke A Victorian Tragedy* (London: Collins, 1958), 235–40, 245–53.

12. Beal, *The Trial of Adelaide Bartlett*, 234–71, 287–311; *Dundee Courier*, April 20, 1886.

13. Beal, *The Trial of Adelaide Bartlett*, 312; *Dundee Courier*, April 20, 1886; *Dundee Evening Telegraph*, April 19, 1886; *Dumfries and Galloway Standard*, April 21, 1886.

14. Pamela Horn, *The Rise and Fall of the Victorian Servant* (Stroud: Sutton Publishing, 1995), 18, 22, 76.

15. Ben Griffin, *The Politics of Gender in Victorian Britain: Masculinity, Political Culture and the Struggle for Women's Rights* (Cambridge: Cambridge University Press, 2012), 83, 4–5, 38, 40, 43, 45, 71.

16. Judith Flanders, *The Victorian House: Domestic Life from Childbirth to Deathbed* (London: Harper Perennial, 2004), 302; Miriam Bailin, *The Sickroom in Victorian Fiction: The Art of Being Ill* (Cambridge: Cambridge University Press, 1994), 6, 26, 28; Sandra Hempel, *The Inheritor's Powder* (New York: W.W. Norton, 2013), 52–6; Roy Porter, *Bodies Politic: Disease, Death and Doctors in Britain, 1650–1900* (London: Reaktion Books, 2001), 89–90, 130–1, 151, 257; Janet Oppenheim, *"Shattered Nerves": Doctors, Patients and Depression in Victorian England* (Oxford: Oxford University Press, 1991), 19, 21, 140.

17. Victoria Blake, *Mrs. Maybrick* (Kew: The National Archives, 2008), 29–30; Kate Colquhoun, *Did She Kill Him? A Victorian Tale of Deception, Adultery and Arsenic* (London: Little, Brown, 2014), 77; Mike Covill, *Jack the Ripper and the Maybrick Family* (Milton Keynes: Amazon, 2015), 14.

18. Blake, *Mrs. Maybrick*, 29–30; Colquhoun, *Did She Kill Him?*, 71; Trevor L. Christie, *Etched in Arsenic: A New Study of the Maybrick Case* (London: George G. Harrap & Co., 1968), 308; Bernard Ryan, *The Poisoned Life of Mrs. Maybrick* (London: Penguin Books, 1989), 29.

19. Colquhoun, *Did She Kill Him?*, 85; Christie, *Etched in Arsenic*, 59–60.

20. Blake, *Mrs. Maybrick*, 35; Colquhoun, *Did She Kill Him?*, 102, 113, 123–6; Christie, *Etched in Arsenic*, 61; *Liverpool Mercury*, May 15, 1889; Taylor, *Cruelly Murdered*, 132.

21. *Daily News*, June 7, 1889; *Norwich Post*, June 18, 1889; *Reynolds's Newspaper*, June 16, 1889; *Liverpool Mercury*, June 13, 14, 1889; *Sheffield Independent*, June 13, 14, 1889; Ratcliff to Aunspaugh, June 7, 1889, Christie Papers, AHC.

22. *Liverpool Mercury*, June 14, 19, 1889; *Liverpool Echo*, June 14, 1889; Maybrick, *Mrs. Maybrick's Own Story*, 46–7.

23. O'Brien, *Lord Russell*, 213–5, 229–42; *Colchester Gazette*, February 27, 1889; *Lancaster Gazette*, July 2, 1890; *Preston Herald*, December 5, 1885; *Sporting Life*, September 3, 1887; Maybrick, *Mrs. Maybrick's Own Story*, 46–7; H.B. Irving, ed., *Trial of Mrs. Maybrick* (Edinburgh: William Hodge & Company, 1912), 3, xxvi, 3–23; Joseph Hiam Levy, *The Necessity of Criminal Appeals: As Illustrated by the Maybrick Case and the Jurisprudence of Various Countries* (London: P.S. King, 1899), 21–2, 51–2; *Liverpool Daily Post*, August 9, 1889; *Belfast News-Letter*, August 6, 1889; Crim 6/9, National Archives (NA).

24. Irving, *Trial of Mrs. Maybrick*, 99–112; Levy, *The Necessity of Criminal Appeal*, 122–35; *Pall Mall Gazette*, August 3, 1889.

25. *Lloyd's Weekly Newspaper*, August 11, 1889.

26. *Tablet*, September 3, 1859; Irving, *Trial of Mrs. Maybrick*, 314–55; Levy, *The Necessity for Criminal Appeal*, 356–401; G. Lathom Browne and C.G. Stewart, *Reports of Trials for Murder by Poisoning by Prussic Acid, Strychnia, Antimony, Arsenic, and Aconitia* (London: Stevens and Sons, 1893), 15.

27. Hartman, *Victorian Murderesses*,

218; *Gloucester Citizen*, August 8, 1889; *Derby Daily Telegraph*, August 10, 1889; *Staffordshire Chronicle*, August 17, 1889; *Exeter and Plymouth Guardian*, August 16, 1889: Russell to Matthews, August 7, 1889, HO 144/1638/5078, NA.

28. Andrew Roberts, *Salisbury: Victorian Titan* (London: Weidenfeld & Nicolson Ltd., 2000), 108; *Portsmouth Evening News*, August 23, 1889; *Staffordshire Sentinel*, August 23, 1889; *Sheffield Independent*, August 23, 1889; *Hull Daily Mail*, August 23, 1889; Whorton, *The Arsenic Century*, 278–83.

Chapter Eight

1. Martin J. Wiener, *Reconstructing the Criminal: Culture, Law and Policy in England, 1830–1914* (Cambridge: Cambridge University Press, 1990), 53; Hugh McLeod, *Religion and Society in England 1850–1914* (London: MacMillan Press, 1996), 23, 62; Picard, *Victorian London*, 96; Gordon and Nair, *Public Lives*, 133–5; Wiener, "Victorian Convicted Murderers and the Press Idolatration," www.atmostfear-entertainment.com.

2. Knelman, *Twisting in the Wind*, 36–7; Wiener, "Victorian Convicted Murderers and the Press Idolatration," www.atmostfear-entertainment.com.

3. Wiener, *Reconstructing the Criminal*, 49, 145; Watson, *Poisoned Lives*, 208, 42–3; John Parascandola, *A History of Arsenic* (Washington, D.C.: Potomac Books, 2012), 14, 78; Walsh, *Domestic Murder in Nineteenth-Century England*, 138.

4. Wilson, *Murderess*, 136–43; Croft, *Murderesses in Victorian Britain*, 144–5; Knelman, *Twisting in the Wind*, 50–1, 126–7; *The Dial*, January 2, 1864; *Morpeth Herald*, January 2, 1864; *Gravesend Reporter*, January 2, 1864.

5. Croft, *Murderesses in Victorian Britain*, 32–3; Wilson, *Murderess*, 143; *Kentish Gazette*, April 3, 1866.

6. Wilson, *Murderess*, 144–5; Croft, *Murderesses in Victorian Britain*, 34; *Liverpool Courier*, March 31, 1866; *Kentish Gazette*, April 3, 1866; *Dundee Advertiser*, April 3, 1866; *Sussex Advertiser*, March 20, 1866; *Derbyshire Courier*, April 7, 1866; *Sherborne Mercury*, April 3, 1866; V.A.C. Catrell, *The Hanging Tree Execution and the English People 1770–1868* (Oxford: Oxford University Press, 1994), 610.

7. *Lincolnshire Chronicle*, January 2, 1869; *Liverpool Mercury*, December 16, 1868; *Reynolds's Newspaper*, November 1, 1868; *Pontypool Free Press*, October 31, 1868; Jakobi, *Misjudged Murderesses*, 94; "Priscilla Biggadyke—The Stickney poisoner," www.capitalpunishmentuk.org/Biggadyke.html.

8. Jakobi, *Misjudged Murderesses*, 94, 100–2, 104, 106.

9. Wiener, "Victorian Convicted Murderers and the Press Idolatration"; *London Sun*, December 23, 1868; Gatrell, *The Hanging Tree*, 589–90; "Priscilla Biggadyke: The Stickney Poisoner"; Croft, *Murderesses in Victorian Britain*, 38.

10. *The Times*, June 12, 1869; *Sheffield Daily Telegraph*, July 26, 1869.

11. *Morning Advertiser*, July 26, 1869; *London Sun*, August 3, 1869; *Daily Telegraph*, July 22, 26, 1869; *Birmingham Daily Post*, August 2, 1869; *The Echo* (London), July 28, 1869; *Birmingham Daily Post*, August 2, 1869; *Western Morning News*, August 4, 1869.

12. Martin Connolly, *Mary Ann Cotton, Dark Angel: Britain's First Female Serial Killer* (True Crime [Pen and Sword], Barnsley, 2016), 1–32.

13. Simon Webb and Miranda Brown, *Mary Ann Cotton: Victorian Serial Killer* (Bolton, ON: The Langley Press, 2016), 21–32.

14. Connolly, *Mary Ann Cotton, Dark Angel*, 61–71; David Wilson, *Mary Ann Cotton: Britain's First Female Serial Killer* (Eastbourne: Gardeners Books, 2012), Kindle, 1534, 1660.

15. Wilson, *Mary Ann Cotton*, Kindle, 1794, 2142, 2212.

16. Emsley, *The Elements of Murder*, 154; *Newcastle Chronicle*, July 18, 1896; *Berwick Advertiser*, March 28, 1873; Wilson, *Murderess*, 204; Whorton, *The Arsenic Century*, 57.

17. *Western Times*, October 11, 1883; Angela Brabin, *The Black Widows of Liverpool: A Chilling Account of Cold-Blooded Murder in Victorian Liverpool* (Lancaster: Palatine Books, 2003), 32, 35–9.

18. *Harborne Herald*, October 20, 1883;

Derby Daily Telegraph, October 16, 1883; *Manchester Evening News*, October 30, 1883; Brabin, *The Black Widows of Liverpool*, 43–4.
 19. *Liverpool Echo*, February 15, 1884; *Morning Post*, February 16, 1884; *Densbury Chronicle*, February 23, 1884.
 20. *Bath Chronicle and Weekly Gazette*, February 21, 1884; *Maidstone Journal and Kentish Advertiser*, March 3, 1884; Brabin, *The Black Widows of Liverpool*, 114, 108, 104.
 21. *Lancaster Gazette*, May 28, 1884; *Sun* (Antigua), December 8, 1913; *Newry Telegraph*, May 12, 1892; *Belfast News-Letter*, May 5, 1892; Wilson, *Murderess*, 209–14, 216; Jakobi, *Misjudged Murderesses*, 189–99, 202–3.
 22. *Shepton Mallet Journal*, August 13, 1886; Wilson, *Murderess*, 217–8.
 23. *Blackburn Standard*, July 17, 1886; *Bradford Daily Telegraph*, July 12, 1886; *York Herald*, May 29, 1886; *St. James's Gazette*, July 24, 1886.
 24. *Liverpool Mercury*, July 24, 1886; *London Evening Standard*, July 24, 1886; *Grantham Journal*, July 31, 1886; *Morning Post*, July 24, 1886.
 25. *Stalybridge Reporter*, April 1, 1892; *Blackpool Gazette and Herald*, October 1, 1886; *Sheffield Daily Telegraph*, September 1, 1886.
 26. Wilson, *Murderess*, 219–20; *Manchester Courier*, February 23, 1887.
 27. *Langpost and Somerset Herald*, March 5, 1887; *Bury and Suffolk Standard*, March 1, 1887; *Brecon County Times*, March 4, 1887; *Nottingham Evening Post*, February 24, 1887; *Manchester Courier*, February 23, 1887.
 28. *Sunderland Daily Echo*, February 24, 1887; *Manchester Evening News*, February 23, March 14, 1887; *Brecon County Times*, March 4, 1887; *Tamworth Herald*, March 5, 1887.

 29. *Western Times*, July 28, 1899; Croft, *Murderesses in Victorian Britain*, 93; *Dover Express*, April 14, 1899; Wilson, *Murderess*, 242, 244.
 30. *Echo* (London), June 29, 1899; *Morning Leader*, April 11, 1899.
 31. *Dover Express*, April 14, 1899; *Morning Leader*, April 11, 1899; *Morning Post*, April 11, 1899; Walsh, *Domestic Murder in Nineteenth-Century England*, 139–43.
 32. *Western Gazette*, April 14, 1899; *Echo* (London), April 7, June 29, 1899; *Dublin Evening Mail*, April 13, 1899; *Newcastle Courant*, July 22, 1899; Wilson, *Murderess*, 244; Croft, *Murderesses in Victorian Britain*, 94–5.
 33. *South Wales Echo*, July 10, 1899; *Western Gazette*, July 21, 1899; Croft, *Murderesses in Victorian Britain*, 94; Wiener, "Victorian Convicted Murderesses and the Press Idolatration," 4/43, 5/43.
 34. Croft, *Murderesses in Victorian Britain*, 94; *Taunton Courier and Western Advertiser*, July 26, 1899; *Newcastle Courant*, July 22, 1899; *Western Gazette*, July 21, 1899; *Bridport News*, July 21, 1899.

Conclusion

 1. David Bentley, *English Criminal Justice in the Nineteenth Century* (London: Hambledon Press: 1998), 8–9; James Fitzjames Stephen, *A General View of the Criminal Law of England* (London: Macmillan & Co: 1863), 233; John H. Langbein, *The Origins of the Adversary Trial* (Oxford: Oxford University Press, 2003), 261–2; John Q. Quitman, *The Origins of Reasonable Doubt* (New Haven: Yale University Press, 2008), 2–4.

Bibliography

Primary Sources

• **American Heritage Center, Laramie**
Trevor L. Christie Papers
Ratcliffe to Aunspaugh, 7 June 1889

• **National Archives, Kew**
Conviction of Florence Maybrick
Russell to Matthews, 7 August 1889
HO 144/1638/5078

• **National Archives of Scotland, Edinburgh**
Trial of Madeleine Smith
AD 14/57/255/1
AD 14/57/255/5
AD 14/55/255/13
AD 14/57/255/20

• **National Library of Scotland, Edinburgh**
Legal Notebooks of John Inglis
38.1.17; 38.2.17
Watt, John Crabb. *John Inglis Lord Justice-General of Scotland. A Memoir.* Edinburgh: William Green & Sons, 1893.

Contemporary Sources

Ballantine, William. *Some Experiences of a Barrister's Life.* London: Richard Bentley & Sons, 1883.
Beal, Edward. *The Trial of Adelaide Bartlett for Murder, Held at the Central Criminal Court (1886).* London: Stevens & Haynes, 1886.
Brown, G. Lathom. *Report of Trials for Murder by Poisoning.* London: Stevens and Sons, 1883.
Circumstantial Evidence: The Extraordinary Case of Eliza Fenning with a Statement of Facts Since Developed Tending to Prove Her Innocence of the Crime. London: Cowrie and Strange, n.d.
Clarke, Edward. *The Story of My Life.* London: John Murray, 1918.
Clarke, Percy, and Charles Meymott Tidy. *Medical Law for Medical Men.* London: Bailliere, Tindall, and Cox, 1890.
Creighton, M. *Memoir of Sir George Grey.* London: Longmans Green, and Co., 1901.
Crispe, Thomas Edward. *Reminiscences of a K. C.* London: Methuen, 1909.
Davies and Company. *Extraordinary Life and Character of Mary Bateman: The Yorkshire Witch.* Leeds: Stanhope Press, 1811.
Important Results on an Elaborate Investigation into the Mysterious Case of Elizabeth Fenning. 1815.
Irving, H.B., ed. *Trial of Mrs. Maybrick.* London: William Hodge & Company, 1912.
Levy, Joseph Hiam. *The Necessity of Criminal Appeal: As Illustrated by the Maybrick Case and the Jurisprudence of Various Countries.* London: P.S. King, 1899.
Marshall, John. *Five Cases of Recovery from the Effects of Arsenic Relative to the Guilt of Eliza Fenning.* London: C. Chapple, 1815.
Maudsley, Henry. *Responsibility in Mental Diseases.* New York: Appleton and Company, 1896.
Maybrick, Florence Elizabeth. *Mrs. Maybrick's Own Story: My Fifteen Lost Years.* New York: Funk & Wagnall, 1905.

Bibliography

"The Proceedings of the Old Bailey." www.oldbaileyonline.org.
Stapleton, Joseph Whitaker. *The Great Crime of 1860.* London: E. Marlborough & Co., 1861.
Taylor, Alfred S. *A Manual of Medical Jurisprudence.* 2nd ed. London: John Churchill, 1846.
Taylor, Alfred Swaine. *On Poisons in Relation to Medical Jurisprudence and Medicine.* 2nd and revised edition. Philadelphia: Blanchard & Lea, 1859.

A selection from national and provincial newspapers

Bath Chronicle and Weekly Gazette
Belfast News-Letter
Birmingham Daily Post
Bradford Daily Telegraph
Brecon County Times
Brighton Gazette
Daily News
Daily Telegraph
Dover Express
Dublin Evening Mail
Dundee Advertiser
Kentish Gazette
Liverpool Daily Post
Liverpool Echo
Liverpool Mercury
Lloyd's Weekly Newspaper
London Evening Standard
London Sun
Manchester Evening News
Morning Advertiser
Morning Herald
Morning Leader
Morning Post
Paisley and Renfrewshire Gazette
Pall Mall Gazette
Reynolds's Newspaper
South London Press
The Times

Secondary Sources

Appignanesi, Lisa. *Mad, Bad and Sad: A History of Women and the Mind Doctors from 1800 to the Present.* London: Virago Press, 2009.
Bailin, Miriam. *The Sickroom in Victorian Fiction: The Art of Being Ill.* Cambridge: Cambridge University Press, 1994.
Berry-Dee, Christopher. *Female Serial Killers: Up Close and Personal.* Berkeley, CA: Ulysses Press, 2019.
Blake, Victoria. *Mrs. Maybrick.* Kew: The National Archives, 2008.
Brabin, Angela. *The Black Widows of Liverpool: A Chilling Account of Cold-Blooded Murder in Victorian Liverpool.* Lancaster: Palatine Books, 2003.
Bridges, Yseult. *How Charles Bravo Died: The Chronicle of a Cause Célèbre.* London: Reprint Society, 1957.
_____. *Poison and Adelaide Bartlett: The Pimlico Poisoning Case.* London: Macmillan & Co., 1970.
_____. *Saint—With Red Hands? The Chronicle of a Great Crime.* London: Jarrolds, 1954.
Briggs, John, Christopher Harrison, Angus McInnes, and David Vincent. *Crime and Punishment in England: An Introductory History.* London: UCL Press, 1996.
Brown, Antony M. *Poisoned at the Priory: The Notorious Death of Charles Bravo.* London: Mirror Books, 2020.
Burney, Ian. *Poison, Detection and Victorian Imagination.* Manchester: Manchester University Press, 2006.
Christie, Trevor L. *Etched in Arsenic: A New Study of the Maybrick Case.* London: George G. Harrap & Co., 1968.
Clarke, Kate. *In the Interests of Science: Adelaide Bartlett and the Pimlico Poisoning.* London: Mango Books, 2019.
_____, ed. *Trial of Eliza Fenning.* Notable British Trials Series 88. London: Mango Books, 2020.
Clifford, Naomi. *Women and the Gallows, 1778–1837: Unfortunate Wretches.* Barnsley: Pen and Sword, 2017.
Colquhoun, Kate. *Did She Kill Him? A Victorian Tale of Deception, Adultery and Arsenic.* London: Little Brown, 2019.
Connolly, Martha. *Mary Ann Cotton, Dark Angel: Britain's First Female Serial Killer.* Barnsley: Pen and Sword, 2016.
Croft, Christina. *Murderesses in Victorian Britain.* Monee, IL: 2021.
D'Cruze, Shani. *Crimes of Outrage: Sex, Violence and Victorian Working Women.* DeKalb: Northern Illinois University Press, 1998.

Diamond, Michael. *Victorian Sensation: Or, the Spectacular, the Shocking, and Scandalous in Nineteenth-Century Britain.* London: Anthem Press, 2003.

Dixon, Rachel. *Infanticide: Expert Evidence and Testimony in Child Murder Cases, 1688–1955.* London: Routledge, 2022.

Emsley, John. *The Elements of Murder: A History of Poison.* Oxford: Oxford University Press, 2005.

Farrington, Karen. *Murder, Mystery and My Family.* London: BBC Books, 2019.

Flanders, Judith. *The Invention of Murder: How the Victorians Revelled in Death and Detection and Created Modern Crime.* London: Harper Press, 2011.

_____. *The Victorian House: Domestic Life from Childbirth to Deathbed.* London: Harper Perennial, 2004.

Gatrell, V.A.C. *The Hanging Tree: Execution and the English People, 1770–1868.* Oxford: Oxford University Press, 1994.

Gordon, Eleanor, and Gwyneth Nair. *Murder and Morality in Victorian Britain: The Story of Madeleine Smith.* Manchester: Manchester University Press, 2009.

_____, and _____. *Public Lives: Women, Family and Society in Victorian Britain:* New Haven, CT: Yale University Press, 2003.

Griffin, Ben. *The Politics of Gender in Victorian Britain: Masculinity, Political Culture and the Struggle for Women's Rights.* Cambridge: Cambridge University Press, 2012.

Hammerton, A. James. *Cruelty and Companionship: Conflict in Nineteenth-Century Married Life.* London: Routledge, 1992.

Harrison, J.F.C. *The Early Victorians 1832–1851.* St. Albans: Panther Books, 1973.

Hartman, Mary. *Victorian Murderesses.* London: Robin Books, 1985.

Hempel, Sandra. *The Inheritor's Powder.* New York: W.W. Norton, 2013.

Hendry, Sally. *Mother and Murder: The Sad True Tale of Rebecca Smith.* Gloucester: Hobnob Press, 2022.

Heslop, Paul. *Murderous Women from Sarah Dazley to Ruth Ellis.* Stroud: History Press, 2009.

Horn, Pamela. *The Rise and Fall of the Victorian Servant.* Stroud: Sutton Publishing, 1995.

Hostettler, John. *Thomas Erskine and Trial by Jury.* London: Waterside Press, 2010.

Jackson, Sophie. *Death by Chocolate: The Serial Poisoning of Victorian Britain.* Stroud: Fonthill Media, 2015.

Jakobi, Stephen. *In the Mind of the Serial Killer.* Barnsley: Pen and Sword, 2017.

_____. *Misjudged Murderesses: Female Injustice in Victorian Britain.* Barnsley: Pen and Sword, 2019.

James, Lawrence. *The Middle Class: A History.* London: Little, Brown, 2007.

Jenkins, Brian. *Madeleine Smith on Trial: A Glasgow Murder and the Young Woman Too Respectable to Convict.* Jefferson, NC: McFarland, 2019.

Jenkins, Elizabeth. *Dr. Gully: A Novel.* London: Michael Joseph, 1972.

Jenkins, Roy. *Sir Charles Dilke: A Victorian Tragedy.* London: Collins, 1958.

Jones, Kaye. *The Case of the Chocolate Cream Killer: The Poisonous Passion of Christiana Edmunds.* Barnsley: Pen and Sword, 2016.

Keeton, G.W. *Guilty but Insane: Four Trials for Murder.* London: MacDonald, 1961.

Knelman, Judith. *Twisting in the Wind: The Murderess and the English Press.* Toronto: University of Toronto Press, 1998.

Leckie, Barbara. *Culture and Adultery: The Novel, the Newspaper, and the Law, 1857–1914.* Philadelphia: University of Pennsylvania Press, 1999.

Lee, Alan J. *The Origins of the Popular Press in England, 1855–1914.* London: Croom Helm, 1976.

Maunder, Andrew, and Grace Moore, eds. *Victorian Crime, Madness and Sensation.* London: Ashgate, 2004.

McGowan, Douglas. *The Strange Affair of Madeleine Smith.* Glasgow: Mercer Press, 2007.

McLeod, Hugh. *Religion and Society in England 1850–1914.* London: Macmillan Press, 1996.

Muscutt, Robert. *The Life, Trial and Hanging of Mary Ball.* Milton Keynes: Broadlands Books, 2011.

O'Brien, R. Barry. *The Life of Lord Russell of Killowen.* London: Thomas Nelson and Sons, 1980.

Oppenheim, Janet. *"Shattered Nerves": Doctors, Patients and Depression in Victorian England.* Oxford: Oxford University Press, 1991.

Parascandola, John. *King of Poisons: A History of Arsenic.* Washington, D.C.: Potomac Books, 2012.

Perkin, Joan. *Victorian Women.* London: John Murray (Publishers), 1993.

Pettegree, Andrew. *The Invention of News: How the World Came to Know About Itself.* London: Yale University Press, 2014.

Porter, Roy. *Bodies Politic: Disease, Death and Doctors in Britain, 1650–1900.* London: Reaktion Books, 2001.

Roberts, Andrew. *Salisbury: Victorian Titan.* London: Weidenfeld & Nicolson Ltd., 2000.

Rose, Lionel. *Massacre of the Innocents: Infanticide in Great Britain 1800–1939.* London: Routledge & Kegan Paul, 1986.

Roughead, William. *Malice Domestic.* Garden City, NY: Doubleday, Doran and Company, 1929.

Rowbotham, Judith, Marianna Muravyeva, and David Nash, eds. *Shame, Blame and Culpability: Crime and Violence in the Modern State.* London: Routledge, 2013.

Ruddick, James. *Death at the Priory: Love, Sex, and Murder in Victorian England.* New York: Grove Press, 2001.

Ryan, Bernard. *The Poisoned Life of Mrs. Maybrick.* London: Penguin Books, 1989.

Shpayer-Makov, Haia. *The Ascent of Detective Police Sleuths in Victorian and Edwardian England.* Oxford: Oxford University Press, 2011.

Smith, Roger. *Trial by Medicine: Insanity and Responsibility in Victorian Trials.* Edinburgh: Edinburgh University Press, 1981.

Stevens, Mark. *Broadmoor Revealed: Victorian Crime and the Lunatic Asylum.* Barnsley: Pen and Sword, 2020.

Stratmann, Linda. *The Secret Poisoner: A Century of Murder.* London: Yale University Press, 2016.

Summerscale, Kate. *The Suspicions of Mr. Whicher.* London: Bloomsbury, 2009.

Taylor, Bernard. *Cruelly Murdered: Constance Kent and the Killing at Road Hill House.* London: Grafton Books, 1989.

_____, and Kate Clarke. *Murder at the Priory: The Mysterious Poisoning of Charles Bravo.* London: Grafton Books, 1988.

Telfer, Torie. *Lady Killers: Deadly Women Throughout History.* New York: Harper Collins, 2017.

Van De Warker, Ely. "The Relations of Women to Crime." In *Women Who Killed: Murderous Women from 18th and 19th Century.* Redditch: Read Books Ltd., 2020.

Vronsky, Peter. *Female Serial Killers: How and Why Women Become Monsters.* New York: Berkley Books, 2007.

Walsh, Bridget. *Domestic Murder in Nineteenth-Century England: Literary and Cultural Representations.* London: Routledge, 2016.

Ward, Roger. *Henry Matthews, Viscount Llandaff: The Unknown Home Secretary.* Stroud: Fonthill Media, 2018.

Watson, Katherine. *Poisoned Lives: English Poisoners and their Victims.* London: Hambledon and London, 2004.

Webb, Simon, and Miranda Brown. *Mary Ann Cotton: Victorian Serial Killer.* Bolton, ON: Langley Press, 2016.

Whorton, James C. *The Arsenic Century: How Victorian Britain Was Poisoned at Home, Work, and Play.* Oxford: Oxford University Press, 2011.

Wiener, Martin J. *Reconstructing the Criminal: Culture, Law and Policy in England, 1830–1914.* Cambridge: Cambridge University Press, 1990.

Williams, John. *Suddenly at the Priory.* London: Penguin, 1989.

Wilson, Ben. *The Laughter of Triumph: William Hone and the Fight for the Free Press.* London: Faber & Faber, 2005.

_____. *The Making of Victorian Values: Decency and Dissent in Britain 1789–1937.* London: Penguin Books, 2007.

Wilson, David. *Mary Ann Cotton: Britain's First Female Serial Killer.* Hampshire: Waterside Press, Ltd., 2012.

Wilson, Patrick. *Murderess: A Study of Women Executed in Britain Since 1843.* London: Michael Joseph, 1971.

Articles

Burney, Ian A. "A Poisoning of No Substance: The Trials of Medico-Legal

Proof in Mid-Victorian England." *Journal of British Studies* 38 (1999).

Holloway, S.W.F. "The Apothecaries' Act, 1815: A Reinterpretation." *Medical History* 10 (1966): 107–29.

Kiel, Kent A., and Morrie B. Hoffman. "The Criminal Psychopath History. Neuroscience, Treatment, and Economics." *Jurimetrics* 51 (2011).

Morton Alison. "The Female Crime: Class and Female Criminality in Victorian Representation of Poisoning." *Midland Historical Review* 5 (2021).

Swinton, William E. "The Hydrotherapy and Infamy of Dr. James Gully." *Canadian Medical Association Journal* 123 (1980).

Wiener, Martin. "Victorian Convicted Murderers and the Press Idolatration." https://www.atmostfear-entertainment.com/culture/criminology/victorian-convicted-murderers/.

Index

adultery 156, 158, 162, 167, 179
Adulteration of Food and Drink Act, 1860 122
Alienists 84; and M'Naghten rules 84
Allen, Mary 36–37
Alley, Peter, barrister 21–23, 29
Ansell, Mary Ann 186–189
Apothecaries Act, 1815 19
arsenic 10, 13, 16, 18, 21, 25, 29, 31, 34, 171; rudimentary analysis 19, 24, 31–33
Arsenic Act, 1851 74–76; limited effects 75–77, 171
arsenic eaters 10, 72
arsenical poisoning 13, 26, 29, 34, 47, 56, 58, 73, 172, 175
Ashford, Mary Ann 172–173

Ball, Mary, 63–64
Ballantine, William, barrister 82; defense of Vyse 116; prosecutor Christina Edmunds 125–126
Bartlett, Adelaide 143–149
Bartlett, Edwin, Sr. 143–145
Bartlett, Edwin Thomas 143–147
Bateman, John 12, 15
Bateman, Mary 11–14, 30; trial 13–14, 16
Baxter, Edwin, grocer 143
Beard, Dr. Charles, 121–123, 130
Bedlam Asylum 43–45
Bellingham, John, assassin 43
Berry, Elizabeth 184–186
Bethlem Royal Hospital 87–88, 127
Biggadyke, Priscilla 173–175
Bloody Code 6, 12, 28–29
Blythe letters 13–14
Bodkin, William Henry, barrister 85–87
Bravo, Charles 132–138, 140, 143
Brierley, Alfred 156, 158
Briggs, Matilda 154–156, 158, 161
Brighouse, Samuel 158–160

Britain, and industrialization 1, 3, 4, 97
Britland, Mary Ann 182, 184
Brough, Mary Ann 85–89
Burdock, Mary Ann 35, 48; execution 39; trial 37–38
burial clubs 32, 57–62
Bryning, Isaac, superintendent 159–160

Cage, Mary Emily 76–77
Calcraft, William, hangman 172–173
capital punishment 2, 58, 65
Carter, Dr. William 158–159, 167
Carter, William, coroner for East Surrey 138–140
Chesham, Sarah 69–71, 73, 77, 74
childbirth and insanity 45
Christison, Robert 34, 97, 99–100, 106; and Treatise on Poisons 34
Christmas, Celestina 81–83
circumstantial evidence 24, 28, 31, 53, 61, 68, 174–175
Clarke, Edward, barrister 151–153
closing address 152
Cockburn, Alexander 43–44
Cotton, Mary Ann 176–179
Cox, Jane Cannon 132, 134–135, 137, 139–141
criminology 171
curtailment of access to dangerous drugs 171; Pharmacy Act, 1868 171

Davies, Edward, public analyst 164–165
deadly poisons 10; mercuric chloride 10–11, 14–16; prussic acid 10, 67, 171; strychnine 10, 74, 84, 97, 171; tartar emetic 171
Dickens, Charles 28, 76
Dillon, Garrett, surgeon 32–33
Doggett, Frederick, registrar births and deaths 145, 147
Dyson, George 145–151

211

Edmunds, Christiana, 120–125, 128–130
Edney, Sophia 47–48
Ellenborough, Lord 11, 49; Malicious Shooting and Stabbing Act 11, 16
English criminal law 6, 12, 29
epidemic diseases 4, 16
Erle, Sir William, judge 85, 87–88
Erskine, Thomas, barrister 42–43
expert scientific witnesses 5, 38; doubts of importance 83–84

females and homicide 9–11, 16; opposition to execution 2
Fenning, Eliza 17–26, 28, 30
Fenning, William 23–24, 26
Flanagan, Catherine 179–181
flypapers 158; and arsenic solution 158–159, 163, 181
Freeman, Sarah 57–59
French, Sarah Ann 77–79
Fuller, Charles, surgeon 156–158; trial witness 163

Gadsen, Roger, apprentice 18–20, 23–24, 26
Geering, Mary Ann 62; burial club motive 63; trial 63
Gilmour, Christina 98–101
Gully, Dr. James Manby, water therapist 130–131, 133, 140

Hadfield, James 41–43
Hale, Jane 40–41
Harris, Charlotte 64–65
Haslam, Betty 60–61
Herapath, William, chemist 5, 36–39, 48–49, 52, 58, 83, 173
Higgins, Margaret 179–181
Hill, Frederick 3, 5
Holt, Alice 171–172
Hone, William, journalist 26–27, 29
Humphreys, Richard, surgeon 157–158

infanticides 7, 9, 11, 39–41, 50–51; childbirth insanity 41, 51, 53
inquests 6, 33, 50, 52, 58
Irish famine, victims 3, 5

James, Edwin, Q.C. 85–87
Joyce, Eliza 55–56
juries 6–7, 44–45, 52, 64, 67, 81, 98; reluctance to commit females poisoners 79, 83

L'Angelier, Pierre Emile 101–106
laudenum poisoning 56, 137

Leach, Dr. Alfred 146–147
Leavesden Asylum 186
Lefley, Mary 181–182
Letheby, Henry, professor of chemistry, 67, 70, 83, 123
lower orders 1–3, 50, 63, 76, 98, 108; and crime 5, 7, 9, 11, 16, 54, 63, 65, 171; and middle class 170
lunacy 42–44, 84, 86–87; and clemency 40–44; Criminal Lunatics Act 74; and insanity defense 74

Married Women's Property Act, 1882 145
Marsh, James, chemist 48–49, 176
Marshall, John, surgeon 17–27
May, Mary 61–62
Maybrick, Edwin 155, 158–159; and brother's health 163
Maybrick, Florence 5, 154–169
Maybrick, James 153–157; postmortem 163
Maybrick, Michael 154–161
McMullen, Betsy 79–81
Medical Witnesses Act 39
Merritt, Anne 66–68, 102
middle class 1, 4–5, 28, 54, 76, 108; expansion 4, 30, 97; expansion of lower middle class 170–171; and patriarchy 30, 155; social attitudes 97–98; women, and murder 1–2, 7, 97–98
milk fever 40–41, 86
Milner, Mary Ann 58–59
M'Naghten, Daniel, assassin 43–44
Morning Post 28, 40

national register of deaths 6
new police 6, 29, 75–76, 98; and statistics 171
not proven 28

Ogilvy, Henry, apothecary 17, 19, 21, 23–25
Old Bailey justice 20–21
Oliver, Fanny 175–176

Palmer, William 4, 99; doubt of expert scientific evidence 84, 97; trial 5, 37
Parry, John Humffreys 125–128
Peel, Sir Robert 29, 43
Peer, Sarah 20, 22–24
penal transportation 28, 51, 65, 68, 75, 81–82
Perrigo, Rebecca 13–14
Perrigo, William 13–15
Pickford, William, barrister 180

plea of the belly 15, 51, 65, 126
poisoning hysteria 68–69
press 2, 7–8, 69; Anne Merritt case 68; and criminal justice 2, 7, 72; Eliza Fenning case 25; expansion 49–50, 68; Sarah Chambers case 72, 74
public executions: bungled 1, 33–34, 47, 58, 74, 77, 79, 172; celebratory events 34, 39, 47, 55, 68, 77

Queen Victoria 2; attempted assassination 6, 76

Reinsch, Hugo, chemist 49
Ricardo, Florence 130–142
Rowland, Betty 46–47
Russell, Sir Charles 150–151; and Cotton case 178; and Maybrick case 168

Sandys, Anne 59–60
Sandys, George 59–60
Sandys, Honor 59–60
Sandys, Robert 59–60
Saville-Kent, Francis 109–111
Saville-Kent, Samuel 108–110
serial killers 54–55
Sherrington, Ann 39–40
Silvester, Sir John, judge 21, 23–25, 27–28
Smith, Clara Ann, poison victim 35–38
Smith, Madeleine 28, 101–107
Smith, Rebecca 51–53
Smith, Thomas 39–40

Stephen, James Fitzjames, judge 167–168
Stevenson, Thomas, Home Office scientific expert 148–149, 152, 164–165

Taylor, Alfred Swaine 5, 11, 61–63, 69, 71, 78, 83, 86, 94, 97
Thorpe, Mary 9, 30, 41
Tidy, Charles Meynott, Home Office expert 165
Toulmin, Francis, surgeon 66–67
Turner, Charlotte 17–21, 23, 25–26
Turner, Orlibar 25; suspicion of poisoning 17–19, 21
Turner, Robert 17, 22, 25, 28
Turner family 16–17, 25–27

Voce, Mary 9–11, 30
Voce, Thomas 9–10
Vyse, Ann Cornish 112–118

Wade, Edward, surgeon 48
Wansborough, Thomas, chemist 25–26
Wetherell, Sir Charles, recorder 35, 38–39
Wilson, Catherine, serial killer 89–95
Winslow, Forbes 86–87, 118, 188
Wittenback, Mary 32–33
Woodman, Mary 31–32
Wright, Charles William, surgeon 32–33

Yapp, Alice, nursemaid 155, 158, 161

www.ingramcontent.com/pod-product-compliance
Lightning Source LLC
Chambersburg PA
CBHW021856230426
43671CB00006B/413